THE GRAND DUCHY OF WARSAW

By G.F.Nafziger and M.T.Wesolowski

THE GRAND DUCHY OF WARSAW
By George Nafziger and M. T. Wesolowski
Cover design by Vincent Rospond
This edition published in 2019

Nafziger Collection, in conjunction with

Pike and Powder Publishing Group LLC
1525 Hulse Rd, Unit 1 1 Craven Lane, Box 66066
Point Pleasant, NJ 08742 Lawrence, NJ 08648-66066

ISBN 978-1-9454308-1-7
LCN

Published by The Nafziger Collection, Inc.
PO Box 1522, West Chester, OH 45071-1522
E-mail: Drnafziger@yahoo.com
On-line Catalog: http://www.nafzigercollection.com/

Bibliographical References and Index
1. Poland. 2. History. 3. Napoleonic Military

For more information on Pike and Powder Publishing Group, LLC,
visit us at www.PikeandPowder.com & www.wingedhussarpublishing.com

twitter: @pike_powder
facebook: @PikeandPowder

The Grand Duchy of Warsaw

By G.F.Nafziger and M.T.Wesolowski

The Seal of the Grand Duchy of Warsaw

TABLE OF CONTENTS

The Duchy of Warsaw

1733 -1795 Old Poland

In order to understand the Grand Duchy of Warsaw it is necessary to review the history of Poland prior to the Napoleonic wars. On the Death of August II in 1733, Stanislaw Leszczyski who was elected and deposed in 1709 and the father-in-law to Louis XV of France attempted to regain his throne with the aid of a small French force under Louis de Bréhan. Because the King of Poland was elected, he solicited and received the assistance of the Czartoryski family. He was shortly later re-elected King.

Subsequently, Poland factionalized and the Lithuanians (the Czartoryskis), who favored Friedrich August II of Saxony, son of the late king, invited the Russians to intervene. A Russian army appeared before Warsaw, forced a phantom Sejm (the body that elected the king) and had August III declared king. Stanislaw retired to become Duke of Lorraine and Bar, keeping the title of King of Poland, but leaving August III as the actual king.

August III left running the country to his minister, Heinrich von Brühl, who in turn turned the government of Poland over to the Czartoryskis.

Unfortunately, some of the great families of Poland were obstinately opposed to any reform or violation of their constitution. The francophil Potockis, in particular, whose possessions in southern Poland and the Ukraine covered thousands of square miles, hated the russophil Czatoryskis and successively obstructed all of their efforts. In the Saxon period, every Sejm was dissolved by the hirelings of some great lord or of some foreign potentate.

After a period of cooperation with the Saxon court the Czatorskis broke with the Saxon Court and turned to Russia. Their intermediary was their nephew, Stanislaw August Poniatowski.

Poniatowski adopted the name "August" after he ascended the throne, who they sent as a Saxon minister, to the Russian Court in the suite of the English minister Sir Charles Hanbury Williams, in 1755. The handsome and insinuating Poniatowski speedily won the heart of the Grand Duchess Catherine, but gained nothing else for Poland and returned discredited in 1759.

Under the Saxon Court Poland's decline continued. A general agricultural crisis from the 17th to mid-18th century combined with inflation ruined towns and peasants, as well as the small gentry. Only the large and prominent families improved their situations in this period.

With the death of Augustus III the Czartoryskis began again to manipulate the politics of the Commonwealth. Stanislaw August Poniatowski was elected king with the aid of recommendations and troops from Catherine II of Russia on 7 September 1764. The actual interregnum lasted from 5 October 1763 to 7 May 1764, when the Convocation Diet was assembled.

In late 1763 Prince Nikolai V. Repnin arrived in Warsaw and brought up the question of Polish dissidents. This was done officially again on 4 November 1766. At that time the population of Poland was about 11,420,000, of whom about 1,000,000 were dissidents or dissenters. Half of these were Protestants living in the towns of Polish Prussia and Great Poland. The other half was the Orthodox population of Lithuania. The dissidents had limited political rights and their religious liberties were somewhat restricted. For these persons, mainly agricultural laborers, artisans and petty tradesmen, Repnin, in the name of Catherine II, demanded absolute equality, political and religious, with the Catholic population of Poland. He was well aware that an aristocratic and Catholic assembly like the Sejm would never concede so preposterous a demand.

The Duchy of Warsaw in 1810

In 1767, conservative magnates supported by Repnin, formed a conference at Radom whose first act was to send a deputation to St. Petersburg petitioning Catherine to guarantee the liberties of the republic. With a carte blanche in his pocket, Repnin proceeded to treat the Sejm as if it was totally subservient to Russia.

Despite threats, bribes and the presence of Russian troops outside the doors (as well as inside the Chamber of Deputies) the patriots steadfastily refused Repnin's demands. Only the arrest of the leaders of the resistance by Russian grenadiers stopped further opposition. In addition to removing all restrictions against the dissidents, Russia effectively took over control of the government of Poland.

This led to a Catholic patriotic uprising known as the Confederation of Bar, which started in 1768 in the city of Bar, in the Ukraine. Though supported by the French, this revolt lingered slowly for four years before it died. It also brought to the attention of Berlin and Vienna that Russia was about to absorb all of Poland, so they began to move to expand their own territories at Poland's expense.

On 17 February 1772 the first treaty of partition was signed between Prussia, Austria and Russia. Russia obtained the Palatinates of Vitebsk, Polotsk, Mscislaw, and 1,300,000 new inhabitants. Austria got Malopolska, without Krakow, but it did get Lvov, Tarnopol, and Halicz, which it formed into a new province called Galicia. This territory had 2,650,000 inhabitants. Prussia received the Palatinate of Pomorze, less Gdansk (Danzig); the Palatinate of Chelmno, minus Torun (Thorn); the northern half of Wielkipolska, and the Palatinates of Malbork (Marienburg) and Warmia, calling the new acquisition West Prussia. This territory had 580,000 inhabitants. Poland lost 4.5 million of its 11.4 million inhabitants (39%) and 81,584 of its 283,204 square miles (29%) of territory.

The partitioning powers presented the remains of Poland with a new constitution, but retained the two worst elements of the old constitution, the elective monarchy and the liberum veto (which allowed one dissenting vote to veto any action).

The shock of the partitioning brought much of the petty bickering of the Polish nobility to heel. The "four years Sejm" was convened in 1788. The Permanent Council imposed on it by Russia was abolished, the royal prerogative was enlarged, an army of 65,000 men was raised, and the constitution was reformed. To further ensure its security Poland sought an alliance with Prussia. Friedrich Wilhelm II initially stipulated that Poland must surrender Danzig and Torun (Thorn) to him. The Poles refused and Austrian political intervention prevented this. On 19 March 1791 Prussia and Poland signed a treaty guaranteeing each other's possessions and to render mutual assistance if the other was attacked.

With a series of unusual and decisive political manuvers, on 3 May 1791, the new constitution was instituted. This constitution established a limited, hereditary constitutional monarchy, eliminated the liberum veto and other obstructive machinery of the old system.

Not to be out done, Stanislaw Feliks Potocki, Seweryn Rzewuski and Ksawery Branicki, the three chief opponents of the new constitution, went to Russia. Here they arranged with Catherine II to undertake a restoration of the old system by force of arms. On 14 May 1792 some Polish troops accompanied the three conspira¬tors into the town of Targowica in the Ukraine and declared an end to the new constitution. Four days later the Russian minis¬ter in Warsaw presented a formal declaration of war to the Polish government. Prussia abandoned the Poles, leaving Prince Jozef Antoni Poniatowski, nephew of King Stanislaw II, and Ta¬deusz Kosciuszko to led their 46,000 man army to the east. After winning three pitched battles against the Russians they were obliged to withdraw to Warsaw by Russia's overwhelming numbers.

The king, in a moment of weakness, conceded to the Russian demands and hostilities were suspended. The Polish army was dismattled by treaty with Russian, many officers resigned in disgust and the new constitution was abandoned. The old system was restored and the Russians occupied all of eastern Poland. The Prussians, alarmed at this turn of events, took actions of their own.

After every possible means of coercion was applied to the Poles, the second treaty of partition was signed on 23 September 1793. Russia got all of Poland's eastern provinces between Livonia and Moldava. Prussia got Dobrzyn, Kujavia, Wielkipolska, Tourn, and Danzig. Poland now had only 83,012 square miles of territory and a population of about 4,000,000 inhabitants. Austria did not take part in the second partition.

In an effort to stop the destruction of Poland, if not to restore her lost territories, Kosciuszko, Kollataj, and Ignacy Potocki, among others, began anew to work for Poland. Kosciuszko went to revolutionary France to propose a league of republics to oppose the league of sovereigns. Jacobin France, operating for its own benefit, gave him an evasive reply. When he returned empty handed he found that Polish officers had started a revolt against the imposed limit on the army of 15,000 men. His hand forced, Kosciuszko was declared dictator, on 23 March 1794, in Krakow. He reinstated much of the 1791 Constitution and called the peasants to arms. At first Kosciuszko's army was successful and the Russians were repeatedly defeated. Not only was much of the lost territory recovered from Russia, but Warsaw and Wilno were liberated by popular uprisings.

The overwhelming masses of Prussian and Russian troops, however, proved too much for Kosciuszko's Poland and his army was destroyed on the battlefield at Maciejowice. Kosciuszko was wounded and taken prisoner. Eventually, Warsaw was stormed and captured by Suvarov. A massacre occurred in the Praga suburb.

The remains of Poland were then divided by the three powers. Austria received Lublin, Siedlce, Radom, Kracow and Kielce; Prussia took Suwalki, Bialystok, Lomza and Warsaw. Russia annexed all the rest.

Some of the veterans of the Polish army eventually resurrected Polish units in Italy where they formed three legions. Two legions were eventually lost in Santa Domingo, but the third served as the backbone for a new Polish force to reclaim their homeland.

Grand Duke Frederick Augustus of Saxony and nominal Grand Duke of Warsaw in his red coatee and yellow facings (Vogelstein, 1831)

The Grand Duchy of Warsaw

The Treaty of Tilsit, which was signed 7 and 9 July 1807, formed the Grand Duchy of Warsaw out of parts of the old Polish-Lithuanian Commonwealth. This treaty took back former Polish territories from Prussia the territories taken in the second and third partitioning of Poland to form the "Grand Duchy of Warsaw." There were three exceptions; Danzig became a free city, the district of Bialystok was given to Russia and the Notec district annexed by Prussia in the first partition was added to the Duchy.

Its new constitution was dictated by Napoleon and presented to the Poles on 22 July 1807. It was organized on the French model along very advanced lines. Equality before the law, absolute religious tolerance, and a highly developed bureaucracy were its principal features.

Instead of a free, independent Poland under a Polish sovereign it was placed under the guardianship of the King of Saxony, who Napoleon made its Duke in keeping with the old 3 May Constitution. Its formal government was placed in Warsaw with Stanislaw Malachowski as the President of its State Council and Prince Poniatowski as its Minister of War, but its administration was largely controlled by the French. In spite of being subjected to the most burdensome financial and military exigencies for the purpose of supporting Napoleon's continuous warfare, the economy of the Duchy is reputed by some sources to have prospered, while others indicate it constantly on the brink of financial ruin.

On 21 September 1807 Friedrich August, King of Saxony and the new Grand Duke of Warsaw, arrived in Warsaw to personally supervise the organization of the state. As the King of Saxony spoke Polish this was a very wise selection by Napoleon and a questionably popular decision with the Polish people. There were period jokes about the Duchy having "a Saxon King, French laws, Polish army and Prussian currency." It was under Friedrich Au-gust's direction that the Grand Duchy was organized along the French model with departments established as the second level of government throughout the country. In addition, it had a state treasury which was heavily financed by France. This was not without compensation to France.

With Napoleon's defeat in Russia Poland once again saw herself invaded by a Russian army. The vestiges of the Duchy's army withdrew to the west eventually joining the main French armies and began reforming for the 1813 campaign. Despite the successes in the spring campaign, the Duchy remained occupied by the Allies. The disastrous fall campaign sealed the Duchy's fate and though its soldiers continued to fight in the French army through 1815 the independent Polish nation was to vanish until it was restored by Pilsudski after World War I.

The Polish Army Reborn

After western Poland was liberated from Prussia in 1806 General Dombrowski was recalled from Italian service and was directed to begin establishing the new Polish army beginning on 16 November 1806. On 29 November Napoleon directed him to form eight regiments of infantry, each with two battalions. Four were to be raised in Posen and four in Kalisz. On 10 December he directd that a draft of one man per every ten households be made in the Warsaw region and that the resulting men be used to organize two more regiments. By December General Dombrowski had a force of approximately 11,000 men in Posen and an honor guard of 100

Jan Henryk Dombrowski (19th century, artist unknown)

light cavalry, which was presented to Napoleon.

The Posen Honor Guard was organized on 7 November 1806 by General Dombrowski under the commanded of Colonel J. M. Uminski, but it ceased to exist after 15 December 1806. On that day, while leaving Posen for Warsaw, Napoleon ordered Dombrowski to give the officers of this guard commissions in the newly form¬ing Polish regiments. Eventually a large number of these men ended up in the Polish General Staff and Uminski took command of a newly forming uhlan regiment.

The Warsaw Honor Guard was formed by Dombrowski from members of the "Society of the Friends of the Fatherland" some time in early December 1806. It was commanded by Wincenty Krasinski and became the nucleus of the Polish Lancer Regiment of the Imperial Guard.

Between 23 October and 3 November 1806 Napoleon held a series of audiences with General Dombrowski in Berlin and Dessau. In these audiences, Dombrowski promised Napoleon that he would raise a force of 40,000 Poles in the newly liberated Polish-Prussian districts.

On 6 November Dombrowski arrived in Posen. On the next day he organized the Polish authorities in Poznań and Kalisz, territories which were already free of Prussian forces. On 16 November he issued a decree ordering the Polish population of the Poznań, Kalisz and, later, Warsaw Departments to provide one infantry recruit from every ten households, one cavalry recruit from every 45 households, and one light infantryman (chasseur) from every estate. These latter men were usually gamekeepers. The forces to be raised were:

Department	Infantry	Cavalry	Chasseurs
Poznań Department	8,684	1,800	100
Kalisz Department	6,844	1,800	100
Warsaw Department	5,300	1,800	200

The quotas for the departments still under Prussian control were as follows:

Department	Infantry	Cavalry	Chasseurs
Bromberg & Marienwerder	800	1,800	100
Plock	5,300	1,800	100
Bialystok	8,200	2,000	150

These quotas were, however, quite unrealistic. The quota for Bromberg and Marienwerder was too small and that for Bialystok was too large. As for Warsaw, the city was liberated three weeks after Poznań and the local government was preoccupied with urgent administrative tasks. As a result the conscription was not announced until 15 December. By mid-January the Warsaw Department had raised less than 3,000 men, while Poznań and Kalisz had provided a total of about 18,000 men. The total strength of the Polish units in January 1807 was 20,528 regular soldiers and another 2,500 to 3,500 volunteers.

At first, Dombrowski planned to organize the infantry into three battalion regiments, with nine companies per battalion similar to the old Polish army. A company was to consist of:

1 Captain	1 Fourrier
1 Lieutenant	8 Corporals
1 Sous-lieutenant	2 Drummers
1 Sergeant major	106 Privates
4 Sergeants	125 Total

The battalion staff contained one lieutenant colonel and one adjutant. On 1 December 1806, Dombrowski decided that two battalion regiments were more practical in wartime and organized accordingly. This would have set the organization of a regiment at 63 officers and 2,210 men. According to Colonel J. Weyssenhoff, at the beginning of 1807 the infantry of Dombrowski's went into Pomerania organized in six company battalions. Each company had a strength of 150 men.

As for the regular cavalry, before the reorganization of 26 January 1807, a regiment theoretically numbered 40 officers and 772 men organized into four squadrons.

The artillery is not well documented at this time, and details are quite scarce. It is known that three companies were formed by the time of Friedland and two of those batteries, under Captains Gugenmus and Kobylanski, took part in the battle.

The order of 2 January 1807 directed that the first battalions of the 1st through 8th Regiments should be organized in Bromberg, raised to a strength of 800 men each, and organized into a division to serve under General Dombrowski. The second battalions were to join them as soon as they were raised to a strength of 800 men each.

On 26 January 1807 the Governing Committee ratified the official structure with three legions. Each legion was to have a staff, four infantry regiments, one light cavalry regiment with six squadrons and a battalion of artillery and engineers. The number of companies in an infantry battalion remained at nine, but the number of soldiers per company was fixed at 140.

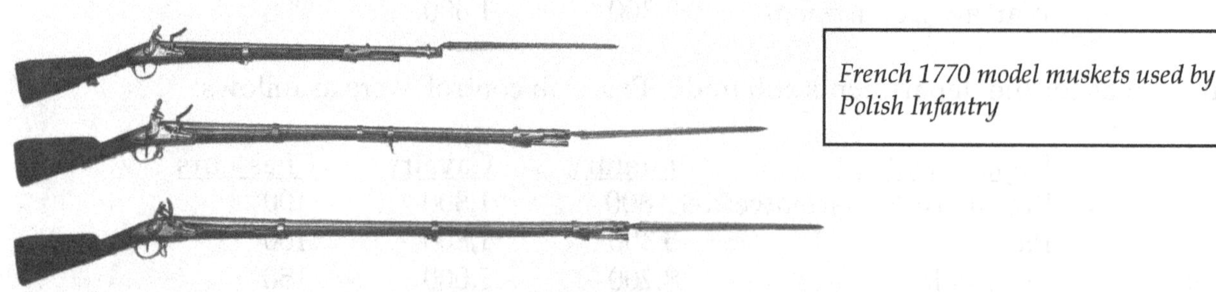

French 1770 model muskets used by Polish Infantry

In addition, on 26 January 1807 it was directed that the legions be renumbered.

Before 26 January		After 26 January
1st Legion	became	3rd Legion
1st Infantry		9th Infantry
2nd Infantry		10th Infantry
3rd Infantry		11th Infantry
4th Infantry		12th Infantry
1st Chasseurs		5th Chasseurs
2nd Uhlans		6th Uhlans
1st Artillery Battalion		3rd Artillery Battalion
3rd Legion		1st Legion
9th Infantry		1st Infantry
10th Infantry		2nd Infantry
11th Infantry		3rd Infantry
12th Infantry		4th Infantry
5th Chasseurs		1st Chasseurs
6th Uhlans		2nd Uhlans
3rd Artillery Battalion		1st Artillery Battalion

The actual reorganization occurred on 1 March 1807 and the Polish Army was organized into three legions. The 1st Legion (Division) under Poniatowski and the 3rd Legion (Division) under Dombrowski were described above, while the 2nd Leigon (Division) under Zayonczek contained the 5th, 6th, 7th and 8th Infantry Regiments, the 3rd Uhlan Regiment, the 4th Chasseur à Cheval Regiment and the 2nd Artillery Battalion.

The Poznań (Dombrowski) Legion

The legion staff was organized on 20 November 1806 and consisted of:

Legion Commander:	Général de division J. H. Dombrowski
Chief of staff:	Colonel M. Hauke
Chefs de brigade:	Général de brigade A. Kosinski
Général de brigade:	W. Axamitowski
Adjutants-General:	Lt. Colonel P. Tremo
	Lt. Colonel C. Pakosz
	Lt. Colonel J. Weyssenhoff
Adjuncts:	Lt. Colonel C. Godebski
	Lt. Colonel A. Cedrowski
	Sous-lieutenant J. Hauke.

Three days later, General Kosinski was sent to Bromberg to supervise the organization of the army there. His brigade was taken over by Général de brigade Stanislaw Fiszer. Fiszer, in his turn, as sent to Kalisz with a similar task on 29 December 1806.

The legion absorbed conscripts from he Poznań and Bromberg Departments. They were to be organized into 12 provisional battalions (eight from Poznań, four from Bromberg) and later converted into eight regular battalions. The surplus was equally divided into four regimental depots. In practice, the recurits came almost exclusively from the Poznań Department. Bromberg was under threat by Prussian forces, so it kept its recruits at home and organized them into units there. The majority of the latter were grouped into the 11th Regiment in Swiec and commanded by Colonel Dzerer. The regiment, numbering six companies (600 men), accompanied by Dombrowski, went into Pomerania and in March 1807 was converted into the divisional depot of the Poznań Legion.

The 1st Infantry Regiment was organized in Gniezno (Gnessen), the 2nd Regiment was organized at Rogzno, the 3rd at Poznań, and the 4th at Koscian. The auxiliary regimental depots were established at Leszno, Zduny, Pawlowice and Rawicz. The cavalry units were formed in Koscian, Wschowa, and Bromberg.

As was the old way of raising troops, the commanders of the infantry regiments were not profes¬sional soldiers, but wealthy landowners, who made great financial contributions to the organization of their units. The actual field command was, therefore, in the hands of the regimental majors, with the exception of the 2nd Regiment, whose acting colonel was a veteran. The majors were veterans of the Polish Legions in Italy.

Regiment	Colonel	Major
1st	A. Sulkowski	S. Galubowski
2nd	T. Lecki (honorary) A. Downarowicz (acting)	P.Tremo
3rd	S. Mielzynski	J.Sierawski
4th	S. Poninski	A.Darewski

The organization of the infantry regiments in the Poznań Department went very smoothly due to the presence of a large number of Polish conscripts in the local Prussian units, which the Prussians had not been able to mobilize in time for the 1806 campaign. These men, along with the numerous deserters from the other Prussian Regiments, reputedly over 3,000 men by 20 December 1806, formed the first battalions of the four infantry regiments. They began their training during the second half of December. The second battalions were generally fleshed out from new conscripts. Apart from these units, Dombrowski was organizing a company of light infantry under Captain Golaszewski, which was designated as a reconnaissance force.

In contrast, the organization of the cavalry went quite slowly due to the lack of horses. Most of the horses had already been taken by the mass levy. By the end of December 1806, a two company squadron, 180 riders, under Colonel J. N. Uminski, was ready at Koscian. Another group of 150 men under Colonel F. Garczynski, was organized in Wschowa.

In Bromberg, Major D. Dziewanowski gathered 80 troopers from the dispersed Prussian Towarczy Uhlan Regiment. The unit grew slowly and by the end of December it had 125 men.

On 3 January 1807 Dziewanowski was nominated as colonel and commander of a light cavalry regiment, which became the 2nd (later the 6th) Uhlan Regiment. In a show of defiance, Dziewanowski's uhlans decided to retain their Prussian uniforms, which were patterned after the customary Polish cavalry dress, despite the fact that if they were captured they faced certain execution. They did, however, add horsehair plumes to their czapkas and changed the black Prussian eagles to white Polish eagles.

The first company of foot artillery was completed in Poznań on 29 December 1806. It seems that it was not ready to go to the field, because when Dombrowski moved into Pommerania he was accompanied by a company of French artillery and a battery of six Polish guns, sent to his division from Warsaw, which were manned by improvised crews.

The Kalisz (Zayonczek) Legion

Prior to mid-December the organization of this legion was supervised by the Poznan Legion staff through its local representative General P. Skorzewski. Afterward, Général de division J. Zayonczek, recently transferred from the command of the Légion du Nord, became its commanding officer. General H. Wolodkowicz acted as his chief of staff. Apart from these two men, the provisional and incomplete staff of the Kalisz Legion included Généraux de brigade S. Fiszer, serving as infantry commander, and Généraux de brigade J. Niemojewski and I. Krasinski, who jointly supervised the cavalry.

The legion's infantry units, after 6 March 1807, were located as follows:

Regiment	Commander	Garrison
5th	Colonel I. Zioelinski	Kalisz
6th	Colonel M. Sobolewski	Kolo
7th	Colonel W. Skorzewski	Radomsk
8th	Colonel C. Godebski	Lutomierz

The chasseur company, commanded by General J. Stokowski, was located in Kalisz.

By the end of December 1806 the Kalisz Legion had already organized 3,200 men in the first battalions of its four assigned infantry regiments. Its cavalry consisted of noble levy units scattered over the department that had very inconsistent structures. On 6 April 1807 elite companies, grenadiers and voltigeurs, were established in the Kaliz Legion infantry regiments.

The 3rd Uhlan Regiment went into the field in January 1807, fighting in East Prussia with Zayonczek's observation corps until July 1807. The 4th Chasseur Regiment, organized from the Krakow irregular cavalry units, joined the 3rd Uhlans in June 1807. The 3rd Uhlans were commanded by Colonel J. Laczynski and the 4th Chasseurs were commanded by Colonel W.Mecinski.

The artillery of the Kalisz Legion was organized in December 1806 in the captured fortress of Czestochowa. At first it had only 40 men, but by January 1807 it had risen to a strength of 160. After the issuance of the 26 January 1807 organizational decree, which assigned a three company artillery battalion to each legion, Lt. Colonel A. Gorski received 460 men from the 2/8th Infantry Regiment. From these men he formed three artillery companies, a sapper company and a train company. The artillery battalion received a further 50 men from the 6th Infantry Regiment in the Fall of 1807.

The Warsaw (Poniatowski) Legion

This legion was initially organized by Generals Onufry, Dombrowski and I. Gielgud, but they were replaced on 26 January 1807 by Prince J. Poniatowski. Its incomplete staff consisted of Généraux de brigade L. Kamieniecki and S. Woyczynski, and Colonels J. Rautenstrauch and F. Paszkowski.

The legion was recruited from the Warsaw and Plock Departments. Its infantry consisted of:

Regiment	Commander	Garrison
9th	Colonel M. Grabowski	Warsaw
10th	Colonel S. Potocki	Warsaw
11th	Colonel E. Zoltowski	Lenczyca
12th	Colonel F. Potocki	Plock

The legion also had a light infantry company. The organization of the 10th and 12th Regiments went very quickly, as opposed to the 9th, which did not take shape until mid-January 1807. The 11th Regiment was even slower and was not truly a regiment until the end of March 1807. It was finally brought to regimental strength by the incorporation of the light infantry companies from Poznań, Kalisz and Warsaw. These companies were formed into a weak, 400 man battalion that was finally absorbed into the 11th Regiment on 31 March 1807.

The first battalions of the Warsaw infantry regiments, 3,200 men, were more or less ready for combat by the end of January 1807.

Napoleon's order of 28 January 1807 directed the six battalions to be united into a legion under Poniatowski's command. One battalion was raised in Lenczyca and Lowicz and four were raised in Warsaw. This legion served as the garrison of Warsaw and Praga. Starting 2 February 1807 these battalions began departing for the front, leaving their regimental depots and administration in Warsaw. The 9th and 11th Regiments fought in Zayonczek's observation corps after mid-March 1807. The 12th Regiment participated in the blockade of Graudnez from May to July 1807, while the 10th Regiment fought with the Lemarrois division, and later joined the siege of Graudenz.

The 1st Chasseur is discussed in the following section on the Noble Levy. The 2nd Uhlans were organized in Plock in 1806 as the 2nd Light Cavalry Regiment under the command of W. Kwas¬niewski. In May 1807 the regiment joined the Lemarrois division and fought against the Cossacks on 9 May 1807 at Zatory.

The Legion's artillery started forming in January 1807 with seven guns supplied by the French. By June 1807 Poniatowski had two artillery companies. The 1st Company was under Captain I. Bielicki and the 2nd was under Captain I. Hauschild.

The Mass/Noble Levy of November 1806-January 1807

The first call for the traditional Noble Levy occurred on 11 and 13 November 1806 when the reactivated palatinate councils of Lenczyca and Sieradz called for one fully equipped rider from each estate and every 40 town households. A total of 3,000 men were anticipated to be organized in this conscription.

On 2 December 1806 the palatine (voivode) of Gniesno, J. Radziminski, issued a manifesto calling the nobility from the left bank of the Vistula to gather in Lowicz by 25 December for the purpose of forming a Noble Levy. In his organizational decree, which accompanied the manifesto, General Dombrowski nominated "rotmistrz" (cavalry leaders - a term incorporated into Polish from the German "rittmeister") for the nine palatinates, giving them the rank of major generals and specifying the structure of the palatinate cavalry units. These units were called "choragiew" (literally "banner" or "standard"). A "chora¬giew" was to consist of:

1 Porucznik ("Lieutenant", but in fact a captain)
1 Podporucznik ("Sous-lieutenant", in fact a lieutenant)
2 Chorazy ("standard bearers", actually sous-lieutenants)
5 Namiestnik (Brigadiers)
1 Namiestnik pisarz (Fourrier or company clerk)
60 Rycerz and Pocztowy ("knights & squires")

A "choragiew" was supposed to have its own military band or, at least, one or two trumpeters. Each rider was to be armed with a saber and a pistol or carbine. If firearms were not available they were to have three meter long lances.

On 1 January 1807 over 6,000 riders appeared at Lowicz. Four hundred were chosen to form the 1st National Cavalry Regiment under the command of Colonel J. M. Dombrowski, the general's son. It had three squadrons, each of 120 men. After Colonel Dombrowski was severely wounded at Dirschau (Tczew) the command passed to Colonel K. Przebendowski. The regiment was later renamed the 1st Chasseur à Cheval Regiment.

Immediately after the New Year Review, about half of the Noble Levy simply went home. The 2,840 cavalry remaining included:

143 – from the Lenczyca Palatinate
137 – Gnieszno
314 – Rawa
858 – Sieradz
206 – Wielun
560 – Kalisz
182 – Kujawy
206 – Inowroclaw
234 – Mazovia

These units went, for the most part, with General Dombrowski into Pommerania, while the others joined the Grande Armée to protect their winter quarters. Among the latter, 500 men were present with Lasalle's division during the battle of Eylau. The Poznań levy joined Dombrowski's division during its operations in Pommerania.

The Noble Levy was dissolved by the Governing Committee on 20 January 1807, but the majority of its men decided to stay with the army, gradually joining its cavalry regiments.

The Dombrowski Division - 2 January - 27 May 1807

On 2 January 1807 Napoleon ordered the formation of a Polish division under the command of General Dombrowski. Its 1st Brigade, under General W. Axamitowski, was formed from the first battalions of the Poznań Legion and concentrated around Gnieszno. The 2nd Brigade, under General S. Fiszer, contained the first battalions of the Kalisz Legion and was concentrated around Konin. Its decreed strength was 6,400 men, but it probably contained 6,600 men, since it was accompanied by Captain Golaszewski's light infantry company and some loose volunteer groups.

The 3,000 cavalry assigned to the division consisted of the 1st Chasseurs, under Colonel Garczynski (150 men), one squadron of the 2nd Uhlans under Colonel Uminski (150 men), one squadron of Dziewanowski's uhlans (125 men), the 1st National Cavalry Regiment (400 men in 3 squadrons) and most of the Noble Levy units from Lowicz. They were commanded by General Axamitowski. The division was accompanied by a French artillery company under Captain Charelot. It had four cannons and two howitzers. The division departed for Bromberg on 7 January and arrived by 21 January.

On 23 January Maréchal Berthier ordered the division broken into two parts. The Kalisz battalions went to Graudenz to join its blockade force under Bernadotte. All the cavalry and the Poznań battalions were sent to Danzig. General Kosinski took over command of the irregular cavalry. The regular forces went under General Axamitowski. The infantry was organized into two provisional regiments. The 1/1st and 1/2nd Regiments were under Colonel J. Sierawski and the 1/3rd and 1/4th Regiments were under Colonel J. Wasilewski. In addition, the division passed into the X Corps of Maréchal Lefebvre.

On 27 January the Poles encountered the retreating Prussians. Though militarily successful, their vanguard was surprised by about 400 Prussians at Dirschau and suffered substantial losses. Colonel Uminski was taken prisoner in this action. Colonel Dziewanowski assumed command of the 2nd Uhlans and incorporated his Towarczy into it. Captain Golaszewski was killed and his light infantry were absorbed into Sierawski's regiment.

A pause occurred in the offensive between 29 January and 12 February. during that time, the second battalions of the Poznań Legion joined their regiments and the second battalions of the Kalisz Legion were temporarily assigned to Dombrowski's command, which held the line of the Vistula between Thorn and Neustadt. In addition, there were over 3,000 cavalry and six guns with 66 gunners (plus the French artillery company of Captain Charelot). On 7 February, General Kosinski took command of the vanguard and General M. Sokolnicki assumed command of the irregular cavalry.

On 14 February, the Poles took Mewe (Gniew) and contacted Ménard's division, which included the Légion du Nord. This division passed under General Dombrowski's command. On 20 February, Sokolinicki and his irregular cavalry, plus two infantry companies stormed and took Stolpen (Slupsk), cutting off the Prussian lines of communication between Danzig and Kolberg.

On 23 February the main body of Dombrowski's division, assisted by a force of Baden infantry and the Légion du Nord, stormed and took Dirschau (Tczew). This assault was the baptism of fire for the Poznań troops. General Dombrowski was wounded and command passed to General Kosinski. Thirteen Poles and Captain Charelot, of the French artillery company, accompanying the division, were awarded crosses of the Légion d'Honneur for their parts int his battle.

By the end of the month, Sokolnicki reorganized the irregular cavalry, abandoning the loose "choragiew" structure and forming three regiments. Each regiment had two squadrons, formed with two companies of 80 men. On 3 March the entire cavalry of the division was sent to the right bank of the Vistula under the command of General Zayonczek. However, only the 1st National Cavalry Regiment and a few loose units of the Noble Levy, attached to various infantry groups operating outside the main body of the division, joined Zayonczek as a cavalry group under General Niemojewski. The Sokolnicki group, consisting of the 1st Chasseurs and the 2nd Uhlans remained with the Polish division.

The second battalions of the Kalisz Legion, temporarily attached to the Dombrowski Division, now joined their first battalions, under Zayonczek. Accompanying them were the irregular cavalry units from the Kalisz Department, i.e. from the Kalisz, Sieradz and Wielun Palatinates. It is possible that these are the "loose units" of Noble Levy refered to earlier.

During the first week of March, in preparation for the siege of Gdansk, Lefebvre allocated various Polish units to the differ¬ent divisions of his corps. The 1/2nd, 1/2/3rd and 1/2/4th Infantry joined the 1st Division under General Kosinski. The 2/2nd Regiment went to the 4th Division. The 1st Regiment was detached and sent to the blockade of Kolberg. The Légion du Nord remained with Ménard's 1st Division. The remaining cavalry joined the French cavalry division under the Saxon General von Polenz. This temporarily disbanded Dombrowski's division, but these assignments kept changing during the course of the siege.

The siege of Gdansk (Danzig) lasted from 10 March to 27 May. A total of 9,000 Poles participated, of which 1,600 were killed and 400 were wounded.

The Légion du Nord was at the siege of Danzig in early March 1807. At this time Napoleon also merged the 1st and 2nd Legions and reorganizing them into two regiments. On 6 March Zayonczek proposed Colonels M. Radziwill (who commanded the Legion in his absence) and M. Sobolewski as commanders of these two regiments. Poniatowski and Davout approved the recommendations and they occurred some time later. These units were enti¬tled the 5th Chasseurs and 6th Fusiliers respectively.

Between February 1807 and February 1808, the fate of the now combined legions was still officially undecided. Napoleon wanted to transfer them into Polish service, which resulted in Zayonczek's inclusion of it in his corps, but the Duchy was unable to pay for it, so Davout delayed the transfer as long as possible. After the capitulation of Gdansk, the Legion garrisoned the Weichselmünde fortress where its strength was down to about 2,000 men. In September 1807 the Legion marched to Poznań and was placed under the command of Dombrowski. Finally, at Gnieszno on 13 February 1808, the Legion took an oath of fidelity to Friedrich August. On 7 March it moved to Warsaw, where it was disbanded and its soldiers distributed between the 5th and 6th Infantry Regiments. All but one of the French officers in the Legion, nearly 2/3rds of all the Legion's officers, elected to return to French service.

As to the original 5th Infantry Regiment, on 9 March 1808, it had only 51 officers and 1,315 men. The actual incorporation of the Légion du Nord did not occur until 1 April 1808.

Poles in Lemarois' Division

On 28 January 1807, Napoleon sent two battalions of the Warsaw Legion to join Lemarois' division. In addition, once the Warsaw Legion uhlans were formed and operational, they also joined Lemarois. The division operated southeast of Zayonczek's divi¬sion in much the same role.

The End of the 1807 Campaign

When Gdansk fell on 27 May the Dombrowski division was reassigned to the newly organized corps under Maréchal Mortier. Its 1st Infantry Regiment had been detached and was blockading Kolberg. Though Zayonczek's was unable to join the Grande Armée for Friedland, Dombrowski's forces did.

Dombrowski's infantry and artillery stood on the left flank of Mortier's corps while the 1st Polish Chasseurs and the 2nd Polish Uhlans stood with the French cavalry on the corps' front. Though suffering from artillery fire, the infantry did not engage in the battle. However, the cavalry attacked the Russian Guard several times, earning Napoleon's praise and several decorations.

After Friedland, Napoleon concentrated the Polish forces at hand into a single corps under Dombrowski and dispatched it to Grodno. They were to remain there during the talks at Tilsit.

After the 1807 Campaign

On 22 July 1807 Napoleon gave the Grand Duchy of Warsaw its constitution in a ceremony in Dresden. The Governing Committee was replaced by a State Council and the Council of Ministers. Prince Poniatowski was made Minister of War and the constitution established the Duchy's army at 30,000 men. In fact, by mid-July the strength of the army was to increased to about 31,800 men, of whom 9,000 were in hospital. This force contained a huge percentage of officers who had no positions within the structure of the newly forming army. In order to employ them a corps of veterans was formed under the command of Poniatowski.

In addition, there were problems with the discrepancy between the army structure (39,321 men) set forth in the organizational decree of 26 January 1807 and the constitutional limit of 30,000 men. The Légion du Nord had been officially incorporated into the army in February 1808 and the demands of the new campaign had brought more men into the army. In order to resolve this problem the army was kept in a permanent state of under strength. That is, many cadres were formed and kept at full strength, but the numbers of soldiers was kept at about half the normal ratio of soldiers to cadre. As a result, on 1 October 1808 the 5th Infantry lacked 886 men, the 6th - 773 men, and the 8th - 731 men.

After July the cavalry was reorganized and brought into conformance with the January organizational decree. The 1st National Cavalry Regiment, 1st Chasseur Regiment and the 2nd, 3rd and 4th Cavalry were brought up to full strength by absorbing irregular units. The 5th and 6th Regiments (formerly the 1st and 2nd) also absorbed some irregulars.

From 22 July 1807 to the beginning of the 1809 campaign the nominal strength of the army of the Grand Duchy of Warsaw was nominally set at 30,000 men. However, by the end of the 1809 campaign it was to reach a strength of 59,500 men and was still growing.

The army consisted of the three divisions. Each division consisted of four two battalion infantry regiments, two light cavalry regiments and three artillery batteries organized into a single battalion. Their organization, strength and commanders on 27 November 1807 were:

Division or Legion	Regiment	Regimental Commander	Strength
1	1st Artillery	Colonel Doberski	354
2	2nd Artillery	Lt. Colonel A. Gorski	597
3	3rd Artillery	Lt. Colonel J. Hurtig	389
1	1st Infantry	Colonel M. Grabowski	1,518
	2nd Infantry	Colonel S. Potocki	1,746
	3rd Infantry	Colonel E.Zoltowski	696
	4th Infantry	Colonel F. Potocki	1,466
2	5th Infantry	I. Zielinski	1,088
	6th Infantry	Colonel M. Sobolewski	1,087
	7th Infantry	Colonel P. Skorzewski	1,558
	8th Infantry	Colonel C. Godebski	1,552
3	9th Infantry	Colonel A. Sulkowski	1,339
	10th Infantry	Colonel A. Downarowicz	1,606
	11th Infantry	Colonel S. Mielzynski	1,477
	12th Infantry	Colonel S. Poninski	1,316
	Independent Force	Prince M. Radziwill	1,361
1	1st Cavalry	Colonel J. M. Dombrowski	725
	2nd Cavalry	Colonel W.Kwasniewski	571
2	3rd Cavalry	Colonel K. Laczynski	857
	4th Cavalry	Colonel W. Mecinski	823
3	5th Cavalry	Colonel K. Turno	943
	6th Cavalry	Colonel D. Dziewanowski	996
	Independent Force	Lt. Colonel Wiener	116

The King of Saxony signed a convention on 10 May 1808 which directed that a force of 8,000 men be drawn from the army of the Grand Duchy of Warsaw for service in the French army. The 4th, 7th and 9th Regiments were chosen. They were organized with two battalions each. Each battalion was to have nine companies, including one of grenadiers and one of voltigeurs. In addition, the infantry was supplimented by the addition of a 140 man artillery company and a 190 man sapper company. Napoleon took this force into French service on much the same basis as the Hessians served the British in the American Revolution. They were promptly sent to Spain where they engaged in considerable combat. The actual strengths of these regiments were as follows:

Date	Unit	Officers	Soldiers	Total
August 7	4th Infantry	65	2,494	2,559
July 19	7th Infantry	65	2,465	2,530
August 2	9th Infantry	64	2,351	2,415
August 1	Artillery Co.	4	145	149
July 2	Sapper Co.	4	186	190

The organization of the army of the Grand Duchy became more formal in its structure after a period of peace and its overall structure settled down into the following form:

1st Division:

Commander:	General J. Poniatowski	
Division Major:	General L. Bieganski	
Chief of Staff:	Colonel F. Paszkowski	
Brigade Commanders:	General W. Axamitowski	
	General S. Woyczynski	
Adjutant of the Divisional Commander:	Colonel J. Rautenstrauch	
à la suite:	General L. Kamieniecki	
1st Regiment:	Colonel K. Malachowski	Warsaw
2nd Regiment:	Colonel S. Potocki	Modlin
3rd Regiment:	Colonel E. Zoltowski	Warsaw
4th Regiment:	Colonel F. Potocki	Plock
1st Chasseurs	Colonel M. Dombrowski	Piaseczno
(Acting commander was	Major K. Przebendowski)	
2nd Uhlans:	Colonel T. Tyszkiewicz	Warsaw
Artillery & Sappers	Lt. Colonel J. Redel	Warsaw

2nd Division:

Commander:	General J. Zayonczek	
Division Major:	General P. Skorzewski	
Chief of Staff:	Colonel K. Kossecki	
Brigade Commanders:	General J. Niemojewski	
	General I. Krasinski	
Adjutant of the Divisional Commander:	Colonel A. Radziminski	
5th Infantry:	Colonel M. Radziwill	Czestochowa
6th Infantry:	Colonel J. Sierawski	Czestochowa and Kalisz
7th Infantry:	Colonel M. Sobolewski	Kalisz
8th Infantry:	Colonel C. Godebski	Konin
3rd Uhlans:	Colonel J. Laczynski	Sieradz
4th Chasseurs:	Colonel W. Mecinski	Warta
Artillery & Sappers:	Lt. Colonel A.Gorski	Kalisz

3rd Division:

Commander:	General J. H. Dombrowski	
Division Major:	Colonel M. Hauke	
Chief of Staff:	Colonel C. Pakosz	
Brigade Commanders:	General M. Sokolnicki	
	General M. Grabowski	
Adjutant of the Divisional Commander:	Lt. Colonel A. Cedrowski	
9th Infantry	Colonel A. Sulkowski	Leszno
10th Infantry	Colonel A. Downarowicz	Lenczyca
11th Infantry	Colonel S. Mielzynski	Danzig
12th Infantry	Colonel J. Weyssenhoff	Rawicz
5th Chasseurs	Colonel K. Turno	Rawa
6th Uhlans	Colonel D. Dziewanowski	Radziejow
Artillery & Sappers	Lt. Colonel J. Hurtig	Posen

The staff of the army consisted of:

3 Général de division
13 Général de brigade
35 Adjutants
1 Adjutant-commandant
3 Inspecteurs aux revues
6 Sous-inspecteurs
3 Commissaire de guerre
3 Paymasters

It was in August 1808 that the 4th, 7th and 9th Infantry Regiments, one regiment from each division, plus an artillery and sapper company were sent to Spain. At the same time the 10th Regiment joined the 11th in Danzig. The 4th Chasseurs à Cheval went to Stettin on 21 February 1809 where they formed part of the garrison. Twelve companies of the 5th Regiment were also detached to the garrison of Glogau. This so stripped the organization that the 3rd Division, now lacking three infantry regiments, was placed on a reduced standing and General Dombrowski went on leave until April 1809.

From mid-July 1807 to August 1808 the actual general command of the Poles was in the hands of Maréchal Davout. He did not initially trust Poniatowski, but after a very candid interview in late August he changed his opinion and, when he left Warsaw in early September 1808, he turned command over to Poniatowski. On 21 March 1809 Poniatowski was nominated Commander-in-Chief by the King of Saxony, who was also the Grand Duke of Warsaw. Despite that, he still was, theoretically, subordinated to Maréchal Bernadotte.

During this period, the only major development in the army was the organization of static artillery companies organized in the fortresses of Serock, Thorn, Praga, and Modlin. In addition, a horse artillery company with four officers, 58 gunners, four 6pdrs and two howitzers was organized by Captain W. Potocki. A second horse battery was formed in January 1809, bringing the total strength of this unit to 7 officers and 112 men serving 8 guns.

On 1 January 1809 the army of the Grand Duchy was as follows:

Regiment	Location	Strength	Colonel
1st Regiment	Praga	1,707	K. Malachowski
2nd Regiment	Warsaw	1,707	S. Potocki
3rd Regiment	Warsaw	1,707	E. Zoltowski
4th Regiment	Spain	1,808	F. Potocki
5th Regiment	Kustrin/Glogau	1,933	M. Radziwill
6th Regiment	Serock/Pultusk	1,635	J. Sierawski
7th Regiment	Spain	1,817	M. Sobolewski
8th Regiment	Modlin	1,539	C. Godebski
9th Regiment	Spain	1,945	A. Sulkowski
10th Regiment	Danzig	1,500	A. Downarowicz
11th Regiment	Danzig	1,649	S. Mielzynski
12th Regiment	Thorn	1,178	J. Weyssenhoff

Regiment	Location	Strength	Colonel
1st Chasseurs	Gora/Czersk	745	K. Przebendowski
2nd Uhlans	Warsaw	880	T. Tyszkiewicz
3rd Uhlans	Piaseczno	719	J. Laczynski
4th Chasseurs	Stettin	625	W. Mecinski
5th Chasseurs	On Niemen R.	596	K. Turno
6th Uhlans	Blonie	691	D. Dziewanowski

Artillery			
1st Foot Bn.	Warsaw	409	J. Redel
2nd Foot Bn.	Serock/ Czestochowa	137	A. Gorski
3rd Foot Bn.	Praga/Modlin/Thorn	266	J. Hurtig
1st Horse Bn.	Warsaw	119	W. Potocki
1st Sapper Co.	Warsaw	79	J. Lubiewski
2nd Sapper Co.	Praga/Modlin	103	J. Sternberg
3rd Sapper Co.	Czestochowa/Serock	91	W. Dombrowski
Train Battalion		402	
Pontooneer/ Artisan Co.	Thorn	67	

The 2/5th Infantry (585 men) served as the garrison of the Czestochowa fortress.

Because of the wide distribution of Polish forces, from Spain to the Grand Duchy, the divisional organization had become obsolete. In an effort to organize functional tactical formations, Poniatowski proposed changes to the divisional structure. As a temporary measure the infantry of the 1st, 2nd and 3rd Regiments was brigaded under Général de brigade L. Kamieniecki and the 1st Chasseurs, 2nd Uhlans and 5th Chasseurs were brigaded under Général de brigade A. Rozniecki. In addition to implementing this temporary restructuring, Poniatowski made pr-

Prince Jozef Poniatowski (based on Jozef Grassi, 1810)

posals to Napoleon, who decided to reorganize the Polish forces into three new divisions. Each division was to consist of four line infantry regiments, two cavalry regiments and two light infantry battalions.

Napoleon determined that the infantry regiments should be increased to a three battalion strength. Each company was raised from 95 to 140 men each.
Although the theoretical strength of a company at this time was already at 140 men, the economic policies of maintaining units at the lower strength level of 95 had prevented this number from being reached.

In addition, the cavalry regiments were increased to 1,047 men, growing from three to four squadrons each. The battalions were reorganized and the nine company structure reduced to six, as set forth in Napoleon's famous Decree of 18 February 1808, which addressed the organization of the French infantry. A draft in the spring of 1809 brought the company strengths up from 95 to 140 men each.

The results of this effort are not clear. Indications are that before the start of the 1809 campaign, this reorganization to six companies was completed only for the 10th and 11th Infantry Regiments. The third battalions of these regiments were sent to Thorn to replace the 12th Regiment, which was sent to Warsaw. However, in a letter dated 8 April Poniatowski informed Marshal Davout that the increase in company strength to 140 men had been completed. Before the outbreak of the 1809 campaign only the 1st, 2nd and 3rd Infantry Regiments had their companies raised to the new strength, which is why their two battalions show a strength of 1,707 men each.

Polish Lancers in Spain (Juliusz Kossak)

It should be noted that the 4th, 7th and 9th Infantry Regiments, then in Spain, had already raised their company strengths to 140 men, but retained the two battalion organization. Indeed, they retained the 9 (later 8) company organization up to May 1812.

As with the infantry, the cavalry had not had time to implement these changes and no fourth squadrons existed by the commencement of the 1809 campaign.

Immediately before the 1809 campaign the army of the Grand Duchy, less various detachments, stood at 18,634 men. Line regiments, garrison troops and their assigned artillery numbered 74 staff officers, 486 regimental officers, 14,857 rank and file and 246 guns. In addition there was a 2,000 man Saxon corps.

On 19 April, at Raszyn, about 14,000 Poles and Saxons, with 39 guns, faced the Austrian VII Corps, which had 33,000 men and 90 guns. After a pitched battle the Poles were forced to withdraw and temporarily abandon Warsaw.

In May the Poles began an offensive campaign taking the war into Austrian territories and seizing the fortresses of Sandomierz, Zamosc, and Krakow. One unusual unit was raised during that period was the Guides of Poniatowski. This was a personal bodyguard raised by the order of 8 May 1809. All of the non-commissioned officers and troopers were volunteer noblemen serving without pay. The company was very short lived and was disbanded on 27 November 1809. Most of its troopers were then commissioned as sous-lieutenants in the various line regiments.

In the course of the 1809 campaign Poniatowski liberated western Galicia, taken by the Austrians in 1795, and advanced as far as Lvov and Tarnopol. After the peace treaty of Schönbrunn (14 October 1809) western Galicia and the Zamosc district of eastern Galicia were incorporated into the Grand Duchy.

In order to improve his situation, Poniatowski began to recruit more men. By the end of the 1809 campaign he had raised a total of six new infantry regiments (13th through 18th) and ten new cavalry regiments (7th through 16th). These new regiments were organized both in the Grand Duchy of Warsaw and in the newly liberated regions of Galicia. The latter were financed by local landowners who often became their colonels. These Galician regiments formed the "Galician-French Army" and had a separate numbering until October 1809. The infantry was numbered 1 - 4 and the cavalry 1 - 7. The regiments formed in the Grand Duchy of Warsaw received temporary numbers that were later changed. The new Grand Duchy regiments were the 14th and 15th Infantry Regiments, the 7th and 9th Uhlans, and the 10th Hussars. The Galician-French regiments became the 13th, 16th, 17th and 18th Infantry Regiments, the 8th, 11th, 12th, 15th, and 16th Uhlans, the 13th Hussars, and the 14th Cuirassiers in October.

The new regiments were to be organized on the French model, with four line battalions of six companies each and a fifth depot battalion with four companies. In fact, only a few of these regiments actually reached this organizational strength. On 30 March 1810 the number of battalions was reduced to three. By the end of 1809 there were a total of 18 infantry regiments, 16 cavalry regimetns, 3 battalions of foot artillery, a horse artillery battalion with two companies, and a company of engineers.

The strength of the Polish army on 14 November 1809 was:

Regiment	Commanding Officer	Effectives	Location
1st Regiment	Colonel K. Malachowski	2,690	Praga
2nd Regiment	Colonel S. Potocki	3,030	Warsaw
3rd Regiment	Colonel E. Zoltowski	2,647	Modlin
4th Regiment	Colonel M. Wierzbinski	2,241	Spain
5th Regiment	Colonel M. Radziwill	2,104	Kustrin
6th Regiment	Colonel J. Sierawski	2,673	Serock
7th Regiment	Colonel S. Jakubowski	1,905	Spain
8th Regiment	Colonel K. Stuart	2,302	Warsaw
9th Regiment	Colonel A. Sulkowski	2,050	Spain
10th Regiment	Colonel B. Wierbzicki	1,996	Danzig
11th Regiment	Colonel S. Mielzynski	2,145	Danzig
12th Regiment	Colonel J. Weyssenhoff	2,614	Krakow
13th Regiment	Colonel A. Szneyder	3,435	Zamosc
14th Regiment	Colonel E. Siemianowski	2,852	Plock
15th Regiment	Colonel K. Miaskowski	3,422	Krakow
16th Regiment[1]	Colonel J. Keszycki	2,338	
17th Regiment	Colonel K. Czartoryski	2,561	Warsaw/Rawa
18th Regiment	Colonel J. Hornowski	1,985	Plock

[1]The 16th Regiment, shown above, was disbanded and its soldiers were incorporated into the other regiments. The 17th and 18th Regiments were then redesignated as the 16th and 17th Regiments, respectively. On 14 March 1810 Colonel J. Keszycki took command of the 13th Infantry Regiment.

Regiment	Commanding Officer	Effectives	Location
1st Chasseurs	Colonel K. Przebendowski	937	Warsaw
2nd Uhlans	Colonel T. Tyszkiewicz	1,163	Warsaw
3rd Uhlans	Colonel J. Laczynski	1,015	Krakow
4th Chasseurs	Colonel W. Kwasniowski	687	Westphalia
5th Chasseurs	Colonel K.Turno	1,097	Rawa
6th Uhlans	Colonel D. Dziewanowski	1,009	Posen
7th Uhlans	Colonel A. Zawadzki	840	Kalisz
8th Uhlans	Colonel K. Rozwadowski	954	Krakow
9th Uhlans	Colonel F. Przyszychowsk	936	Konin
10th Hussars	Colonel J. Uminski	803	Pultusk
11th Uhlans	Colonel A. Potocki	899	Zolkiew
12th Uhlans	Colonel G. Rzyszczewski	943	Biala
13th Hussars	Colonel J. Tolinski	1,048	Siedlce
14th Cuirassiers	Colonel S. Malachowski	610	Konskie
15th Uhlans	Colonel A. Trzecieski	916	Ostrolenka
16th Uhlans	Colonel M. Tarnowski	661	Lublin

On 7 December 1809 King Friedrich August changed the official state of the army to 60,000 men, which was, in fact, a reduction in the actual strength as it stood at that time. Two further decrees were issued that furthered this process, the first being on 10 March 1810 and the second on 30 March 1810. The new organization of the army was:

General Staff

8	Généraux de division, including
1	Commander-in-Chief
4	Military District Commanders
3	Inspector Generals
15	Généraux de brigade
2	Command Adjutants (with the Grand Duke)
1	Command Adjutant, Sous-Chef of the General Staff
4	Command Adjutants, Chiefs of the Divisional Staffs
9	Chefs d'escadron, Adjutant Generals
24	Captains, Adjutant Generals
4	Lieutenant-Colonels - assistants
8	Captains - assistants
12	Lieutenants - assistants
17	Infantry Regiments, 3 battalions each
15	Cavalry Regiments, 4 squadrons each
1	Cuirassier Regiment, 2 squadrons

The Decree of 20 March 1810 reorganized the Grand Duchy of Warsaw into four military districts. They were as follows:

District	Commander
I Warsaw	Général de division J. Zayonczek
II Posen	Général de division J. H. Dombrowski
III Lublin	Général de division L. Kamieniecki
IV Radom	Général de division M. Sokolnicki

In September 1810, the Polish Army raised a third battalion for the 13th through 17th Regiments. On 1 October 1810 the strength of the army was:

Regiment	Commanding Officer	Effectives
1st Regiment	Colonel K. Malachowski	2,388
2nd Regiment	Colonel J. Krukowiecki	2,322
3rd Regiment	Colonel E. Zoltowski	2,267
4th Regiment	Colonel T. Wolinski	2,211
5th Regiment	Colonel M. Radziwill	2,496
6th Regiment	Colonel J. Sierawski	2,275
7th Regiment	Major W. Borowski	1,832
8th Regiment	Colonel K. Stuart	2,357
9th Regiment	Colonel M. Cichocki	1,990
10th Regiment	Colonel M. Wierzbicki	2,403
11th Regiment	Colonel A. Chlebowski	2,410
12th Regiment	Colonel J. Weyssenhoff	2,379
13th Regiment	Colonel J. Keszycki	2,228
14th Regiment	Colonel E. Siemianowski	2,163
15th Regiment	Colonel K. Miaskowski	2,398
16th Regiment	Colonel K. Czartoryski	2,361
17th Regiment	Colonel J. Hornowski	2,076
1st Chasseurs	Colonel K. Przebendowski	799
2nd Uhlans	Colonel T. Tyszkiewicz	813
3rd Uhlans	Colonel J. Laczynski	786
4th Chasseurs	Colonel S. Dulfus	777
5th Chasseurs	Colonel Z. Kurnatowski	839
6th Uhlans	Colonel M. Pagowski	795
7th Uhlans	Colonel A. Zawadzki	770
8th Uhlans	Colonel K. Rozwadowski	818
9th Uhlans	Colonel F. Przyszychowski	891
10th Hussars	Colonel J. Uminski	843
11th Uhlans	Colonel A. Potocki	722
12th Uhlans	Colonel G. Rzyszczewski	787
13th Hussars	Colonel J. Tolinski	782
14th Cuirassiers	Colonel S. Malachowski	814
15th Uhlans	Colonel A. Trzecieski	915
16th Uhlans	Colonel M. Tarnowski	777

On 6 April 1811 Poniatowski proposed organizing two gun regimental batteries to Napoleon. This was approved on 17 May. The actual organization took place after the issuance of the Royal Decree of 25 May 1811.

On 17 May 1811 Napoleon ordered the alteration of the regimental strength from 18 to 19 companies. The 19th Company was to be 200 men strong and serve as a depot and reserve. These depots were grouped together in the fortresses of Thorn and Modlin, where they served as a garrison as well as depots. In case of war the strength of these companies was to be raised to 300-400 men.

In June 1811 the army of the Grand Duchy consisted of 17 infantry regiments, three of which had been serving since 1808 in Spain. From among the remaining 14 regiments, another three were stationed in Danzig. Each of these 14 regiments was composed of three battalions (18 companies of 136 men each) and a staff of 39 men, giving the army a theoretical strength of 34,818 infantry. The actual strength was probably around 32,000. The three regiments in Spain, who had a theoretical strength of 7,590 men in 54 companies and their staffs, had been reduced by combat, etc., to a strength of about 5,000 men. There were also 16 cavalry regiments, all of whom, except for the cuirassiers, had four squadrons. This gave the Poles a total strength of 12,764 men organized in 62 squadrons and regimental staffs. Several of the regiments, most notably the 10th Hussars, only had three squadrons, and their total strengths were probably 500 short of the prescribed strength.

In addition, there was a two-squadron regiment of horse artillery with a theoretical total of 691 men, a foot regiment with a staff, 12 field companies and four static companies (theoretically 2,685 men), a sapper/miner battalion (756 men) and an artisan company (123 men). The infantry regiments in Spain had with them an artillery company of about 140 men and a sapper company, also of about 140 men.

This gave the Duchy a total strength of 60,000 men (52,00 in the Duchy and Danzig and 8,000 in Spain), but efforts were already underway that would raise this to 75,000 within the Duchy alone.

In 1811 each infantry regiment raised a depot battalion that had four companies and the cavalry raised depot squadrons, each having two companies. All of the artillery's depot needs were attended to by a single depot battalion, which had six companies

The 1st, 4th, and 5th Cavalry Regiments were chasseurs à cheval, the 10th and 13th were hussars and the 14th was a cuirassier regiment. The other regiments, numbering up to the 16th Regiment, were uhlan or lancer regiments.

The regimental commanders of the army of the Grand Duchy of Warsaw in June 1811 were:

Regiment	Commander	Regiment	Commander
1st Regiment	Col. K.Malachowski	1st Chasseurs	Col.K.Przebendowski
2nd Regiment	Col. J.Krukowiecki	2nd Uhlans	Col. T.Tyszkiewicz
3rd Regiment	Col. E.Zoltowski	3rd Uhlans	Col. B.Laczynski
4th Regiment	Col. T.Wolinski	4th Chasseurs	Col. S.Dulfus
5th Regiment	Col. M.Radziwill	5th Chasseurs	Col. Z.Kurnatowski
6th Regiment	Col. J.Sierawski	6th Uhlans	Col. M.Pagowski
7th Regiment	Col. P.Tremo	7th Uhlans	Col. Z.Zawadzki
8th Regiment	Col. K.Stuart	8th Uhlans	Col. D.Radziwill
9th Regiment	Col. M.Cichocki	9th Uhlans	Col. F.Przyszychowski
10th Regiment	Col. B.Wierzbicki	10th Hussars	Col. J.N.Uminski
11th Regiment	Col. A.Chlebowski	11th Uhlans	Col. A.Potocki
12th Regiment	Col. J.Weyssenhoff	12th Uhlans	Col. G.Rzyszczewski
13th Regiment	Col. F.Zymirski	13th Hussars	Col. J.Tolinski
14th Regiment	Col. E.Siemianowski	14th Cuirassiers	Col. S.Malachowski
15th Regiment	Col. K.Miaskowski	15th Uhlans	Col. A.Trzecieski
16th Regiment	Col. K.Czartoryski	16th Uhlans	Col. M.Tarnowski
17th Regiment	Col. J.Hornowski		
Foot Artillery	Col. A.Gorski		
Horse Artillery	Col. W.Potocki		
Sapper Battalion	Commandant M.Kubicki		

By November 1811 the infantry regiments were ordered to raise a fourth battalion.

The internal situation in the Grand Duchy was not good. A letter from Davout to Napoleon, dated 26 November 1811, states that the state of commerce was bad and that property holders were not able to make the required contributions. He states that the pay of the army was eight to nine months in arrears and that the military finances were destitute. There were no funds to pay for the repairs and improvements of the fortifications at Modlin, Thorn and Zamosc and "if it were not for the love of thier country and the general enthusiasm for the Emperor and his cause, the entire machine would have siezed up long ago".

On 1 January 1812 Napoleon took into French pay the 5th, 10th, and 11th Infantry Regiments, the 9th Uhlans and the artillery company stationed in Danzig and Kustrin. These three infantry regiments were to be brought up to full strength for the existing three battalions and a fourth battalion was to be raised. In the fall of 1811, the 5th lacked 200 men, the 10th lacked 389 men, and the 11th lacked 233 men from their theoretical full strength.

On 25 February 1812 a convention was signed by France and the Grand Duchy that stated that the three infantry regiments in Danzig were to bring their companies up to 140 men each and that a 25th or depot company was to be raised. This was intended to bring the regimental strengths to over 3,500 men.

This convention also directed that the 11 infantry regiments in the Duchy were to bring the strength of their companies up to 160 men, bringing their strength to 3,119 men per regiment. Similarly, the 15 cavalry regiments were to bring the company strengths up to 120 troopers, giving them a new field strength of 983 men per regiment. The modification to the cavalry regiments probably did not include the 14th Cuirassier Regiment.

By 1812 the army of the Grand Duchy consisted of 75,000 men and 165 cannon. It provided the forces that formed the V Corps of the Grande Armée during the 1812 campaign. This force was joined by all the Poles serving in the French army at that time, including the Vistula Legion and the 4th, 7th, and 9th Polish Regiments, though they served in other corps.

During the invasion of Russia Napoleon liberated portions of ancient Lithuania which had been part of Poland in the not too distant past. There was sufficient pro-Polish sentiment there to cause Napoleon to form a provincial government there on 1 July 1812 and to make it part of the Grand Duchy.

The Decree of 1 July raised the Vilna National Guard (2 battalions), which was slowly fleshed out with men drawn from the recently captured territories. To police the countryside, Napoleon raised a gendarmerie in the Vilna, Grodno, Minsk, and Bialystock Districts. This force consisted of a single company of 107 men posted in each county. There were four districts with a total of 33 counties (*powiaty*), so the strength eventually reached six squadrons.

In addition, Lithuania was the organizing grounds for the 18th to 22nd Infantry Regiments and the 17th to 21st Uhlan Regiments. On 13 July Napoleon named the colonels for these regiments:

Regiment	Commanding Officer
18th Infantry	Colonel A. Chodkiewicz
19th Infantry	Colonel K. Tyzenhauz
20th Infantry	Colonel A. Biszping
21st Infantry	Colonel K. Przezdziecki- Later Col. A. Gielgud.
22nd Infantry	Colonel S. Czapski
17th Uhlans	Colonel M. Tyszkiewicz
18th Uhlans	Colonel J. Wawrzecki
19th Uhlans	Colonel K. Rajecki
20th Uhlans	Colonel X. Obuchowicz
21st Uhlans	Colonel J. Lubanski

In August Colonel K. Przezdziecki was named colonel of the 18th Uhlan Regiment, leaving the 21st Infantry Regiment. In addition, a Lithuanian hussar regiment was being organized under Colonel Abramowicz as was a Franco-Polish Regiment under Prince A. Sapieha. However, neither regiment appears to have materialized. A Lithuanian Tartar squadron was being organized by Mustapha Murza Achmatowicz and assigned to the 3rd Regiment of Guard Lancers.

The 21st Uhlans were organized by the end of 1812 by merging Colonel I.Moniuszko's Chasseur à Cheval Regiment with the uhlans being formed by Colonel J. Lubanski.

The Army of Lithuania, as it was called, was placed under the direct command of Napoleon and not made part of the army of the Grand Duchy's field forces. Initially, it did not receive its orders from the Polish general staff.

Because the territory had been ravaged by the retreating Russians, it was impossible for the Lithuanian army to be raised without active French financial support. Napoleon provided finances, but not sufficiently to do the job completely. In order to fully provide the finances for the fledgling army the regimental commanders were selected from the most eminent and wealthy families of the country. They were expected to provide a great deal of the funds necessary for the organization of their regiments. Money was not the only problem. There were insufficient weapons, uniforms were hard to acquire, and horses were quite scarce.

Approximately 40,000 muskets were provided by the French, but the lack of organization and the shortness of time prevented a complete distribution of these arms. In addition, the recruitment and organization went very slowly. By the end of July the only standing unit was the 1/18th Infantry Regiment in Vilna. It was formed from volunteers and 354 Polish prisoners of war. A conscription was finally declared on 5 August for the infantry and on 15 August for the cavalry. Up to then, the actual number of volunteers was only about 2,400 men. For unknown reasons, many of the Lithuanian recruits were sent to the French 129th Line Regiment and the Illyrian Regiment instead of joining their national units. In addition, volunteers joined the Imperial Guard's 1st Chevauléger-lancer (Polish) Regiment and the 3rd (Lithuanian) Guard Chevalegers.

On 24 August Napoleon named General Hogendorp as President of the Commission of the Lithuanian Government and charged him with completing the organization of the Lithuanian army. Hogen¬dorp promised Napoleon that he would have the army completed by the beginning of January, but the outcome of the campaign pre¬vented this from happening.

On 30 September the strengths of the Lithuanian infantry regiments were as follows:

18th	- 1,650 men
19th	- 929
20th	- 1,014
21st	- 1,197
22nd	- 1,133

In the beginning of August it was decided that an additional six battalions, all of light infantry, would be raised. The commanding officers and their cadres were quickly selected.

Unit	Commanding Officer
1st Light Battalion	J. Kossakowski
2nd Light Battalion	Rokicki
3rd Light Battalion	K. Plater
4th Light Battalion	Kurczewski
5th Light Battalion	Obuchowicz
6th Light Battalion	Lochowski

These battalions were formed from foresters and other outdoorsmen who had experience with weapons. They were to act as scouts and to control the incursions of Cossacks, apprehend vagabonds, and act as a police force. They were organized from volunteers and the expense of their outfitting was to be absorbed by the proprietors of the forests in which they had worked prior to their volunteering.

In September it was decided to incorporate these six battalions into the regular army. In November the government of Lithuania resolved to form these troops into two regiments of light infantry, each with three battalions but, recruitment was very slow. Only one regiment was actually formed and it had only two battalions. It was commanded by Colonel Kossakowski. On 4 November it had a total of 624 men.

The first two battalions were raised in the Minsk district. Eventually a third battalion was raised near Vilna, but it did not join the regiment. It remained as an independent body for the rest of its existence. There is some indication that a fourth light battalion was raised, but very little documentation was found to provide details of its service.

A total of 15,000 Lithuanians were brought into active service by the French administration. These men and their regiments were distributed throughout the province and with the retreat of the French army from Moscow they quickly found themselves in combat. Some units participated in the battles during the passage of the Berezina and along with approximately 6,000 others, withdrew with the French into Germany. The others simply vanished.

The 18th, 20th and 21st Infantry Regiments, and the 18th and 20th Uhlan Regiments arrived in Warsaw relatively intact, as did the cadre of the 22nd Infantry. In addition the embryo of Tyzenhauz's Lithuania Horse Artillery Regiment, the debris of the Tartar Squadron, a squadron of the Moniuszko Chasseurs à Cheval, the 4th Light Infantry Battalion, detachments of the Horse Gendarmes, detachments from the National Guard and the debris of the 3e Regiment de Chevau-légers de la Garde also arrived in Warsaw.

The 17th and 19th Uhlan Regiments retired to Königsberg with part of the 19th Infantry Regiment. The total Lithuanian force that escaped was 6,000 infantry and 2,000 cavalry.

In order to defend the Grand Duchy after Napoleon's defeat in Russia the government announced on 20 December 1812 a mass/noble levy under Poniatowski, who would act as its "regimentarz" or commander-in-chief. This effort was a dismal failure that pro¬duced only a few hundred horsemen that were incorporated into the existing regiments.

The next effort was the execution of the conscription of 25,000 men decreed by the Duchy's government in November 1812. In addition, an extraordinary draft of one horsemen per 50 rural households and one light infantryman for every 20 rural households was declared. The results fell below the goal, but were better than the previous attempt to raise troops. A further attempt occurred on 25 January 1813, when Friedrich Augustus decreed a draft for the National Guard of one soldier for every 20 rural and urban households, and ten riders from every county (subdivisions of the districts). The steady encroachment of the Russian armies into Poland reduced this draft to well below the anticpated 13,000 men. There were further problems of increasing desertions among the conscripts.

Poniatowski began forming third battalions of the infantry regiments from the National Guard and incorporated the mounted guardsmen into the cavalry regiments, despite the semi-legality of these moves. By mid-January the Duchy's army reached 12,000 men, 1,105 veterans in hospital, and 4,000 conscripts on their way to the depots.

The 1813 Campaign

The Decree of 18 January 1813 issued by the King of Saxony, directed the reorganization of the Polish Army. A total of 1,145,557 florins were initially issued for its reorganization. Eventually a total of 6,499,919 florins were spent. By 25 March 1813 the 4th, 5th, 7th, 9th, 10th and 11th Infantry Regiments and the 9th Uhlan Regiment were in French service as a form of French military subsidy.

As the 1813 spring campaign developed the situation in the Grand Duchy of Warsaw was largely in the hands of Schwarzenberg's Austrian Corps and it was, though nominally still an ally, was steadily defecting from the French ranks. Poniatowski began withdrawing southwards across Poland as Schwarzenberg's treacherous maneuvers exposed him to the approaching Russians. His 8,000[2] man army was joined by about 6,000 light cavalry from the four south-

[2]The army totaled 8,000 men after detaching various garrisons.

western departments, but due to the lack of proper supervisions, the force suffered a very high desertion rate. Those that remained were incorporated into the infantry or used to form the 1st Krakus Regiment under Major K. Rzuchowski.

While Poniatowski's forces in Krakow were growing back to 15,000 men, a second group under Zoltowski moved out of Malopolska into Saxony with Reynier's VII Corps. Zoltowski commanded consisted of the 2nd, 14th and 1/15th Infantry Regiments, 2nd Uhlans and 4th Chasseurs, a company of gendarmes, a veteran company and the depots of the 5th, 6th, 7th, 8th, 10th, 14th and 15th Cavalry Regiments. This force was reorganized by the Imperial Decree of 18 April into a Polish corps under the command of General Dombrowski.

The third force of Poles reforming at this time were the old 5th, 10th and 11th Infantry Regiments (233 officers and 3,438 men), the 6th and 16th Foot Batteries and a horse artillery company (10 officers and 301 men), a sapper company (3 officers and 68 men) and the 9th Uhlan Regiment (30 officers and 413 men). This force was in Danzig forming part of the city's garrison.

The survivors of the 28th (Polish) Division of IX Corps (the 4th, 7th and 9th Infantry Regiments) had gathered in Poznań. Between 16 January and 12 February they were joined by the remains of the Vistula Legion and about 200 cavalry, mostly of the 2nd Uhlan Regiment. They were organized into a division under Generals Girard and Bronikowski.

The 4th Infantry Regiment was eventually sent to Wittenberg to form part of the garrison. The 7th and 9th were initially assigned to the garrison of Spandau. When the fortress capitulated to the Prussians they were sent to Erfurt. The Imperial Decree of 18 June merged the 4th, 7th and 9th Infantry Regiments into a new 4th Polish Infantry Regiment with two battalions of about 450 men each.

The Vistula Legion's survivors returned from Russia and had about 200 men in Poznań in early 1813. The 4th Vistula Legion Regiment arrived shortly later with 22 officers and about 800 men. In February the 1st, 2nd and 3rd Vistula Legion Regiments moved to Spandau and on 25 May they totaled 78 officers and 365 men. The 4th Regiment moved to Wittenberg where it was besieged. There was a slow, but steady trickle of men into the legion and the end of May the four regiments had grown to 133 officers and 1,190 men.

The 18th, 20th and 21st (Lithuanian) Infantry Regiments withdrew from Russia and in January 1813 found themselves in Modlin. Here they took part in the year long siege. The 19th (Lithuanian) Infantry was annihilated near Vilna. Its survivors withdrew into the Grand Duchy and Modlin. In June, they were merged into the 21st (Lithuania) Regiment. The 22nd (Lithuanian) Infantry Regiment was badly beaten up at Koidanovo on 15 November. Its survivors withdrew to Modlin. The Chasseur à pied Regiment was also mauled at Koidanovo. It took further beatings at Berezina and Vilna. Eventually it joined the 17th Uhlan Regiment and withdrew into Germany with them.

In Poniatowski's corps the artillery was reformed and consisted of a six gun horse battery, six foot companies, and a train battalion. In addition a company of sappers, a company of military equipage and a company of gendarmes were reorganized. In Dombrowski's corps a second horse battery was raised by the Decree of 18 April 1813.

Beyond the forces already mentioned, the Imperial Decree of 18 April also reorganized Dombrowski's corps. This force had the 2nd and 14th Infantry Regiments and the 2nd and 4th Uhlan Regiments. The infantry regiments had two six company battalions each and the cavalry, reformed in the French pattern had four squadrons per regiment.

In Poniatowski's corps, six cavalry regiments (1st, 3rd, 6th, 8th, 13th, and 16th Regiments were organized into two cavalry divisions. The cuirassiers and the Krakus formed an advanced guard cavalry brigade. On 29 June the 1st and 5th Chasseurs were used to reform the 1st Chasseur à Cheval Regiment. The 3rd Uhlans were reformed from the 3rd and 11th Uhlans, the 6th was reformed from the 6th Uhlans and the 18th Lithuanian Uhlans, the 8th was reformed with the 8th and 12th Uhlans, the 13th Hussars was reformed with the 10th and 13th Hussars and their depot. The 16th Uhlans were reformed from the 16th Uhlans and the 20th and 21st Lithuanian Uhlans. The 14th Cuirassiers were reformed with only two squadrons totaling 180 men. During this process, the cuirassiers absorbed their depot. The 17th (Lithuanian) Uhlans absorbed the 19th Uhlans on 20 April 1813 and joined the XIII (Davout) Corps in Hamburg. All of the other regiments were reorganized with the old four squadron strength and their internal structure was identical to that of the French chasseurs à cheval.

On 12 March 1813 the forces Poniatowski organized in Krakow were designated by Napoleon as the VIII Corps of the Grande Armée. They departed Krakow during the second week of May 1813, marching through Bohemia to Saxony, where they arrived in mid-June.

The Horse Gendarmerie, at its height, had six squadrons. A squadron of the Minsk Gendarmes had fought under General Doumerc and Stachov. The Lithuanian Gendarmes had fought at Vilna on 9 December. About 60 gendarmes were incorporated into the 1st Guard Chevauléger-lancier (Polish) Regiment and the rest went to the French 7th and 8th Lancer Regiments.

On 23 May 1813 the reorganized army of the Grand Duchy of Warsaw stood as follows:

Regiment	Regimental Commander	Off	Men	Regimental Regiment	Commander	Off	Men
1st Infantry	Col. Piotrowski 59			1st Adv. Guard*[3]	Maj. Suchecki	22	317
2nd Infantry	Maj. Szymanowski	?		2nd Adv Guard	Maj. Nosarzewski	20	32
3rd Infantry	Maj. Hoffman 46			3rd Adv Guard	Maj. Korytowski	18	431
4th Infantry				15th Uhlans	Maj. Dwernicki		
5th Infantry				1st Chasseurs	Cde Hryniewicz	28	312
6th Infantry	Maj. Kossecki 44	774		2nd Uhlans	Col. Rzodkiewicz		
7th Infantry				3rd Uhlans	Maj. Rzuchowski		
8th Infantry	Col. Stuart	55	636	4th Chasseurs	Col. Kurnatowski		
9th Infantry	Col. Cichocki			5th Chasseurs	Col. Kurnatowski	15	233
10th Infantry				6th Uhlans	Col. Suchorzewski	22	405
11th Infantry				7th Uhlans	Col. Zawadzki		
12th Infantry	Col. Wierzbinski	61	847	8th Uhlans	Col. Potocki	22	474
13th Infantry	Maj. Obertynski 25	525		9th Uhlans	Col. Oborski		
14th Infantry	Maj. Winnicki ?	848		11th Uhlans	CdB Hryniewicz	28	
15th Infantry	Col. Straszewski	37	619	Train Battalion			
16th Infantry	Maj. Nosarzewski	59	784	12th Uhlans	Cde. Zabielski		
17th Infantry	Col. Koszarski			13th Hussars	Maj. Gutakowski		
18th Infantry	Col. Chodkiewicz			14th Cuirassiers	Maj. Skarzynski		
19th Infantry	Maj. Pawlowski			16th Uhlans	Col. Tarnowski		
20th Infantry	Col. Biszping			17th Uhlans			
21st Infantry	Col. Gielgud			18th Uhlans	Col. Przezdziecki		
22nd Infantry	Col. Czapski			19th Uhlans			
Foot Art. Regt	Col. Redel			20th Uhlans	Col. Obuchowicz		
Pontooneer Coy	Capt. Bujalski			Horse Art. Regt.	Col. Hurtig		
Sapper Bn	CdB Rakowiecki			Sup. Art. Bn	CdB Weysflog		

[3]Also known as the Krakus Regiment.

In June 1813, in Zittau, the forces of the Grand Duchy were reorganized into two infantry divisions containing a total of five infantry regiments (1st, 8th, 12th, 15th and 16th). The depots of the 3rd, 6th and 13th Infantry were absorbed into the other regiments in an effort to bring them up to full strength.

Dombrowski's forces had joined the Grande Armée in February. The Imperial Decree of 18 April set the strength of this force at two cavalry regiments (3,000 men), two infantry regiments, each with two battalions, and a horse battery. On 25 April this force consisted of 211 officers, 2,813 men and 1,492 horses. The corps' cavalry consisted of the 2nd Uhlans and the 4th Uhlans, which had been converted from the earlier chasseur regiment. The rest of the corps consisted of the 2nd and 14th Infantry Regiments and a horse battery with six guns under Chef d'escadron J. Szweryn.

The Imperial Decree of 7 June directed that it, and the 4th, 7th, and 9th Infantry Regiments and the Vistula Legion, were to be merged into the VIII Corps, but this decree was countermanded shorty later because of fears of mass desertions that might result from Austrian actions.

On 18 June the four Vistula Legion Regiments were merged into one regiment, known as the Vistula Regiment.

On 27 June 1813 Napoleon issued a decree organizing the Polish VIII Corps. In this decree he stated that Poniatowski was to be rendered the same honors as the French marshals. Earlier, on 24 June, Napoleon sent the proposed reorganization of the VIII Corps to Poniatowski. Poniatowski opposed the complete disbanding of the 7th and 9th Infantry Regiments and the organization of separate depots for his and Dombrowski's corps. He also pointed out the impossibility of fitting the cuirassiers and the Krakus into the proposed cavalry scheme. When Napoleon issued the Decree of 27 June Napoleon had chosen only to accept Poniatowski's comments on the cavalry.

The Vistula Legion in Spain (Bellange)

The 27 June Decree established the Krakus or "régiments d'avant-garde" with four squadrons of 220 men each. Initially, the 1st Krakus consisted of the departmental riders who marched with Poniatowski from Warsaw to Krakow. The 2nd and 3rd Krakus were formed from those recruited during the army's stay in Krakow. This was the source of the regiments' name and their dress. Shortly later all three regiments were combined into a single Krakus Regiment, which was organized with a theoretical strength four squadrons, each squadron having 220 men. It was then brigaded with the 14th Polish Cuirassier Regiment.

The provisions of this decree relating to the incorporation of Dombrowski's forces into the VIII Corps were never executed. Dombrowski's forces were renamed an observation corps and posted near Wittenberg under the general command of Maréchal Oudinot. They were short of horses and were unable to mount all of their troopers. The 2nd Uhlans had 1,125 men and 880 horses, while the 4th Uhlans had 1,032 men and only 713 horses on 14 July. Portions of Dombrowski's forces were later engaged at Hagelsberg, where Girard was defeated and driven back to Wittenberg. At that time the 4th Polish Infantry Regiment was incorporated into Dombrowski's corps.

As a result, of the change in Dombrowski's corps only the Vistula Regiment joined the VIII Corps. On 6 July 1813, the VIII Corps stood as follows:

VIII Corps: Général Poniatowski
- 26th Division: Général de division Kamieniecki
  - 1st Brigade: Général de brigade Sierawski
    - 1/1st Polish Infantry Regiment (30/528)[4]
    - 2/1st Polish Infantry Regiment (24/512)
    - 1/16th Polish Infantry Regiment (31/538)
    - 2/16th Polish Infantry Regiment (24/528)
    - 1/2/Vistula Regiment (detached to Wittenberg)
  - 2nd Brigade: Général de brigade Malachowski
    - 1/8th Polish Infantry Regiment (29/549)
    - 2/8th Polish Infantry Regiment (24/530)
    - 1/15th Polish Infantry Regiment (31/542)
    - 2/15th Polish Infantry Regiment (24/523)
  - Artillery: Orzinski
    - 5th Polish Foot Artillery (7/132)
    - 7th Polish Foot Artillery (6/129)
    - 18th Polish Foot Artillery (6/133)
- 27th Division:
  - 2nd Brigade: Général de brigade Grabowski
    - 1/2/4th Polish Infantry Regiment (detached to Wittenberg)
    - 1/12th Polish Infantry Regiment (32/560)
    - 2/12th Polish Infantry Regiment (24/549)
  - Artillery: Chef de bataillon Weisflog
    - 10th Polish Foot Artillery (6/136)
    - Det. 14th Polish Foot Artillery (3/61)
- 27th Light Cavalry Brigade: Général de brigade Uminski
    - 1/14th Cuirassier Regiment (8/147)
    - 2/14th Cuirassier Regiment (1/83)
    - 1/Krakus Regiment (17/208)
    - 2/Krakus Regiment (8/195)
    - 3/Krakus Regiment (9/199)
    - 4/Krakus Regiment (4/114)
- Artillery Park: Colonel Bontemps
    - 11th Polish Foot Artillery (6/129)
    - Det. 14th Polish Foot Artillery (3/62)
    - 1st Polish Sapper Company (5/135)
  - Polish Military Equipage (9/98)
  - Polish Gendarmes (4/90)

[4] Numbers are officers and men.

At the same time Napoleon organized the IV Cavalry Corps from the large force of Polish cavalry. The strength and organization of the IV corps, as of 6 July 1813, was as follows:

IV Corps: This organization for the IV Corps was prepared 10 days prior to Poniatowski's arrival in Zittau and, as a result, does not reflect the final organization of the corps. Krukowiecki's brigade remained with Dombrowski and Uminski was to command the advanced guard cavalry brigade in the VIII Corps.

7th Light Cavarly Division: Général de division Sokolnicki
- Brigade: Général de brigade Krukowiecki (Detached to I Corps)
  - 2nd Polish Uhlan Regiment
  - 4th Polish Chasseur à Cheval Regiment
- Brigade: Général de brigadeTolinski
  - 1/3rd Polish Uhlan Regiment (19/208/276)[5]
  - 2/3rd Polish Uhlan Regiment (8/195/232)
  - 3/3rd Polish Uhlan Regiment (9/199/237)
  - 4/3rd Polish Uhlan Regiment (4/144/112)
  - 1/13th Polish Hussar Regiment (19/164/221)
  - 2/13th Polish Hussar Regiment (7/102/109)
  - 3/13th Polish Hussar Regiment (8/105/120)
  - 4/13th Polish Hussar Regiment (8/127/138)

8th Light Cavalry Division:Général de division Sulkowski
- Brigade: Général de brigade Uminski
  - 1/1st Polish Chasseur à Cheval Regiment (20/181/262)
  - 2/1st Polish Chasseur à Cheval Regiment (7/119/140)
  - 3/1st Polish Chasseur à Cheval Regiment (8/141/163)
  - 4/1st Polish Chasseur à Cheval Regiment (11/98/106)
  - 1/6th Polish Uhlan Regiment (20/182/272)
  - 2/6th Polish Uhlan Regiment (8/141/166)
  - 3/6th Polish Uhlan Regiment (9/148/168)
  - 4/6th Polish Uhlan Regiment (11/126/87)
- Brigade: Général de brigade Weissenhoff
  - 1/8th Polish Uhlan Regiment (20/231/298)
  - 2/8th Polish Uhlan Regiment (11/167/202)
  - 3/8th Polish Uhlan Regiment (11/170/203)
  - 4/8th Polish Uhlan Regiment (15/164/161)
  - 1/16th Polish Uhlan Regiment (19/193/262)
  - 2/16th Polish Uhlan Regiment (11/130/159)
  - 3/16th Polish Uhlan Regiment (11/118/143)
  - 4/16th Polish Uhlan Regiment (12/129/162)
- Artillery:
  - 1st Polish Horse Battery (8/161)

[5] Numbers are officers, men and horses.

On 29 August Napoleon directed that those Austrian prisoners of war known to be Polish were to be sent to the four Polish depot companies which were in Dresden. Each company was to be brought to a total strength of 500 men each. They were to be commanded by Polish majors. One more company was formed for the 4th Polish Infantry Regiment, one for the Vistula Legion and two for the regiments of General Dombrowski whose depots were stationed in Düsseldorf. A total of 4,000 men were organized into these eight companies. The last four were commanded by Major J. Regulski.

7th Regiment Chevau-Legers (Jan Chelminski)

The Poles were severely handled at Leipzig. Most of the Polish survivors of the battle at Leipzig were captured when a bridge over the Elster was destroyed prematurely. In an attempt to swim the river Prince Poniatowski was drowned. He had received his marshal's baton only three days before.

Shortly before the battle of Leipzig, on 2 October 1813, Napoleon ordered the raising of a Polish Battalion of the Imperial Guard. The unit was raised before 2 October and it can be found on official orders of battle, but its actual strength is much in question. Admission to the battalion required 10 years of service, participation in one campaign and the soldier must have been decorated. The commanding officer of the battalion was Lt. Colonel S. Kurcjusz, who had served in the 1809 and 1812 campaigns. The battalion was organized and equipped in Dresden where it was barracked with the Saxon Grenadier Garde.

The soldiers selected for this battalion were all at least 23 years old with two years of service in the other Polish regiments. They were hand picked. The battalion was attached to the Old Guard Division.

It appears to have disintegrated and by 18 December 1813 only 15 officers and 80 soldiers remained. The officers of the regiment, with three exceptions, and all the men went to Paris and served in the 3e Eclaireurs de la Garde.

After Leipzig

With the death of Prince Poniatowski the Army of the Grand Duchy began to fall apart and individual soldiers wandered back to Poland or followed the retreating French westwards. The VIII Corps had ceased to exist, only about 500 men escaping Leipzig. The four cavalry regiments of the IV Corps and Krukowiecki's Brigade, though weakened, retreated westward with little trouble. The Krakus were in an acceptable condition, but the 14th Cuirassiers were reduced to a few score men. When Dresden capitulated and the Allies reneged on their agreement, the 7th Chevaulégers[6], 13th Hussars and 16th Polish Uhlans passed into captivity.

Dombrowski's tiny corps withdrew to the west without much difficulty either. The Polish general officers then began a bout of serious infighting and politicking, most notably General Krukowiecki. In addition, the simple Polish soldiers began to desert because they were moving further and further from their homeland. Napoleon intervened personally and restored order, but General Sulkowski, though innocent, found himself compromised and obliged to retired to Poland. Shortly thereafter all the remaining Poles were placed in a single, united force under the command of Dombrowski.

On 20 November 1813 the remains of the Polish cavalry were drawn together in Sedan. They totaled about 221 officers, 1,761 men, and 1,851 horses, not including the Gardes d'honneur.

Initially, Napoleon entertained thoughts of completely disbanding the infantry and organizing four uhlan regiments and two regiments of Polish Cossacks.

The Imperial Decree dated 18 December 1813, reorganized them into the Polish Army Corps. This corps consisted of two regiments of lancers, each with four 125 man companies, one regiment of Krakus with six squadrons of 250 men, a single infantry regiment known as the Vistula Regiment (organized with two battalions, each battalion having six 140 man companies), a horse artillery battery, four foot artillery batteries and a sapper company.

All excess officers were organized into four companies of Gardes d'honneur. The French encouraged those officers to remain with the French army, which was terribly short of trained offi¬cers. To sweeten the incentive, they were offered a promotion of one rank. However, very few accepted the offer. On 1 January 1814 the Polish Corps in Sedan had:

	Officers	Soldiers	Total	Troop Horses
1st Uhlans	25	505	530	399
2nd Uhlans	25	505	530	336
Eclaireurs (Krakus)	78	997	1,075	360
Horse Artillery	5	120	125	47
Vistula Regiment	47	807	854	13
4 Foot Batteries	20	500	520	-
Sapper Company	4	64	68	-

The eclaireurs were short 576 men and the Vistula Regiment was short 854 men. The corps was short a total of 1,471 horses. In the uhlan regiments 196 horses were unfit for service.

[6]The 7th Chevaulégers was the Polish lancers who had earlier been part of the Vistula Legion and had been absorbed into the French line cavarly, though remaining entirely Polish in their make-up.

In the beginning of February the remnants of the Polish Guard Battalion were incorporated into a 3rd Eclaireur Regiment of the Guard. With the abdication, all of the Poles still in French service found themselves released and returned to Poland.

On 20 November the following Polish cavalry forces were in Sedan:

	Officers	Men	Horses
2nd Uhlan Regiment	45	384	392
3rd Uhlan Regiment	32	221	230
4th Uhlan Regiment	26	203	229
8th Uhlan Regiment	48	369	402
16th Uhlan Regiment	4	27	10
1st Chasseur Regiment	28	191	188
Krakus Regiment	21	257	288
13th Hussar Regiment	17	113	112
1st Gardes d'honneur	93	-	139
2nd Gardes d'honneur	60	-	97
Total	374	1,765	2,087

ORGANIZATION

Internal Organization of The Polish Army in 1807

The legions or divisions formed in 1807 consisted of a divisional staff, four infantry regiments, two cavalry regiments (either uhlans or chasseurs) and a battalion of artillery and sappers. The term "legion" was to remain in use until the end of 1807 and was later replaced by the term "division". The legion or divisional staff consisted of:

1 Général de division
1 Major of the Legion (Général de brigade or Colonel)
2 Brigade commanders (Généraux de brigade)
1 Chief of staff (Général de brigade or Colonel)
2 Engineering Officers
1 Commissaire de la guerre
1 Adjunct
1 Paymaster
1 Inspector of Reviews
3 Under Inspectors of Reviews
3 Adjutants to the Legion Commander
1 Personal Adjutant to the Legion Commander
1 Adjutant to the Major of the Legion
(only if he was a Général de brigade)
2 Adjutants for the brigade commanders.

The staff of the infantry regiments consisted of:

1 Colonel
1 Major (ranking as a Lt. Colonel)
2 Chefs de bataillon (also Lt. Colonels)
1 Adjutant-major (Captain)
1 Quartermaster (Captain)
1 1st Class Surgeon
1 2nd Class, Sous-Surgeon
1 Chaplain
1 Master Tailor
1 Master Cobbler
1 Master Armorer
1 Drum Major
8 Musicians

Each battalion had a staff formed with:

1 Chef de bataillon (shown in regimental staff)
1 Adjutant-major (Lieutenant)
1 Surgeon
2 Adjutant NCOs
1 Battalion Drummer

The battalion was organized with nine companies. The 1st Battalion had the odd numbered companies, i.e. the 1st Grenadier, 1st Voltigeur, 3rd, 5th, 7th, 9th, 11th, 13th and 15th Fusilier Companies. The even numbered companies were in the 2nd Battalion. The companies were organized very close to the organization established by the French Imperial Decree of 18 February 1808.

Each company had:

1 Captain	1 Fourrier
1 Lieutenant	8 Corporals
1 Sous-lieutenant	2 Drummers
1 Sergeant-major	120 Soldiers
4 Sergeants	1 Sapper or Clerk
	140 Total

Each company was organized into three platoons, commanded by a lieutenant, sous-lieutenant and sergeant major. One of the four sergeants was designated as the chef de compagnie and the other three were assigned as second in command to each of the platoons. Each platoon was organized with three sections, each with a corporal and 13 privates. There was also one sapper and one clerk assigned for every two companies.

Initially, the War Directory Decree of 26 January 1807 assigned the legion a single cavalry regiment with six squadrons. This regiment was to consist of:

1 Colonel	48 Sergeants
6 Chefs d'escadron	12 Brigadiers Chefs (Lance corporals)
1 Adjutant Major, Captain	96 Brigadiers (Corporals)
2 Adjutant NCOs	24 Trumpeters
12 Captains	12 Blacksmiths
12 Lieutenants	1,800 Troopers
12 Sous-lieutenants	2,050 Total
12 Sergeant majors	

However, the organization of the cavalry had progressed such that many regiments stood with three full squadrons. There were several advantages to having two smaller regiments, in view of the two brigade structure of the legion. Smaller formations were also more flexible. Thus, in March 1807 each legion was organized with two, three squadron regiments with separate staffs. Their structure was as follows:

1 Colonel	1 Staff Fourrier
1 Major	1 Veterinarian
3 Chefs d'escadron	1 Master Saddlemaker
1 Adjutant Major (Captain)	1 Master Armorer
1 Staff Surgeon 1st Class	1 Master Cobbler
1 Surgeon 2nd Class	1 Master Tailor
1 Paymaster (Captain)	18 Total

Each of the three squadrons was formed with two companies. Each company was divided into three platoons and contained:

1 Captain
1 Lieutenant
1 Sous-lieutenant
1 Sergeant Major
4 Sergeants
1 Fourrier
8 Brigadiers
2 Trumpeters
150 Troopers
170 Total

This gave the squadron a total of 340 men and the entire regiment a total strength of 1,037 men.

A total of three battalions of artillery, three companies of sappers and three train companies were formed. These were divid¬ed between the legions such that each legion's artillery and sapper battalion was formed with three foot artillery companies, a sapper company and a train company. Each company had three platoons and each platoon had three sections. The first two sections of each artillery platoon were gunners and the remaining third were drivers. A company had six guns. These units were organized with:

Artillery Battalion

3 Artillery Companies with:
1 Chef de Battalion (battalion commander)
3 Captains
3 Lieutenants
3 Sous-lieutenants
3 Sergeant majors
12 Sergeants
3 Fourriers
24 Corporals
6 Drummers
3 Artisans
360 Gunners
421 Total

Train Company	Sapper Company
1 Lieutenant	1 Captain
1 Sergeant major	1 Lieutenant
4 Sergeants	1 Sous-lieutenant
1 Brigadier fourrier	1 Sergeant major
8 Brigadiers	4 Sergeants
180 Train Soldiers	1 Fourrier
195 Total	8 Corporals
	1 Artisan
	120 Sappers
	138 Total

Zych provides a variation in the organization of the Sapper Company. Though he states that it was formed like the artillery companies, his breakdown (3 officers, 15 NCOs, and 120 sappers) suggests that there were no artisans or drummers as were found in the artillery companies.

This force was the cadre from which the artillery and engi¬neering forces of the Polish army were eventually organized. The artillery was converged into a three battalion artillery regi¬ment, while the train and sapper companies were converged into battalions. In all three instances this change appears to have been more administrative than a massive shifting of men and material.

The Légion du Nord was not organized in the same manner.
Its staff was formed with:

1 Major-General, Commander	4 Assistant Surgeons
1 Major of the Legion	1 Drum Major
1 Quartermaster-Paymaster	2 Drummers
1 Surgeon Major	8 Musicians
4 Sous-Surgeons	3 Artisans
	26 Total

Each battalion consisted of:

1 Chef de bataillon	7 Chasseur Companies (150 men each)
1 Adjutant-major	1 Voltigeur Company (150 men)
1 Adjutant non-commissioned officers	1 Carabinier Company (139 men)
	1,342 Total

Each company had:

1 Captain	1 Fourrier
1 Lieutenant	8 Corporals
1 Sous-lieutenant	2 Drummers
1 Sergeant-major	131 Chasseurs or Voltigeurs
4 Sergeants	120 Carabiniers

The legion had no cavalry and consisted solely of four battalions and a staff with a total strength of 5,394 men.

Infantry of the Grand Duchy of Warsaw 1809-1814

During March 1809, a new staff organization appeared. The regiments sent two battalions into the field and their staff consisted of:

1 Colonel	2 Adjutant NCOs
2 Chefs de bataillon	1 Drum major
2 Adjutant-majors	1 Drum corporal
1 Eagle Bearer	8 Musicians
4 Surgeons	6 Wagon drivers
	28 Total

The single battalion remaining behind in the depot had a staff that consisted of:

1 Major
2 Surgeons
1 Chef de battalion
3 Artisans
1 Adjutant NCO

In 1810 there was a reorganization of the internal structure of the Polish infantry. Each battalion was now reorganized with six companies. Of these companies one was a grenadier company, one was a voltigeur company and four were fusilier companies. Each regiment was still organized with three battalions, though before 1812 some regiments raised a 4th Bat¬talion. The regimental staff now consisted of:

1 Colonel	6 Adjutant non-commissioned officers
1 Major	2 2nd & 3rd Port-aigle non-commissioned officers
3 Chefs de bataillon	1 Regimental Drum Major
3 Adjutant-majors	1 Drum Corporal
1 Quartermaster treasurer	8 Musicians
1 Port-aigle (Eagle bearer)	1 Master armorer
1 1st Class physician	2 Tailors
2 2nd Class physicians	1 Master Cobbler
3 3rd Class physicians	
1 Chaplain	

Between all the companies of the regiment there were:

6 1st Class Captains	9 2nd Class Lieutenant
9 1st Class Lieutenants	6 3rd Class Captains
6 2nd Class Captains	18 Sous Lieutenants

Each company consisted of:

1 Captain	8 Corporals
1 Lieutenant	2 Drummers (buglers in voltigeur co.)
1 Sous-lieutenant	1 Fourrier
1 Sergeant-major	117 Fusiliers
4 Sergeants	136 Total
	2 *Enfants de troupe*

This set the regiment with a staff of 39 and in the battalions 54 officers, 252 non-commissioned officers, 2,105 soldiers, and 26 drummers nad buglers. The regimental total was 2,4987 men and 36 *enfants de troupe*.

This formation did not remain the standard organization for the Polish infantry throughout the remainder of the existence of the Grand Duchy of Warsaw, but the changes were very minor. The convention between France and the Grand Duke of Warsaw, signed on 25 February 1812, added 20 soldiers to each line company. They were paid for by the French Treasury. On 21 March 1812 Friedrich August added another four soldiers, bringing the company strength to 160 men, from the 136 men per company existing before the February convention.

In 1811 a depot battalion were organized for the first 14 line regiments. Each depot battalion was commanded by a 1st Class Captain and had four fusilier companies organized with:

1 Captain	4 Sergeants
1 Lieutenant	1 Fourrier
1 Sous-lieutenant	8 Corporals
1 Sergeant major	2 Drummers
	140 Fusiliers
	157 Total

The Supplementary Decree of 13 June 1812 specified the number of caissons per infantry regiment as follows:

3 Ammunition caissons
3 Cartridge caissons
3 Bread caissons
1 Ambulance caisson
1 Document caisson

In addition, there was one field forge for every three regiments.

Infantry of the Duchy of Warsaw, 1810 (B. Gembarzewski)

Uniforms of the Polish Infantry

From mid-November 1806 through January 1807 the uniforms for the period consisted of a dark blue uniform with collars, facings, cuffs and side stripes in the departmental color: Poznań - white, Kalisz - crimson, Warsaw - yellow. However, before March 1807 it is difficult to speak of uniformity of dress in the uniforms of the Polish troops, though the tendency was towards a restoration of the old national uniform and colors – dark blue and crimson. On 16 November, General Dombrowski specified that the draftee should wear a dark blue kurtka, white sleeved vest, dark blue or gray pants, and a dark blue or gray czapka. Because of the lack of haversacks and bullet pouches they carried their belongings in canvas bags and their cartridges in their pockets.

Antoni Bialkowski states in his memoirs that the 4th (Poznań) Infantry Regiment was equipped with dark blue czapkas with gold trimming, a tricolor cockade and six inch tall pompons (gold for the fusiliers, poppy red for grenadiers, green for voltigeurs), dark blue kurtkas with yellow facings and cuffs, dark blue pants with yellow side stripes, white sleeveed vests with dark blue collars and shoulder straps, short black gaiters with eight buttons bearing the regimental number, and gray overcoats with yellow collars and shoulder straps. The regimental colors of the Poznań Legion were as follows:

1st Regiment - white with dark blue
2nd Regiment - green with dark blue
3rd Regiment - light blue with dark blue
4th Regiment - yellow with dark blue

Because of supply problems many units wore modified Prussian uniforms or anything that was available, including modified civilian clothes. It was not uncommon for regimental commanders to use artistic license and modify their regiments' uniforms.

On 2 March 1807 the uniform was modified. A divisional uniform was adopted. They were as follows:

Unit	Kurtka	Cuffs & Lapels	Collar	Buttons
1st Division	Dark Blue	Yellow	Poppy Red	Yellow
2nd Division	Dark Blue	Crimson	Crimson	White
3rd Division	DarkBlue	White	White	Yellow

They wore a white cockade on their hat. The pants were dark blue with stripes of the divisional color. The piping on the uniform was the color of the lapels.The grenadiers had poppy red epaulets, the voltigeurs wore light green epaulets. Both officers and soldiers were supposed to wear black felt shakos, but the czapka was commonly used. Pompons and plumes varied - officers wore white ones, the grenadiers wore poppy red, the voltigeurs wore light green and the fusiliers wore black. Though the grenadiers wore bearskin bonnets, there are sources that indicate that in some of the regiments, they wore czapkas with brass plates bearing a grenade.

When the 4th, 7th and 9th Infantry Regiments went to Spain in August 1808 their uniforms were so poor that they were issued some French uniform articles. French shakos were issued to many who lacked head gear. However, despite the issuance of uniforms cut in the French style, they continued to wear the basic Polish colors. This changed with the issuances of the Imperial Decrees of 19 January and 17 February 1812, when they were issues the new French "habit court", shakos with the tricolor cockade, and eliminated the last vestiges of their Polish uniforms. The 4th Regiment wore its 1807 divisional dress until 1813.

The grenadiers wore a wide poppy red band around the top of their shakos and the voltigeurs also probably wore the wide yellow band of the French voltigeurs. The drummers and buglers were issued Imperial livery - light green jackets with dark green and yellow bands, decorated with imperial eagles and ciphers.

In 1809 a large number of Polish troops went into the field wearing a white sleeved vests and linen pants. The newly formed Galician-French regiments were clad as best as could be managed. The 13th Regiment wore uniforms taken from Austrian magazines. They wore shakos and white kurtkas with light blue collars, cuffs and facings.

The Decree of 3 September 1810 directed that all of the infantry uniforms be changed such that they all had the same facings. Despite the decree the 4th Regiment retained its yellow facings and these regulations did not apply to the other regiments in French service either.

Grenadiers of the 5th Infantry 1809 (Jan Chelminski)

The new uniform was a dark blue kurtka (coat) with white lapels. The collar was crimson, though a dark blue collar with crimson piping was often worn by the grenadiers. The cuffs were crimson though yellow cuffs with white piping were worn by the 1st, 2nd and 3rd Regiments and the voltigeurs of the 5th Regiment. The cuff flaps were usually white with crimson piping, though for the 4th, 5th and 9th Regiments they were dark blue with white pipping. The breeches and gaiters were white in the summer. In the winter they wore dark blue breeches.

The grenadiers wore a peaked bearskin bonnet with brass plaque bearing a white metal eagle and the regimental number between two grenades. On the top of the bearskin was a red patch with a white cross. The bonnet was hung with poppy red cords and had a poppy red plume. All the grenadiers wore poppy red epaulets and long mustaches and large side-burns. However, only the bonnets of the 2nd, 4th and 16th Regiments seem to have conformed with regulations. The grenadiers of the 13th Regiment continued to wear the shakos issued in 1809. This shako had a poppy red pompon, cords and tassels. Its brass plate bore the regimental number surmounted by a brass grenade. The black visor was trimmed with brass and there were dark yellow bands around the top and in the "V" on either side. The variations in the other grenadier companies were as follows:

Regiment	Peaked	Plaque	Cords	Tassels	Plume
1st	Yes	Yes[1]	No	Poppy Red on Rt	No
2nd	Yes	Reg. No.	White	Poppy Red on Rt	No
3rd	No	Reg. No.	White	White[2]	No
4th	Yes	No	White	Poppy Red on Rt	Yes
5th	No	Yes	White	Poppy Red on Rt	Yes
6th	No	Yes[3]	White	Poppy Red on Rt	No
7th	No	No	White	Poppy Red on Rt	No
8th	No	No	White	Poppy Red on Rt	No
9th	No	No	White	Poppy Red on Rt	No
10th	No	No	White	None	No
11th	No	No	White	Poppy Red on Rt	No
12th	No	No	White	Poppy Red on Rt	No
13th	See Text	No	White	Poppy Red on Rt	Poppy Red
14th	No	Yes	White	Poppy Red on Rt	Poppy Red
15th	No	Yes	White	Poppy Red on Rt	No
16th	Yes	No	White	Poppy Red on Rt	No
17th	No	Yes	White	Poppy Red on Rt	Poppy Red

In 1812 most of the grenadier companies wore a plume.

The voltigeurs wore a czapka with white cords and a yellow over green plume. The voltigeurs wore green epaulets, yellow collars, and short mustaches. The fusiliers wore a black czapka with a white eagle over a copper plaque. The plaque bore the regimental number. The edges of the square top of the czapka were trimmed with brass. They wore a black pompon and white cords with white and crimson tassels for the non-commissioned officers. The fusiliers wore dark blue shoulder straps and were clean shaven.

The 13th Regiment continued to be an exception with its white and light blue uniforms, black shakos with pompons. Both the grenadiers and voltigeurs had light blue collars. The grenadiers were distinguished by a poppy red pompon, cords and epaulets. There was also a brass grenade on the shako. The uniforms of the voltigeurs had dark green pompons and cords on their shakos, and dark green epaulets. The shako also bore a brass bugle and brass plaque with the regimental number. They did not wear the Polish eagle on their shakos.

[1]Plaque was according to regulation requirements
[2]Tassels were white, right, and on top center only.
[3]Brass grenade with regimental number.

The sappers wore the same bearskin as the grenadiers with a crimson plume and white cords and tassels. They had the red cloth crossed axes and a grenade symbol on their sleeve. Their apron was of white leather and they wore gauntlets. The sapper's axe was carried in a black leather pouch. All sappers carried a saber and a dragoon carbine. Some sources also show the sappers carrying studded maces. They wore the traditional full beards.

The rank distinctions for all grades were the same as those worn by the French.

Polish Guard Infantry Battalion

On 2 October 1813 Napoleon decreed that a battalion of Polish Guard be raised for his Imperial Guard. This battalion was raised and did serve at the battle of Leipzig and Hanau. The battalion consisted of a staff and four companies. The staff consisted of:

1 Battalion Commander	1 Wagon master
1 Adjutant major	1 Drum corporal
1 Sous-adjutant	1 Master armorer
1 Paymaster	3 Mule drivers
1 2nd Class Surgeon	11 Total

Each company contained:

1 Captain	1 Fourrier
1 Lieutenant	8 Corporals
2 Sous-lieutenant	3 Drummers
1 Sergeant-major	183 Grenadiers
4 Sergeant	204 Total

The staff and battalion contained 21 officers and 803 non-commissioned officers and men. Though not part of the decree, there were three servants assigned the battalion commander and a further three mule drivers, bringing the total of the battalion to 830. There had originally been an allowance for a eagle bearer and two assistant eagle bearers, but Napoleon deleted them from the organization.

In addition, in the battalion there were to be eight sap-pers with the rank and pay of corporals, with two assigned to each company.

In theory the grenadiers wore a black Saxon shako with a scarlet pompon and tuft over the Polish cockade. There was no plaque, as the Saxon one was removed, and the chinscales were gilt. Their kurtka was royal blue and in the Polish style. Its collar was royal blue and the kurtka had white demi-lapels. The cuffs were scarlet with white cuff flaps. The turnbacks and piping along the bottom of the jacket were also scarlet. The fringed epaulets were white. The breeches were royal blue with white gaiters. The boots were black. The belts were white. In fact the regiment did not have time to be uniformed in this manner and the soldiers wore the uniforms from their original regiments with bearskin bonnets.

The National Guard of 1807-1809

The first units of the National Guard were organized spontaneously in the Poznań Department. As early as February 1807 the Poznań National Guard had 18 companies, while small towns, such as Wschowa, were able to form up to seven companies each. In Warsaw, the nucleus of the National Guard was the local militia, organized in November 1806, just a few days before the departure of the Prussian garrison. This force served as a police force and was commanded shortly by Prince Poniatowski, then by J. Moszynski and Raszka. In April 1807 the Governing Committee discussed a project of reorganizing the Warsaw Militia into a National Guard. Though the project was approved on 24 April, its implementation was initially limited to Warsaw.

The Warsaw National Guard Regiment was organized like a regular infantry regiment, with two battalions of nine companies. Zych states that it had three battalions, but this seems unlikely as he provides a total strength in 1807 of 2,479.

All property owners in Warsaw, as well as merchants, artisans, and their apprentices (the latter only if sons of property owners), were drafted into the regiment. Priests that were not attached to a parish or a hospital were also incorporat¬ed into the guard and had to pay a contribution towards its upkeeping. Jewish men and public school students were exempt. The guardsmen had to buy their own uniforms and weapons. The guardsmen too poor to afford that expenditure were provided money from the National Guard Treasury. Those funds were, in fact, obtained from citizens who, for some reason, chose to and were able to escape service.

The guard was unpaid unless they had to do service more than two miles from their garrison. The only salaried guardsmen were the officer-instructors from the regular army, i.e., two adjutant-majors (one per demi-battalion) and the junior adjutants (one per demi-battalion and company). The drummers also were paid. These men were paid according to army scales.

On 22 June 1807 the Governing Committee ordered the forma¬tion of National Guard units in all municipalities of the Duchy. They were provided the following guidance by the committee:

No. of Potential Guardsmen	Unit to be Formed	Rank of Commander	Assigned regular Army Instructors
2,400+	Reg. with at least two battalions	Colonel	As in Warsaw
1,200	Battalion	Lt. Colonel	1 Captain/Battalion 1 Lt./company
600	Demi-Battalion	Captain	1 Lt. & 1 Sous-Lt. per Company
120 50+	Company	Lieutenant	1 Sous-lieutenant Salaried NCOs.
Less than 50	None, regions that could not raise 50 men were exempted.		

The National Guard did not have a centralized high command, although it was, on the bottom line, subordinated to the military authorities. In peacetime, it was at the disposal of the admin¬istration and the police, but their orders had to be acknowledged and accepted by the proper military officials. In war they were subordinated to the district commanders or garrison commanders.

On 30 March 1809 the total strength of the National Guard reached 24,557 men and was still growing during the Austro-Polish portion of the war. The breakdown of these men was as follows:

1,973 in the city of Warsaw
12,306 in the Poznań Department
7,332 in the Kalisz Department
2,880 in the Lomza Department
66 in Chelmno (Bromberg Department)

Indications are that it reached about 30,000 men. In March 1809 the State Council created the Sedentary National Guard as a police force. It contained all men between 16 and 60 years of age. They were organized into units of 10, 100, and 1,000. In 1810, the National Guard was organized in the newly acquired territories of Galicia.

The National Guard of 1811-1813

Despite Poniatowski's well-founded arguments that the National Guard was an unnecessary burden on the fragile Polish economy, Napoleon pressed the State Council into reorganizing and expanding it. The Decree of 10 April 1811 drafted all men from 20 to 50 years of age (except clergy, teachers and the handicapped) into the National Guard. Jewish men were included on this occasion, but in practice they were often allowed, on a local basis, to avoid service. The entire force was divided into the Sedentary Guard, the Mobile Guard and the permanent Paid Guard. The Sedentary Guard were property holders, public officials, merchants, artists, licensed artisans and wealthier farmers. They were to form a policing force in the villages and towns and to defend them in case of a direct enemy threat. In large cities, a part of the Sedentary Guard - uniformed at its own expense and divided into regular companies - was kept on a permanent basis, parading on various holidays under the supervision of regular army officers and NCOs assigned according to the need.

Warsaw National Guard (Jan Chelminski)

The Mobile Guard consisted of apprentices, petty farmers, and everyone else. In peacetime, it was divided into " legions" (legie), "banners" (choragwie) and "sections" (roty), while during wartime it was to be organized into battalions and companies with army officers. The Mobile Guard could be used anywhere in the Duchy. If it were sent away from their home departments, the guardsmen were to receive pay on a par with regular army units. The funds for its upkeep came from the civilian administration.

The Paid Guard consisted of volunteers, preferably from among veteran soldiers, commanded by officers on half pay and veterans. They were formed into permanent police units. The idea was to relieve the regular army from having to perform such duties as well as to reduce or eliminate the costs resulting from the employment of other guardsmen in this capacity. The Paid Guard was to be maintained and paid from a 15% increase in the personal tax.

Both Poniatowski and Bignon (Napoleon's resident in Warsaw) were very skeptical about the actual implementation of this decree. Their judgement was to prove correct. The civilian administration, with its notorious slowness and lack of motivation, turned the proposed general restructuring of the guard into a complete mess. Poniatowski demanded a suspension of the April decree, and, on 7 May 1811, ordered the calling-up of part of the existing guard, which according to the April decree, fell under the category of the mobile guard. This half-measure was necessitated by the scarcity of regular army forces in the Duchy. At the same time, National Guard units were being established in the Galician departments. The Sedentary Guard and Paid Guard remained unformed and did not progress beyond a paper organization.

The May decree prescribed the company establishment as follows:

1 Captain	1 Fourrier
1 Lieutenant	17 Sergeants
1 Sous-lieutenant	1 Drummer
1 Sergeant major	177 Guardsmen
	200 Total

The battalion staff consisted of a battalion commander and an adjutant-lieutenant. A battalion contained six companies, including one of grenadiers and another of voltigeurs. The actual organization ordered into existence was as follows:

No. of Men	**Territory**	**Oganizer/Commander**
1,200	City of Warsaw	Lubienski
1,200	Kalisz Department	Biernacki
1,000	Radom Department	Krasinski
1,000	Karkow Department	Krasinski
1,000	Lomza Department	Stögetin
3,000	Poznań Department	Garczynski
1,500	Bromberg Department	Lachocki
300	Plock Department	Poletyllo

The Decree of 22 May organized 400 guardsmen in the Lublin Department and a further 200 in the Siedlce Department under the command of Wieniawski, bringing the total projected strength to 10,800 men organized in 54 companies.

The effects of this partial reorganization, based on the Decree of 22 June 1807 and the Decree of 10 April were mixed. Warsaw functioned satisfactorily since they had an established force. The Radom guard was roughly organized in May 1811, but quickly dissolved. The Bromberg guard was established by the end of June; the Krakow guard was formed in August and the Kalisz guard in September.

The organization of the Lomza guard went smoothly and its men were posted on permanent border guard duty. In the other departments the situation was much worse. The military organiz¬ers encountered numerous obstacles thrown in their way by local civil authorities and the practice of sending unsatisfactory substitutes to the guard was wide spread. In some districts, the administrators treated the guard units as penal institutions and filled their ranks with vagrants, beggars, etc

All in all, the project failed. Poniatowski realized this and on 25 September 1811 he proposed to Friedrich August that a large portion of the existing gurad be incorporated into the army where they could be utilized to better advantage.

This was approved by the Grand Duke on 18 December 1811, with the exception of the guard units in the large cities and the Lomza Department. The remainder of the guard was drafted into the army and their numbers subtracted from the conscription quotas of their departments. Only a few small units were retained by the prefects for police duty and they were absolved from any military duties.

As the year 1812 arrived the National Guard was in a state of considerable chaos. Faced with the approach of war, on 17 March 1812, the Ministry of Internal Affairs decided to reactivate the *April 1811 Decree* and reordered the organization of the Sedentary Guard. They also ordered a census of the Mobile Guard. Both were to be finished by 1 April 1812. The organization of the Paid Guard remained suspended. On 15 April, when it became apparent that executing the decision was impossible, an order was issued to preserve the existing active guard units as in 1811with the Mobile Guard.

The Mobile Guard units were employed along the Russian border. A short time later most of the National Guard units from southern and southeastern parts of the Duchy were assigned to the Kosinski Division. Of these units, only the Krakow Battalion constituted a reliable fighting force. The older units either lacked uniforms and arms or were in a deplorable condition. Kosinski was especially shocked by the sight of the Radom guard, which was formed of vagrants and beggars. He wrote that "even a Cossack would be ashamed to fight against such rabble" who were "so haggard that they couldn't even be used to dig ditches..." As a result, Kosinski left the majority of his guard units in the Zamosc fortress, taking only 7 officers and 156 men of the Krakow guard into the field.

The total number of guardsmen from the Mobile Guard that were activated during the 1812 campaign reached about 3,900. Between February and May 1813 these units were either incorporated into the regular army regiments or simply disintegrated. Those that still remained under arms were used by the Allied occupation authorities for police duty, until the Polish National Guard was finally disbanded by the resolutions of the Congress of Vienna. Only in Krakow, which became an independent republic, did any vestige of the National

Guard remain. Many of the former guardsmen surfaced again in the ranks of the local militia between 1815 and 1836.

National Guard of Warsaw

A Council of Ministers decree dated 15 June 1812 stopped the reorganization of the National Guard directed by the April 1811 decree, causing the organiztion established in May 1811 to be retained. It also increased the number of men being raised. In order to alleviate the load of military duties, additional categories of citizens were drafted. The decree also contained a guarantee that the "National Guard would be used only within the city limits, and solely for the purpose of keeping law and order there."

The ranks wore dark blue kurtkas and the officers wore dark blue tailcoats. They had light blue collars (yellow for the voltigeurs) and pointed cuffs, both of which were piped with white. Their white facings were piped with light blue. The turnbacks were white for the officers and dark blue with light blue piping for the soldiers. The epaulets of the officers were golden, those of the grenadiers were poppy red, the voltigeurs were light green and the fusiliers did not wear them.

The officers wore tight white breeches, while the troops wore white pantaloons. The officers wore black hussar boots with black or golden tassels. The enlisted wore black shoes and white gaiters.

The officers wore bicorns with silver corner tassels, white cockades and agraffes. The ranks wore black shakos with a yellow band around the top of the grenadier shako and orange for the fusiliers. Light blue pompons surmounted with poppy red plumes was worn by the grenadiers. The plumes were light yellow for the voltigeurs and small orange pompons were worn by the fusiliers. The cords were poppy red for the grenadiers, light yellow for the voltigeurs and orange for the fusiliers. The shako had a rhom¬boid brass plaque. The officers wore golden buttons, while the soldiers wore yellow. All of their leather work was white.

The National Guard of Krakow

The National Guard of Krakow was organized in mid-1810 by J. Krasinski, formerly a major in the Warsaw National Guard. The regiment consisted of two battalions, each with six companies. Each battalion had one grenadier, one voltigeur and four fusilier companies. The regiment was formed and operational by 15 August 1810. As Krakow did not have a formal garrison the National Guard was assigned those duties. The only other forces in the city were the depots of 12th Infantry Regiment and the 2nd Uhlan Regiment. In 1812 one battalion was sent to Zamosc and took part in the operations of Kosinski's Division, losing almost half of its strength. The regiment was, as a result, one of the most heavily engaged of the national guard units. In May 1813 it was disarmed by the Russian troops that occupied Krakow and it was disbanded shortly later.

Their uniform consisted of a dark blue kurtka or tailcoat with light blue collars, pointed poppy red cuffs (yellow for the voltigeurs) with white piping, and white facings piped with poppy red. The bottom edge of the uniform and the turnbacks were also piped with white. They wore the same epaulets, legwear and footwear as the Warsaw National Guard, except the officers' boots had no tassels and the soldiers did not wear gaiters.

The officers bicornes had white cockades, golden tassels and agraffes, silver pompons with a short, brush-like plume (white for the fusiliers; light green for the voltigeurs). The grenadier officers wore bearskins with poppy red pompons and long plumes, white cords and tassels. The other ranks wore czapkas with light green pompons topped with plumes as on the officers' hats. The cords were light green for the voltigeurs; white for the fusiliers. The grenadiers' were like those of their offi¬cers, except the top of the plume was white. On the czapkas they had a yellow brass plaque with the Krakow coat of arms. The sappers wore the grenadier uniform with poppy red crossed axes on the left sleeve and long white aprons. All of the leatherwork was white.

National Guard of Lublin

This force was one of the units raised in 1811. Its only notable aspect was its uniform. The grenadiers' officer's uniform consisted of a black bicorn hat with gold tassels in the corners. The coats were navy blue with light blue cuffs and collar. The epaulets, grenades and buttons were blue. The pants and officers sashes were white. The officer sash had a gold fringe.

The National Guard of Vilna

The National Guard of Vilna was formed by the Order of the Day of 1 July 1812, issued in the Imperial camp at Vilna. This orderdirected that two, six company battalions be organized and established them with a complement of 714 men each. It had a staff that consisted of:

1 Commandant	1 Drum major
2 Chefs de bataillon	3 Master Artisans
2 Adjutants-major	1 Surgeon Major
1 Quartermaster	1 Assistant Surgeon Major
2 Adjutant NCOs	8 Musicians
	22 Total

Each company was to have:

1 Captain	1 Quartermaster Corporal
1 Lieutenant	8 Corporals
1 Sous-lieutenant	2 Drummers
1 Sergeant-major	100 Soldiers
4 Sergeants	119 Total

This gave the Vilna National Guard a total strength of 1,450 men. The national guardsmen wore the same uniform as the Polish infantry.

The same decree also directed the raising of a gendarmerie commanded by a colonel in the governments of Vilna, Grodno, Minsk and Bialystok. In Vilna and Minsk there were to be two chefs d'escadron (squadron commanders) and in Grodno and Bialystok one chef d'escadron. Each county was to have a single company consisting of:

1 1st Class Captain commanding	4 Sergeants
1 2nd Class Captain	16 Brigadiers
1 1st Class Lieutenant	80 Gendarmes
2 2nd Class Lieutenants	1 Trumpeter
1 Sergeant major	107 Total

This force was also uniformed like its Warsaw counterpart.

Corps of Veterans and Invalids

The organization of the Corps of Veterans and Invalids is not known. Researches revealed solely its existance and the details of its uniforms. However, though the various veteran and invalid corps throughout Europe at this time did have a "typical" infantry company cadre assigned, they generally took in every veteran or invalid who met their requirements. As a result, their structures were quite variable and generally not mandated beyond indicating the organization of the cadre.

The uniforms of this corps were identical to those of the line infantry units, with the following exceptions. They were of light blue cloth, as was the lining. The collars and cuffs were, depending on the source, either light blue or crimson. The lapels were light blue with crimson piping. The buttons were of white metal and bore the motto "Weterany" or veteran. The czapka was black with a light blue turban piped in crimson, it had a crimson pompon and white plaque with the "Weterany" motto. The czapka plaque occasionally was surmounted by the Polish eagle. The officers wore a bicorn with round crimson pompons, silver tassels and agraffes. Their breeches were either light blue or white. They had hussar style boots. The epaulets, gorgets, worsted knots, czapka cords and galons were in silver or white metal. Rank distinctions were the same as the line infantry.

2nd Infantry Regiment, 1809 (Jan Chelminski)

Standard of the 2nd Infantry Regiment

Tactical Organization of the Infantry

The Polish infantry was organized along the lines of the French reorganization of 1808. The positions of the company officers and non-commissioned officers varied slightly from the *Régle-ment de 1791*. The captain and his sergeant were posted on the right wing of the company. The sergeant seconding the captain was in the third rank. The lieutenant, sous-lieutenant and sergeant-major were posted in the file closers rank where they were to keep the men in the ranks. Two sergeants were posted in the file closers rank, between the sergeant-major and the sous-lieutenant and on the right behind the first file on the wing. When a sapper was designated he was posted behind the captain in the file closers rank.

Grand Duchy of Warsaw Fusilier Company

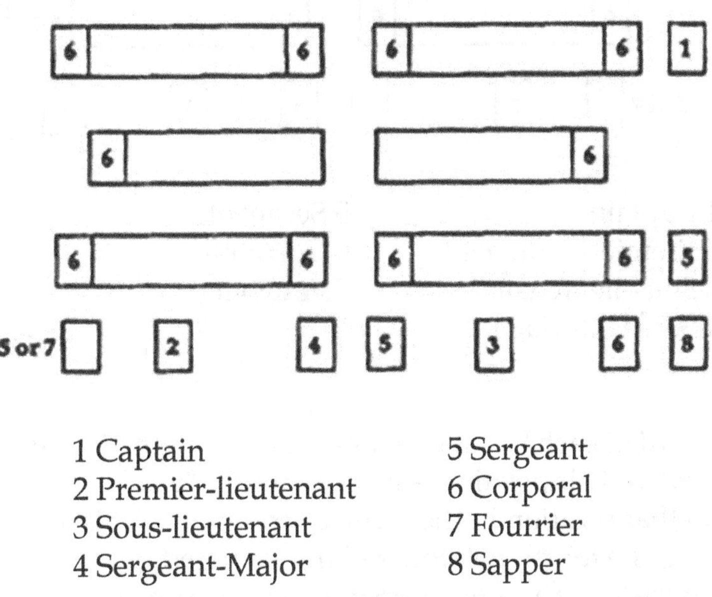

Grand Duchy of Warsaw Grenadier Company

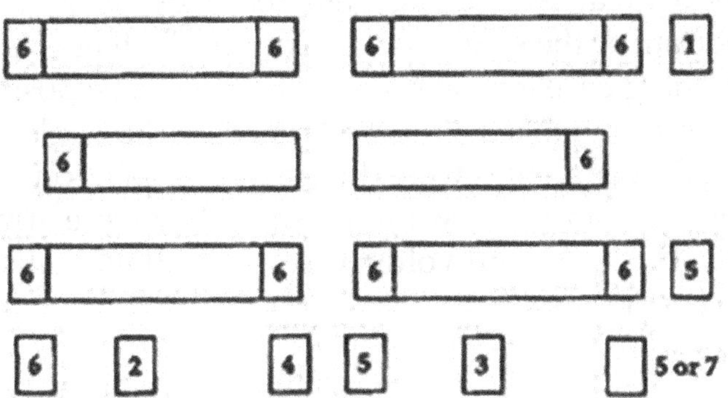

1 Captain
2 Premier-lieutenant
3 Sous-lieutenant
4 Sergeant-Major
5 Sergeant
6 Corporal
7 Fourrier

Grand Duchy of Warsaw Voltigeur Company 1808-1814

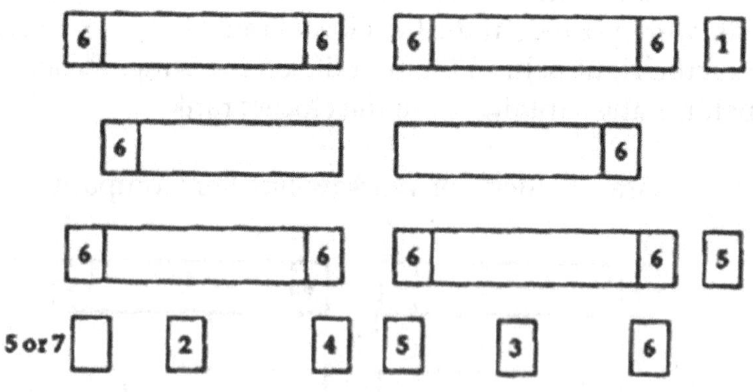

1 Captain
2 Premier-lieutenant
3 Sous-lieutenant
4 Sergeant-Major
5 Sergeant
6 Corporal
7 Fourrier

The standard guard of each battalion was organized with the eight fourriers of the fusilier companies. That is why their position is marked with a "5 or 7", indicating both the sergeant or fourrier could be in that position in the formed company. This detached force of fourriers was posted to the left of the fourth peloton and maneuvered with it.

The first rank consisted of a sergeant-major, who carried the flag and two fourriers who marched on either side of the flag. The two other ranks were formed with three fourriers each. These fourriers as well as the non-commissioned officers (NCOs) posted behind the various officers in the peloton ranks, carried their muskets on their right arm.

The sergeant-major who carried the flag was chosen by the regimental colonel. This position was extremely important as the sergeant who carried the flag was the guide for the entire regiment and set the marching pace for the rest of the unit. The positions of the staff officers in the Polish army was identical to that set for the French by the Réglement de 1791.

When maneuvering the companies were designated as pelotons, each peloton consisting of two sections. When the six companies were present, they were arranged from right to left as follows: grenadiers, 3rd, 1st, 4th, 2nd, and voltigeurs. The battalion always maneuvered by division, a division being two pelotons.

Grand Duchy of Warsaw Infantry Regiment in Line

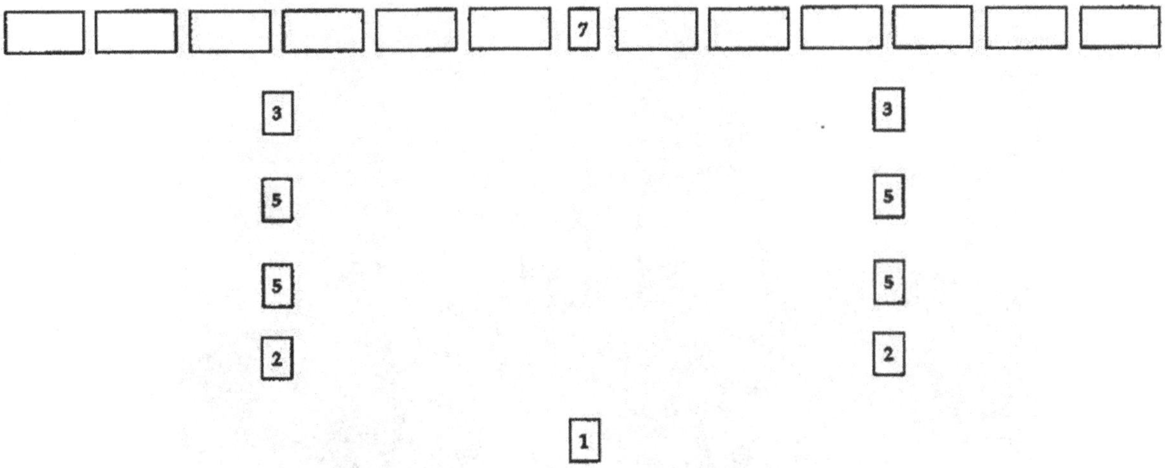

7

3 3

5 5

5 5

2 2

1

1. Colonel
2. Lieutenant Colonel
3. Drum Major
4. Drum Corporal
5. Drummers
6. Musicians
7. Sappers

The 8th Infantry Regiment (Chelminski)

The 3rd Uhlan Regiment (Chelminski)

Uniforms of the Grand Duchy Cavalry

The Uniform Regulations of 2 March 1807 prescribed a single uniform for all of the Polish Cavalry, uhlans or chasseurs. There were absolutely no differences in the uniforming and equipping of these two formations, except that the uhlans carried lances. They were uniformed according to the division to which they were assigned. Those uniforms were as follows:

1st Division: A dark blue kurtka with poppy red collars and cuffs, yellow facings piped with white, a white vest, dark blue breeches with double yellow stripes and yellow buttons. The collars and cuffs were also piped with white. They wore a black shako, though the uhlans often wore a czapka, with black plumes and white cords. In undress the breeches were gray with a double yellow side stripe. The elite companies had their shakos/czapkas sewn around with black lambskin or wore bearskin colpacks. In either instance, the elite companies headdress had a poppy red plume, bag and cords. The senior officers wore white plumes and silver cords.

2nd Division: The collar, cuffs, and facings were crimson with white piping. The side stripes were also crimson, but were not piped. The buttons were white and all other details of the uniform were the same as the 1st Division.

3rd Division: The collar, cuffs, and facings were white with white piping. The side stripes were also white, but were not piped. The buttons were yellow and all other details of the uniform were the same as the 1st Division.

Uniform of the Cuirassiers

The first reference to uniforms for the cuirassier regiment dates from 1809 when it was the Cuirassier Regiment of the Galician-French Army. The steel helmet was of the French pattern. It had a black leather visor and a bearskin turban. The crest, chinscales and metal band around the outer edge of the visor were brass. The houpette (tuft) was of white horsehair and the flowing crest was of black horsehair. A red plume mounted in a yellow metal socket was worn on the left side of the helmet.

The coat was a single breasted habit vest or Kinski of white with a poppy red collar and cuffs. It's lining was poppy red and the coat tails were turned back to show the poppy red lining. The cuffs and collars were piped with white, but the turnbacks were not. The buttons were of yellow metal with the regimental number "1" within a laurel wreath.

The cuirass was bare steel without lining. In its center there was a multi-pointed, yellow metal star.

The breeches were white, worn with black boots reaching above the knees. Steel spurs were worn on the boots. This uniform was worn until December 1809.

On 19 December 1809 the uniform worn by the regiment upon their entry into Warsaw consisted of a dark blue habit-veste lined with red. The collar was poppy red and closed with three hooks. The poppy red cuffs were square cut, and piped with dark blue. The vest, though not visible, was white. Their breeches were of white leather. They wore long black boots extending to the knees with long mobile steel spurs. They had gold/yellow buttons, and gold epaulets for the officers; the NCOs - red-with yellow epaulets; troopers - red epaulets, which allowed them to be distinguished from the French cuirassiers.

Their cuirass was of steel and covered the chest and back. It was trimmed with copper and the straps joining the two plates at the shoulder were scaled copper. The arm holes and waist were trimmed with red cloth in the same style as the French cuirass. Their helmet was of the French model and had a red plume on the left side, with black flowing crest and a yellow houpette or tuft at the peak. In practice, the houpette, being the knotted end of the horse hair crest, was black.

The cuirassiers did not, apparently, have cuirasses for the 1813 campaign. They were reported to have not had them upon their arrival at Zittau nor did they have them after the battle of Leipzig.

The 14th Regiment of Cuirassiers (B. Gembarzewski)

Uniform of the Chasseurs à Cheval

Prior to 1808 the chasseurs wore a dark blue kurtka, but after that it was dark green. There was one exception and that was the 5th Chasseur à cheval Regiment, which continued to wear its blue uniform until 1810. The chasseur's cuffs, collars, piping and turnbacks in the regimental colors (1st Regiment - Poppy Red, 4th Regiment - Crimson, 5th Regiment - Orange). The buttons were yellow. Their breeches were green and were worn over their short black leather shoes.

The soldiers and officers of the elite companies wore col¬packs of black bearskin with a bag of the regimental color and a gold button in its middle. Its cords and plume were red.

The soldiers and officers of the center companies wore a black shako with white cords and a plume of the regimental color tipped with green. It had a metal plaque that bore the regimen¬tal number.

The regimental staff officers wore white plumes. If the officer or trooper wore a colpack it sometimes had a carrot shaped pompon instead of the plume. This would be golden for officers, where if it was worn by a trooper it was poppy red. The officers' cords, if present, were always silver. After 1810 the bags on the colpacks appear to have disappeared. In 1813 the 1st Chasseurs was equipped with lances and the 4th Chasseurs were to have been converted into an uhlan regiment. Only the number remained unchanged. It is interesting to note that, during the 1809 campaign, the chasseurs also carried lances, probably to make up forthe lack of carbines. In 1810 and 1812 they did not carry lances.

4th Regiment Chasseaurs a Cheval (Chelminski)

10th Hussar Regiment (B. Gembarzewski)

Uniform of the Hussars

The hussars wore dark blue pelisses trimmed with black fur for the 10th or white fur for the 13th. On the front it had 18 to 20 rows of buttons according to the size of the wearer. Each row had five buttons and between these buttons was strung yellow (gold for officers) lace for the 10th Regiment and white lace (silver for officers) for the 13th Regiment. The dolman was also dark blue and had a crimson collar. It too was arranged with the same arrangement of buttons and lace as the pelisse. In their dress uniform the breeches were dark blue with yellow (gold) or white (silver) single side stripes and thigh knots. For the undress uniform gray Hungarian breeches with crimson side stripes were worn and the inside of the legs were lined with leather. style boots were worn.

Initially the shakos were black, but later the shako of the 13th was light blue with white cords. They had white chinscales and a black plume. The officers and men of the elite companies wore a black or dark brown colpack with light blue tops, poppy red cords and plumes. The officers wore either gold or silver cords, to match the lace, and white plumes.

The common illustrations of "Polish hussars" in light blue shakos, crimson pelisse and dolman, and light blue breeches are, in fact, not hussars but adjutants of the Commander-in-Chief, Poniatowski, and some of the adjutant-generals.

Uniforms of the Uhlans

The uhlans wore a dark blue kurtka cut in the Polish style. It was decorated with cuffs, collars, turnbacks and piping of the regimental color. The piping was found around the cuffs, collars pockets as well as the outer seams of the sleeves and the back. The regimental colors were:

Regiment	Collar	Piping	Turnbacks	Piping	Cuffs	Piping
2nd	Poppy Red	White	Dark Blue	Yellow	Poppy Red	White
3rd	Crimson	White	Dark Blue	White	Crimson	White
6th	White	Crimson	Dark Blue	Crimson	Dark Blue	Crimson
7th	Yellow	Poppy Red	Dark Blue	Poppy Red	Yellow	Poppy Red
8th	Poppy Red	Dark Blue	Dark Blue	Poppy Red	Poppy Red	Dark Blue
9th	Poppy Red	Dark Blue	Dark Blue	White	Dark Blue	Poppy Red
11th	Crimson	Dark Blue	Crimson	White	Dark Blue	Crimson
12th	Crimson	White	Dark Blue	White	Dark Blue	White
15th	Crimson	White	Crimson	White	Crimson	White
16th	Crimson	White	Dark Blue	Crimson	Crimson	White
17th	Crimson	Dark Blue	Dark Blue	Crimson	Crimson	Dark Blue
18th	Crimson	Dark Blue	Crimson	White	Crimson	Dark Blue
19th	Yellow	Dark Blue	Dark Blue	Yellow	Yellow	Dark Blue
20th	Crimson	Dark Blue	Yellow	Dark Blue	Yellow	Dark Blue
21st	This regiment's distinctive color was orange.					

The kurtka had yellow buttons with the regimental number on them. A white vest was worn under the kurtka. Their breeches were dark blue and worn over the short boots with spurs screwed into the heels. The breeches had a double band of yellow for the 2nd, 3rd, and 7th Regiments, red for the 8th and 9th Regiments and crimson for the other regiments. These stripes were piped with white, except for the 7th and 8th Regiments whose were piped with red.

A black czapka was worn. The edges of the square top were reinforced with yellow metal and cords hung from corner to corner. The cords were golden for officers, white for troopers, poppy red for elite companies. A yellow plaque, known as an "Amazon's Shield", bearing the regimental number was worn. Over the plaque was a white metal eagle. There were regimental variations and some regiments preferred a sunburst plaque with the eagle superimposed on it. The 17th Uhlans (a Lithuanian regiment) and probably several other Lithuanian regiments wore the sunburst plaque with a mounted knight superimposed on it. This was the ancient emblem of Lithuania. Officers wore a two inch wide golden band on their czapkas just above the turban. The troopers had a white band.

A plume was worn on the front peak of the czapka. The plumes were white for staff officers, black for troopers and poppy red for the elite companies. The elite companies,

7th Uhlans with one of Poniatowski's Guides (Jan Chelminski)

however, wore a black lambskin czapka or colpack with poppy red bags, plumes and cords.

The lance pennants of the 2nd, 3rd, 15th and 16th Regiments were red over white. Those of the 7th through 12th were tricolored with a dark blue triangle at the shaft of the lance and the upper portion red and the lower portion white. In the 17th through 21st Regiments, those regiments raised in Lithuania, the pennant was blue over white. Unfortunately this listing is only an approximation, for there were many more color combinations, often within the same regiment. Only the Lithuanian regiments appear to have been fairly consistent on this respect.

Despite this, the 6th Uhlan Regiment continued to wear its old legion/division dark blue uniform with white facings well into 1810, though the collar was changed from white to poppy red. The 11th Uhlans had non-regulation white facings and side stripes and crimson piping on the facings. In addition, several regiments took to wearing non-regulation plumes cut "à la russe" or uncut long horse hair cascading down from the top.

The 21st Uhlan regiment wore chasseur shakos and dark blue uniforms piped with crimson. The 4th Uhlan, converted from the 4th Chasseurs in May 1813, wore dark blue kurtkas with crimson collars, facings and cuffs, crimson breeches with double dark blue side stripes, yellow epaulets and aguilettes on the right shoulder. The collar appears to have been piped with yellow. The czapkas were crimson with yellow piping and trimmings, black turbans topped with yellow bands, yellow cords and white plumes, as well as sunburst plaques. The center of this plaque was white and the sunburst rays were yellow.

Uniform of the Lithuanian Horse Gendarmes

They wore a dark blue "surtout" with poppy red collars, cuffs, piping and turnbacks. Their buttons were white, as were the epaulets, aguilettes on the left shoulder and grenades on the collars. They wore short white breeches and black cuirassier boots. Their headgear consisted of black bicorns with white trim, cockades and agraffes, as well as poppy red carrot shaped pompons. All leather work was white. The lance pennant was poppy red over white. They also carried a lance, carbine, saber and a pair of pistols.

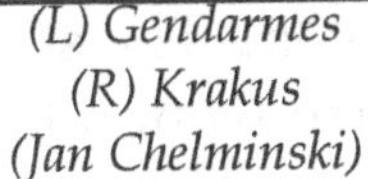

(L) Gendarmes
(R) Krakus
(Jan Chelminski)

Uniform of the Krakus

When formed in 1813 they wore the folk costume of the Krakow region. This consisted of soft, square topped red czapkas with black or white lambskin turbans and without visors. These were known as either "krakuskas" or "konfederatkas". They wore white or brown russet coats with embroidery and appliques, wide pantaloons or tight breeches, long boots, and various overcoats. Later, as the 1813 campaign progressed, they wore Cossack style colpacks and litewkas. The officers usually wore "military style" visored czapkas. The basic uniform colors were dark blue, crimson and white, though there was truly no uniformity to it.

In 1813 they were equipped with a lance, thought it did not always have a pennant. They carried sabers and pistols. Because of the lack of time for proper training, commands were given by waving a handkerchief. In 1814 this function was performed by using a "bunczuk" or horsetail on a pike in the manner of the Tartars.

The Krakus were mounted on small peasant horses, which resulted in Napoleon calling them his "pygmy cavalry." Despite that he was very happy with their performance. Many of the Krakus spoke German or Russian and they provided a tremendous asset in skirmishing and reconnaissance duties.

In 1814 the Krakus adopted an unusual melon-like beret. It had a white spread tassel on top and white lace stripes running from the button to the hat's black sheepskin band. The body of the beret was crimson. A white cockade and plume were worn on the left side of the beret.

They wore a single breasted, full skirted coat, like the litewka worn by the Prussians. It had a crimson collar and cuffs. It had white piping on all edges. A crimson sash was worn at the waist. Their breeches were also blue with crimson side stripes and black leather inserts. They carried pistols, sabers and lances without pennants.

Tactical Organization of the Cavalry

In 1810 the Polish cavalry was reorganized into four squadron regiments. The only exception was the cuirassier regiment, which had only two squadrons and was never raised to a four squadron strength. In contrast to other nations where each type of cavalry was numbered by its type, the Polish uhlans, hussars, cuirassiers and chasseurs were numbered sequentially without regard to the type of regiment involved. The staff of the cavalry regiments was altered in March 1809 and the two squadrons, which went into the field from every regiment, had a staff of:

1 Colonel
2 Chefs d'Escadron
2 Adjutant majors
2 Standard bearers
4 Surgeons
2 Adjutant NCOs
1 Trumpet major
6 Baggage soldiers

The single squadron that remained behind had:

1 Major
1 Chef d'escadron
2 Surgeons
1 Adjutant NCO
3 Artisans

The history of the cuirassiers is sufficiently unusual as to require an indepth review. The 14th Cuirassier Regiment was originally formed as the 1st Cuirassier Regiment of the Galician-French Cavalry. It was organized by S. Malachowski on his estate of Konskie near Kielce on 11 July 1809. Malachowski became the regiment's colonel on 2 September 1809. During the next three months the regimental depot in Konskie received recruits and horses. By 14 November 1809 it had risen to a strength of 610 men. The regiment continued to grow and from July 1809 to July 1810 737 soldiers of all grades passed through its ranks. This would indicate that it was initially intended to form a three or four squadron regiment, but for some undocumented reason, many officers and non-commissioned officers were transferred to other regiments. It was quite possibly the lack of suitable horses that caused this, however, Napoleon felt that the cuirassiers were too expensive and stated a strong preference for either chasseurs or uhlans, rather than cuirassiers.

On 28 December 1809 the Galician-French units were incorporated into the Duchy's army. On 30 March 1810 there was a reorganization that formally established the regiment at a strength of 419 men and 8 enfants de troupe. The regiment was fixed with a strength of two squadrons.

In response to a letter from Napoleon dated 6 October 1810, the King of Saxony issued a decree on 21 November 1810 that directed the reorganization of the cuirassiers as a chasseur à cheval regiment. Apparently Poniatowski tried to persuade the King of Saxony into converting the unit into a dragoon regiment, thus at least preserving its uniforms, because on 20 December 1810 Friedrich August had to repeat his previous decree, adding that, "its transformation into a dragoon regiment would not fulfill the purpose of this change."

On 6 January 1811 Poniatowski issued a farewell address to the regiment, in which he spoke of it as a future chasseur regiment, but the transformation was never executed. Again, the precise reasons for this are not clear. The possession of a cuirassier regiment was a status symbol that separated a second from a third rate power. Poniatowski definitely did not approve of the change and had delayed the transformation repeatedly. In addition, Malachowski's paternal uncle was the President of the Senate. No doubt there was a long series of political machinations that kept the cuirassiers a viable formation.

The internal organization in 1810 of the cavalry was quite consistent. The chasseurs, hussars and uhlans were all organized with a staff and four squadrons, each squadron having two companies. The staff of all but the cuirassiers consisted of:

1 Colonel	1 Standard Bearer
1 Major	2 Adjutant NCOs
2 Chefs d'escadron	1 Trumpet Major
1 Paymaster	1 Veterinarian
2 Adjutant-majors	1 Master Armorer
1 1st Class Physician	1 Master Saddle maker
2 2nd Class Physicians	1 Master Tailor
2 3rd Class Physicians	1 Master Breeches maker
1 Chaplain	1 Master Cobbler

Each of the eight companies in a regiment had:

1 Captain	1 Blacksmith
1 Lieutenant	8 Corporals
2 Sous-lieutenants	2 Trumpeters
1 Sergeant major	79 Troopers
4 Sergeants	100 Total
1 Fourrier	2 Enfants de troupe

Within the regiment there were:

3 Captains 1st Class
5 Captains 2nd Class
4 Lieutenants 1st Class
4 Lieutenants 2nd Class
16 Sous-lieutenants

The regiments, as a result, had a staff of 23, 32 company officers, 112 non-commissioned officers, 8 blacksmiths, 16 trumpeters, and 632 men. The total stood at 823 men and 16 *enfants de troupe*.

The staff of the cuirassier regiment, which had only two squadrons consisted of:

1 Colonel	1 Chaplain
1 Major	1 Standard Bearer
1 Chef d'escadron	1 Trumpet Major
1 Paymaster	1 Veterinarian
1 Adjutant-major	1 Master Armorer
1 Adjutant NCO	1 Master Saddlemaker
1 1st Class Physician	1 Master Tailor
1 2nd Class Physicians	1 Master Breechesmaker
2 3rd Class Physicians	1 Master Cobbler
	19 Total

Within the squadron there were:

2 Captains 1st Class
2 Captains 2nd Class
2 Lieutenants 1st Class
2 Lieutenants 2nd Class
8 Sous-lieutenants

The total theoretical strength of the cuirassier regiment stood at 19 staff, 16 officers, 56 non-commissioned officers, 4 blacksmiths, 8 trumpeters, 316 men. This gave the regiment 419 men and 8 *enfants de troupe*.

Equipment

The equipment of the Polish regiments was quite varied. At first the Poles were issued captured Prussian and Austrian carbines. The legion cavalry in Italy had Austrian 1770-1774 carbines and French Model 1763 and Model 1777 pistols. After 1801 they appear to have been issued the French Model 1786 carbines. The Krakus did not, however, ever carry carbines. Normally the Poles might be expected to have been equipped with French swords, but they proved to be quite scarce. As a result between 1807 and 1809 they were armed with Prussian 1721 Model hussar sabers or straight dragoon "pallasch" of the 1735 and 1797 models. There is some possibility that some were armed with Russian sabers. After 1809 they were equipped with Austrian hussar sabers of the 1769 and 1803 Models and some French sabers of the Models IX, XI and XIII. In addition, after 1810 many were also armed with sabers of Polish manufacture. In 1810 alone New Galicia produced 10,000 sabers, which probably supplanted many foreign sabers in the Duchy's army. The cuirassiers carried the French sabers, Models IX, XI and XIII.

The various cavalry officers carried every type of sword imaginable. Their swords were not covered by regulation and if they were, the regulations would have been ignored. As a result, everything from antiques to captured swords to Oriental swords were worn.

Between 1813 and 1814 the Polish cavalry was armed with French weapons. The 1st and 2nd Uhlans carried the Model XI sabers, the Model XI or XIII pistols and the Model IX carbine. Their lance was the Model 1812, 2.87 meters long.

The uhlans carried a lance and were noted throughout Europe for their prowess with it. In the 1809 and 1813 campaigns the chasseur à cheval regiments also carried a lance. The lance was 265 to 277 cm long (104-109 inches). It was made of ashwood impregnated with a mixture of linseed oil and tar, therefore it was quite light - so much so that one could hold it between the looped forefinger and the middle finger of the right hand raised high above the head, delivering in this manner a very powerful thrust called "par le moulinet". The only metal elements were the spearhead and the heel on the other end. In the hands of an experienced uhlan it was an effective and terrible weapon.

On 18 December 1813, the Polish cavalry was reformed and the organization changed. The staff of the other regiments consisted of:

1 Colonel	2 Adjutant NCOs
1 Colonel en second	2 Chefs d'escadron
2 Adjutant-majors	1 Trumpet Major
1 Quartermaster	1 Master Armorer
1 Chirurgien major	1 Veterinarian (NCO)
1 Chirurgien aide-major	14 Total

The eight companies each had:

1 Captain	1 Quartermaster
1 Lieutenant	8 Brigadiers
2 Sous-lieutenants	2 Trumpeters
1 Sergeant-major	109 Troopers
4 Sergeants	129 Total

This gave the line regiments a strength of 25 officers and 505 rank and file. On 5 January 1814 Napoleon ordered the addition of one lieutenant and one sous-lieutenant per company, which raised the number of officers in each regiment to 33.

The squadron was commanded by the senior captain, who had no designated position. Generally, however, he positioned himself at the head of the squadron, at its center in front of the two brigadiers that formed the junction between the first and second division. The junior captain was in the file closers rank three paces behind the center of the squadron. The lieutenant of the first division stood before the center of the first peloton, the tail of his horse one pace in front of the first rank. The sous-lieutenant of the division stood before the center of the second peloton with his horse one pace in front of the first rank. The lieutenant of the second division stood before the center of the fourth peloton and the sous-lieutenant of the division stood before the third peloton. The second sous-lieutenants were posted at the center of their companies, in the file closers rank.

The senior sergeant major was the file closers rank, in the center of the outer pelotons. The sergeants were posted in the front rank of their companies such that one was on each flank of the peloton. They had a brigadier posted such that one was adjacent to them, inside each peloton and one was behind them in the second rank. The fourrier of each company was posted behind the center of the second peloton.

Grand Duchy of Warsaw Cavalry Squadron 1808-1814

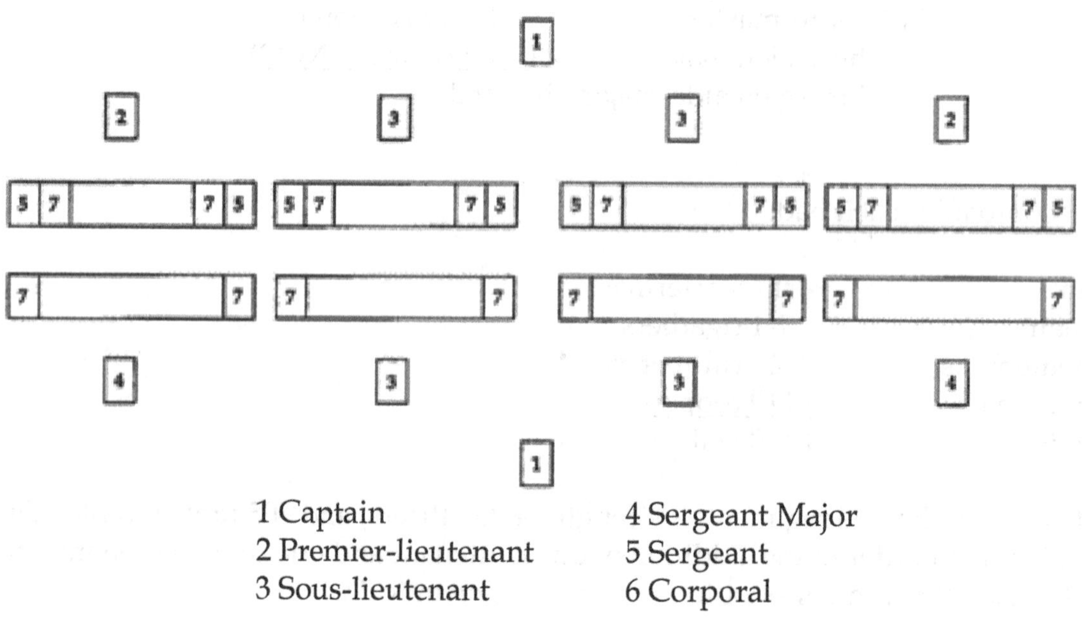

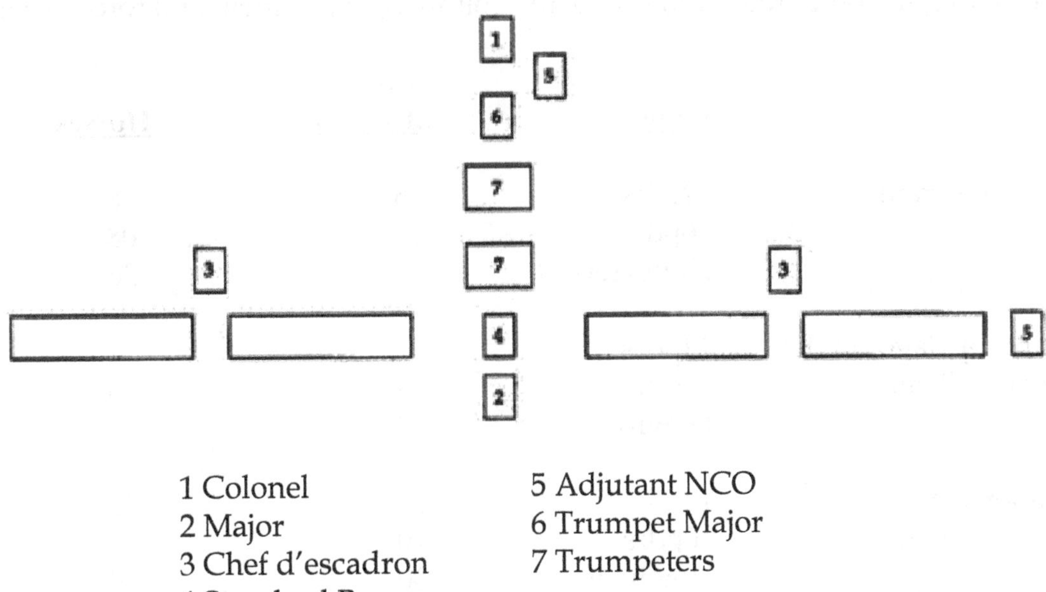
1
5
6
7
7
3
3
4
5
2
1 Colonel
2 Major
3 Chef d'escadron
4 Standard Bearer
5 Adjutant NCO
6 Trumpet Major
7 Trumpeters

Organization of the Artillery and Support Troops

The Polish field army on 18 March 1809 had the following equipment and forces assigned to it:

	Guns	Number of Guns	Horses
Advance Train	12pdrs	6	48
	6pdrs	18	108
	Howitzers	6	36
Spare Carriages in the Advance Train	12pdrs	1	4
	6pdrs	4	16
	Howitzers	2	8
Caissons in the Advance Train	12pdrs	22	132
	6pdrs	40	240
	Howitzers	30	180
	Infantry	70	420
	Park	2	12
	Field Forges	6	36
	Covered Wagons	14	84
	Prolongues	8	48

The personnel assigned to the Polish Artillery Corps consisted of:

Staff	
General Staff	Colonel Pelletier, Commander of artillery & engineers
	Colonel Gorski, Chief of staff
	Captain Jodko, Assistant
Engineering Staff	Captain, Mallet, Commander of engineers
	Captain Gotkowski, Assistant
	Potier, Engineering guard
Artillery Direction	Captain Bontemps, Park director
	2 Assistants
Vanguard	
Officers & Troops	Chef de bataillon Gugemus, commander of the artillery & engineers
	1 Assistant
	1 Horse Artillery Company
	1 Sapper/Pontooneer Company
	6 Artisans
	1 Artificer

Army Corps	
Officers & Troops	Chef de bataillon Hauschild, commander of the artillery & engineers
	1 Assistant
	3 Foot Artillery Companies
	1 Sapper/Pontooneer Company
	8 Artisans
Reserve	
Officers & Troops	Stanisław Potocki, commander of artillery
	1 Assistant
	1 Horse Artillery Company
	1 Foot Artillery Company
	6 Artisans
Park Troops	2 Foot Artillery Companies
	½ company of artisans

The royal decree of 30 March 1810 organized the artillery and engineers. The artillery corps consisted of the Foot Artillery Regiment, the Horse Artillery Regiment, a company of artisans and a battalion of engineers. The general staff of the artillery consisted of:

1 Inspector general
1 Adjutant, Captain to the General Staff
1 Colonel, Director of Powder & Saltpeter, Arms Factories and Gun Foundries
2 Assistant Captains
2 Assistant Lieutenants
1 Colonel, Director of the Engineers
2 Assistant Captains
2 Assistant Lieutenants
1 Colonel Director of Arsenals
1 Assistant Captain
1 Assistant Lieutenant
1 Lieutenant Colonel, Chief of the Topographical Service
1 Assistant Captain
1 Assistant Lieutenant
3 Lieutenant-Colonel, Assistant Directors
7 Captains, Assistant Directors
28 Total

The Engineering Staff consisted of:

4 Captains	10 Assistant Guards
12 Lieutenants	1 Chief Artificer
12 Sous-lieutenants, Students	1 Artificer
10 Guards	50 Total

In addition, a sapper-miner battalion was raised that consisted of 756 men and 180 horses.

The Foot Artillery Regiment consisted of 12 field companies and 4 static companies. The staff of the regiment consisted of:

1 Colonel	1 Master Armorer
2 Adjutant NCOs	1 1st Class Physician
1 Major	1 Master Tailor
1 Regimental Drum Major	1 2nd Class Physician
3 Chefs de bataillon	1 Master Saddlemaker
1 Veterinarian	2 3rd Class Physicians
1 Paymaster	1 Master Cobbler
1 Battalion Drum Major	21 Total[1]
2 Adjutant-majors	

There is some confusion over the actual declaration of the assignment of these personnel. Indications are that the Decree of 30 March 1810 directed the establishment of these positions, but, according to Poniatowski, these positions were not filled until 1812.

Within the field companies of the regiment there were: 12 captains, 24 lieutenants 1st class, and 12 lieutenants 2nd class. Each field company had:

1 Captain 1st Class	2 Harnessmakers
8 Corporals	1 Sergeant-major
(1) Captain 2nd Class[2]	8 Sergeants
4 Artificers	1 Fourrier
2 1st Class Lieutenants	40 1st Class Gunners[3]
2 Blacksmiths	100 2nd Class Gunners
1 2nd Class Lieutenant	2 Drummers
	172 Total[4]

The companies also had the two enfants de troupe assigned to their strength. The four static companies consisted of:

1 Captain 1st Class	4 Artificers
(1) Captain 2nd Class[5]	1 Blacksmith
2 1st Class Lieutenants	1 Harnessmaker
1 2nd Class Lieutenant	2 Drummers
1 Sergeant-major	24 1st Class Gunners
4 Sergeants	76 2nd Class Gunners
1 Fourrier	1 Enfant de troupe
8 Corporals	126 Total[6]

[1]Raised to 22 in 1812 by the addition of an additional master artisan.

[2]Added in 1812.

[3]According to Poniatowski's correspondance this was raised to 48 in 1812, but it also appears in the 1810 decree.

[4]Total of 180 in 1812, or 181 with the additional captain.

[5]Added in 1812.

[6]Total of 127 in 1812

The field company manned a battery of two 6" howitzers and four 6pdr cannons. There appears to have been only one 12pdr battery in the army of the Grand Duchy and it appears to have had six 12pdrs and no howitzers. Most of the equipment was either captured Prussian or Austrian equipment. The Foot Artillery Regiment had a total of 2,685 men and 1,803 horses.

The Horse Artillery Regiment had four horse artillery companies, each with four 6pdr cannon and two 6-inch howitzers. The Decree of 30 March 1810 set the staff of the hrose artillery regiment to:

1 Colonel	1 Regimental Trumpet Major
1 Major	1 Battalion Trumpet Major
2 Chefs d'escadron	1 Veterinarian (Artiste Veterinaire)
1 Paymaster	1 Veterinarian (Maréchal expert)
2 Adjutant-majors	1 Master Saddlemaker
1 1st Class Physician	1 Master Tailor
2 2nd Class Physicians	1 Master Cobbler
2 Adjutant NCOs	19 Total

Poniatowski indicated that the staff of the Horse Artillery Regiment consisted of the following and did not assume the 19 man structure until 1812.

1 Chef de bataillon	1 1st Class Physician
1 Battalion Trumpet Major	1 Master Saddlemaker
1 Adjutant-majors	1 2nd Class Physicians
1 Master Armorer	1 Master Cobbler
1 Paymaster	1 Adjutant NCOs
1 Master Tailor	11 Total

As with the foot companies, the horse companies had always consisted of:

1 Captain 1st Class	2 Blacksmith
(1) Captain 2nd Class[7]	1 Saddlemaker
1 2nd Class Lieutenant	1 Harness maker
1 Sergeant-major	2 Trumpeters
8 Sergeants	48 1st Class Gunners
1 Fourrier	88 2nd Class Gunners[8]
8 Brigadiers (Corporals)	2 Enfants de troupe
4 Artificers	168 Totals[9]

The Horse Artillery Regiment had a total of 691 men and 902 horses.

[7]Added in 1812.

[8]Raised to 100 in 1812.

[9]With the additional captain the strength was 169. The total was raised to 181 in 1812.

In addition, after instructions sent to the King of Saxony and Duke of Warsaw, each infantry regiment had two 3pdr regimental guns manned by a crew consisting of:

1 Lieutenant	2 3pdr cannons
1 Sous-lieutenant	3 Caissons
3 Sergeants	1 Field Forge (for 3 regiments)
3 Corporals	1 Ambulance Caisson
20 Cannoneers	1 Document Caisson
2 Artisans	2 Caissons/battalion for cartridges and bread
40 Train Soldiers	70 Total
	95 Horses

The supplementary artillery battalion, established by the Decree of 26 June 1811, had a staff and eight companies. The staff had:

1 Chef de bataillon	3 Health Officers
1 Quartermaster	2 Adjutant NCOs
2 Adjutant majors	9 Trumpeters, artisans, etc.

Each of the eight companies had:

1 Lieutenant 1st Class	1 Fourrier
2 Lieutenants 2nd Class	1 Blacksmith
1 Sergeant Major	1 Harness maker
4 Sergeants	34 1st Class Gunners[10]
4 Corporals	70 2nd Class Gunners
	120 Total[11]

Poniatowski indicates the single artillery artisan company had:

1 Commanding Captain	1 Fourrier
1 Captain 2nd Class	8 Corporals
2 Lieutenants 1st Class	1 Drummer
1 Lieutenant 2nd Class	24 1st Class Artisans
1 Sergeant major	76 2nd Class Artisans[12]
8 Sergeants	123 Total
	2 Enfants de troupe[13]

[10]Raised to 82 in 1812.

[11]Raised to 132 in 1812.

[12]Raised to 84, probably in 1811, and finally to 96 in 1812.

[13]Total of 132 in 1811 and 144 in 1812.

Other sources indicate it had:

1 Commanding Captain
2 Lieutenants 1st Class
1 Lieutenant 2nd Class
1 Sergeant major
8 Sergeants
1 Fourrier
8 Corporals
1 Drummer
24 1st Class Artisans
76 2nd Class Artisans
123 Total
2 Enfants de troup

The sapper-miner battalion had a staff and six companies. Of the six assigned companies, one was actually a pontooneers company. The staff consisted of:

1 Major
1 Chef de bataillon
1 Quartermaster
2 Adjutant-majors
1 1st Class Health Officer
1 2nd Class Health Officer
2 Adjutant NCOs
3 Master Artisans

The companies consisted of:

1 Commanding Captain
1 Captain 2nd Class[14]
2 Lieutenants 1st Class
1 Lieutenant 2nd Class
1 Sergeant major
4 Sergeants
1 Fourrier
8 Corporals
4 Miners
2 Drummers
24 1st Class Sappers
79 2nd Class Sappers[15]
128 Total[16]
2 Enfants de troupe

Initially the pontooneer company appears to have been organized like the sapper companies. Poniatowski indicates in his correspondence, however, that the pontooneer company, attached to the sapper battalion, had:

1 Colonel, Engineering director
1 Lt. Colonel, Chief of the Topographical Bureau
5 Lt. Colonels, Assistant Directors
10 Engineering Captains
15 Engineering Lieutenants
7 Guards
10 Assistant Guards
9 Porters
24 Caretakers of military equipment
82 Total

[14]Indicated as present only in Poniatowski's correspondance.
[15]This figure is provided by Poniatowski. Other sources indi¬cate it was 76. Poniatowski indicates another 20 added in 1812.
[16]Raised to a total of 149 in 1812. This is as presented by Poniatowski in his correspondance. Other sources indicate 26 1st Class Sappers and no Captain 2nd Class.

Foot Artillery (Jan Chelminski)

Horse Artillery Officer (Jan Chelminski)

Uniforms of the Artillery and Support Troops

Uniforms of the Foot Artillery, Corps of Engineers and Sappers

Between 1807 and 1810 the foot artillery wore dark green infantry kurtkas with black collars, facings, cuffs, cuff flaps and turnbacks. All were piped with red. Their buttons were yellow, their epaulets were poppy red, though the officers wore gold epaulets. Their trousers were black with dark green side stripes. The officers had a double stripe. The trousers covered the short boots of the officers, but the enlisted men wore black gaiters and infantry shoes. The shakos were black with poppy red pompons and cords. Again, the officers wore golden pompons and silver cords.

Between 1807 and 1810 the engineering and sapper officers wore black shakos with a golden band around the top, with silver cords and short tassels. In front they had a golden convex rosette. Their epaulets were golden, their breeches were dark gray with double dark green side stripes and were worn over their short boots. They were, otherwise, dressed like the foot artillery, except they wore no cuff flaps. This uniform was retained until 1811, when they adopted the 1810 foot artillery uniform.

After 1810 the uniform of all three services consisted of a dark green jacket with cuffs, cuff flaps, collar, and lapels of black velvet piped with red. The vest and summer breeches were of white cloth. However, dark green breeches were also worn. If the white breeches were worn, so were white gaiters. If the green was worn, black gaiters were worn.

The buttons were of yellow metal. Their shako was black with a poppy red pompon, plume and cords. It had a brass plaque with the same crest worn on the buttons. Over the plaque was a white metal eagle.

After 25 May 1811 the 2nd Class Gunners were distinguished by breeches covered on the inside of the legs with black leather and by black shoulder straps piped in poppy red. They also appear to have worn pompons rather than plumes. The only significant difference between the uniforms was that the artillery buttons had crossed cannons and a bomb on them. Those of the engineers and the sappers had crossed cannons surmounted by a cuirass in themiddle of a trophy of flags and a helmet.

Uniforms of the Horse Artillery

Between 1808 and 1810 the uniform of the horse artillery consisted of a dark green kurtka cut like those worn by the uhlans. Its collar was of black velvet with poppy red piping. There were two golden grenades embroidered on the collar. The facings and cuffs were also black velvet with poppy red piping. The kurtka had poppy red piping as well and its buttons were gold. Their breeches were dark green with black side stripes. They wore a czapka like that of the uhlans.

In 1810 the czapka was discarded for a colpack with a dark green bag. It had poppy red (gold for officers) cords, pompon and tassels. In undress the officers wore a bicorn.

The breeches were now of dark green cloth with double black side stripes. The gray breeches were used in undress only.

The grenades and buttons were yellow for the soldiers and golden for the officers. The officers' boots were in the Hungarian style with gold trim and tassels. Otherwise they wore uhlan style boots. In undress, the officers wore hussar style breeches, heavily laced vests and sometimes, pelisses and dolmans.

Uniforms of the Train Drivers

The uniform of the drivers of equipment train and ammunition wagons before 1811 consisted of a blue-gray uniform with yellow buttons. The officers wore dark blue uniforms with golden buttons. The czapka was dark blue with a black lambskin turban and rhomboidal brass plaques. The officers' czapkas had a golden band around the top and the plaque and eagle were also golden.

After 1811 the blue-gray uniform adopted light yellow collars and cuffs, black shakos with small light yellow pompons and white eagles. The buttons were white.

The gun team drivers were the 2nd Class Gunners of the artillery companies and their uniforms are discussed above.

Train Driver (Bronislaw Gembarzewski)

Polish Forces in French Service 1795 - 1815

The Lombard/Cisapline Legion and the 1st Polish Legion

When the Third Partitioning occurred in 1795, the last bit of Poland totally disappeared from the map of Europe. When this occurred many of the Polish officers and soldiers fled to Revolutionary France where they felt an ideological compatriotism. One of these Polish officers, General Dombrowski, had hopes of forming a force of Polish troops with those refugees. His proposals were rejected by the French government, which had enacted legislation forbidding the use of foreign troops by France.

It is reputed by Belhomme that the prohibition by the Revolutionary government against foreign troops serving in the French army was first ignored on 1 April 1795 when a Polish battalion was raised in the 21e Demi-brigade by General Kellerman. It consisted of the standard nine companies, one grenadier and eight fusilier companies. It was reportedly recruited from Polish pris¬oners as well as Austrian and Hungarian deserters. Belhomme states that it was commanded by von Tauffen, a former Austrian major. Its officers were Polish, Piedmontese and Italian. The battalion's staff consisted of:

1 Chef de bataillon
1 Adjutant NCO
1 Master tailor
1 Master cobbler

Each of the nine companies had:

1 Captain	1 Caporal-fourrier
1 Lieutenant	8 Corporals
1 Sous-lieutenant	70 Fusiliers or Grenadiers
1 Sergeant-major	2 Drummers
4 Sergeants	89 Total

Dombrowski went to Italy where the Lombard Republic was being formed. In conjunction with Napoleon, he approached the Lombard Council and proposed forming a Polish legion. The proposal was accepted.

On 9 January 1797 an agreement was signed which gave any Pole serving in the Lombard Legion the same pay and privileges as the national troops. Shortly after that agreement was signed Dombrowski issued a proclamation calling all free Poles to join his legion. Within a month approximately 1,200 men were enrolled. Many were exiles, while others were prisoners of war and deserters from the Austrian Galician regiments formed in what used to be Poland.

This second Polish force raised, the Lombard Legion, was formally organized by Napoleon Bonaparte on 7 Ventôse V (25 February 1797). Belhomme suggests that the Polish battalion of the 21e Demi-brigade was used as the cadre around which the Legion was to be formed. However, the nucleus of the Polish legions were two Polish companies in the Lombard (native) Legion and a Polish battalion attached to this legion established by Bonaparte's order of 5 December 1796. The Polish legions proper were created by the convention between Dombrowski and the Lombard Republic, with Napoleon's approval, on 9 January 1797. The first specific organizational decrees are found in Napoleon's order of 17 May 1797. At first they consisted of three battalions and bore the name of the "*Polish Auxiliary Legion in Lombardy*". On their way from Milan to Mantua they fought at Salo (30 March 1797) and afterwards put down local uprisings in Brescia, Rimini and Verona. On 2 June 1797, the Polish Legions stood in Bologna and contained about 6,648 men.

In July 1797 the Lombard Republic was enlarged and renamed the Cisalpine Republic. The new government delayed the signing of a new convention with the Poles until 17 November 1797, however this convention was never formally ratified. The Poles were now renamed as the "*Polish Auxiliary Legions of the Cisalpine Republic*". In November 1798 their name was changed to the "Polish Auxiliary Corps of the Cisalpine Republic".

The legion was to consist of two "demi-légions," each of three battalions, and one artillery company. Its staff was to consist of:

1 Chef de Légion - Brigadier General
1 Adjutant Général - Chef de brigade
1 Aide de camp to the chef de légion
2 Adjoints for the adjutant Général
1 Chef de bataillon - artillery commander
1 Capitaine d'artillerie - charged with organization & material
2 Magazine guards
2 Teamsters

The demi-legion staffs were to consist of:

1 Chef de brigade
1 Major
2 Adjoints
1 Chef de bataillon - to command the grenadiers of the demi-legion

The battalion staffs were to consist of:

1 Chef de bataillon
1 Adjutant major
2 Adjutant NCOs

Napoleon's directive did not specify the number of companies per battalion or any other organizational details of the companies, but he did state that all companies, except the grenadiers were to have ten men trained to act as "éclaireurs" or scouts. These men were to be detached and converged into a separate company that would be directed by a captain, a lieutenant and a sous-lieutenant who were also part of the battalion staff.

The directive went on to state that the artillery companies were to be organized with four 6pdrs and two howitzers each. Each battalion was also to have an infantry munition caisson.

On 9 February a total of 1,128 men were organized and divided into two five company battalions. One of these battalions was a grenadier battalion and the other a chasseur battalion. These battalions consisted of:

1 Chef de bataillon	65 Corporals
1 Captain	5 Drummers
11 Lieutenants	513 Grenadiers
1 Battalion Surgeon	521 Sharpshooters or Chasseurs
10 Sous-lieutenant	1,128 Total

The legion was expanded by a steady stream of Polish volunteers and the legion began to take the form directed by Napoleon. The 1st Fusilier Battalion was raised that April in Mantua, the 2nd, 5th and 6th Battalions and two artillery companies were raised in Milan. By May 1797, there were six full battalions. Each battalion staff consisted of:

1 Chef de bataillon	2 Adjutant NCOs
1 Major	1 Quartermaster
1 Adjutant	

Each battalion was organized with ten companies. The first company was the grenadier company, the second was the "*strzelecka*" or chasseur company, and the last eight were "*fizylierskie*" or fusilier companies. Each company was organized with:

1 Captain	1 Surgeon
8 Corporals	1 Ensign
2 Lieutenants	3 Sappers
3 Drummers	1 Quartermaster Corporal
1 Sergeant	157 Soldiers
	178 Total

Each demi-legion was formed with three battalions and had an artillery company attached to it. In addition, there was an administrative staff assigned to the legion that consisted of the following:

1 Chef de brigade
3 Chefs de bataillon
2 Captains
2 Lieutenants
2 Soldiers

In his decree of 17 May 1797, Napoleon attached the Polish artillery, three batteries strong, to the Lombard Artillery Regiment as one of its four brigades. The Convention of 17 November 1797, however, treated it as part of the Polish force. On the other hand, W. Axamitowski, the battalion commander, stated that his unit was in an organizational limbo until December 1798, when it was finally attached to the Polish Legion. In the meantime, they wore Lombard/ Cisalpine uniforms with French cockades and Polish officer distinctives. A 7th Battalion was raised on 26 February 1797 in Milan.

In addition, the French Directory formed a provisional Polish battalion in Lille with 1,000 Polish prisoners of war taken from the Austrians. This battalion was dispatched to Milan where it arrived on 30 May 1797. It was then attached to the 2nd Fusilier Battalion of the 1st Polish Legion, of the Lombard Legion, and used to form the 2nd Polish Legion. The 1st Legion was commanded by General K. Kniaziewicz and the 2nd Legion was commanded by General J. Wielhorski. The artillery was commanded by Chef de bataillon W. Axamitowski. General Dombrowski was the commander-in-chief of the entire legion Kniaziewicz took command of the 1st Legion in September 1797. Prior to that the 1st Legion was commanded by J. Wielhorski and the 2nd Legion was commanded by F. Rymkiewicz. In July 1798 Wielhorski took over command of the Cisalpine group of the legion. The 2nd Legion was commanded by Rymkiewicz until his death from wounds received in 5 April 1799 at the battle of Magnano. Wielhorski then led the remains of the 2nd Legion to Mantua. The 1st Legion did not participate because it had gone to the Roman Republic.

Both the 1st and 2nd Polish Legions as well as the Lombard Legion were formed with three battalions of ten companies. The companies were organized with 100 men. Each battalion also is reputed to have had a 120 man artillery company attached to it as well, though they probably were still administratively assigned to a separate artillery battalion.

The organization of the Lombard Legion changed in June 1797. Its staff was reorganized and consisted of:

1 Chef du légion
1 Assistant chef, Chef de brigade
1 Major, Battalion Commander
2 Adjutant majors, Captains
3 Adjutant Sous-lieutenants
(assigned to battalions)
1 Chief Surgeon
1 Drum Major

1 Music Director
13 Musicians
1 Tailor
1 Cobbler
3 Gunsmiths

5 Drivers
13 Sappers

The battalion staffs now consisted of:

1 Chef de bataillon
1 Major (paid as a captain)
1 Adjutant Major, Lieutenant
1 Quartermaster, Lieutenant
1 Standard Bearer, Sous-lieutenant
1 Senior Surgeon
1 Drum Corporal
7 Total

The battalion still consisted of ten companies, but each company now had:

1 Captain	1 Quartermaster Corporal
1 Lieutenant	8 Corporals
1 Sous-lieutenant	2 Drummers
1 Sergeant Major	104 Soldiers
4 Sergeants	123 Total

The Lombard Legion was made part of the Cisalpine Republic's army on 4 August 1797. The Cisalpine Army consisted of four legions. The 1st Legion was formed with the 1st, 2nd and 3rd Cohorts of the Lombard Legion in Palmanova. The 2nd Legion was formed with the 4th, 5th and 6th Cohorts of the Lombard Legion in Venice. The 3rd Legion was formed from the Modene Legion's three cohorts and the 4th Legion was formed from the 7th Cohort of the Lombard Legion, the Bergamo Cohort and three companies from Crinsac. Each legion consisted of three battalions, an artillery company and a squadron of chasseurs.

The Lombard Legion was engaged in the battle of Reggio in July 1797 and at Civita Castellana. A cavalry regiment was raised in 1799. It consisted of two squadrons and was furnished with Austrian equipment captured at Gaeta.

A third reorganization of the Lombard Legion occurred on 14 September-October 1798, when they were reformed into the Polish Auxiliary corps of the Cisalpine Republic. The battalion staff now consisted of:

1 Chef de bataillon	1 Quartermaster
1 Staff Fourrier	1 Gunsmith
1 Major	1 Battalion Surgeon
1 Ensign	1 Senior Waggoner
1 Adjutant	2 Waggoners
1 Battalion Drummer	

There were still ten companies per battalion, including one grenadier company, one chasseur company and eight fusilier companies. The total strength of the battalion was 1,230 men, plus 10 supernumerary officers. The company organization con¬sisted of:

1 Captain	1 Surgeon (in every other company)
1 Lieutenant	1 Fourrier
1 Sous-lieutenant	8 Corporals
1 Sergeant-major	2 Drummers
4 Sergeants	86 Soldiers
	106 Total

The artillery battalion had 313 men, 7 in the staff plus three companies of 101 men each and 3 supernumerary officers. The general staff of the Polish Corps contained 8 officers, including one Général de division and one Général de brigade. the staff of a single legion contained 69 men, thus the entire Polish corps, two legions with six battalions and one artillery battalion, contained 7,899 men.

By the end of December 1798 the 1st Legion had captured so many horses that it was possible to begin the organization of cavalry unit in Gaeta, under the supervision of Chef d'escadron Eliasz Tremo. By the beginning of January 1799 two companies of about 100 men had been organized. Their uniforms and weapons were modeled after the national cavalry regiments in pre-1795 Poland, while the organization followed that of the French light cavalry regiments but preserving the Polish nomenclature. A company, therefore, consisted of:

1 Rotmistrz (Captain)	1 Furier (fourrier)
1 Porucznik (Lieutenant)	8 Brygadier (Brigadiers)
2 Podporucznik (Sous-lieutenants)	2 Trumpeters
1 Namiestnik (Sergeant major)	96 Uhlans
4 Wachmistrz (Sergeants)	116 Total

On 9 January 1799 Tremo, with 30-40 uhlans, went to Traetta to prevent a local uprising. The Poles were trapped and about half were killed by gunfire. Tremo and 8 uhlans were captured, mutilated and roasted alive. One officer and a few troopers escaped into an old tower, where they defended themselves for three days by throwing stones. They finally managed to slip out into the night and returned to their base.

Despite this setback, the uhlans' ranks were filling so fast that by 12 February 1799 they were formed into two squadrons, each with two companies. The Polish nomenclature, impossible for the French, was abandoned. The command of the regiment was taken by General A. Karwowski and later passed to Colonel A. Rozniecki.

On 25 November 1799 the regiment had a staff and two squadrons. The staff consisted of:

1 Chef de brigade
1 Chef d'escadron
1 Adjutant Major
1 Quartermaster
1 Adjutant Sous-lieutenant
1 Surgeon
1 Adjutant NCO

In December the regiment was transferred to the Danube Legion, where it eventually grew to a strength of four squadrons.

In May 1799 the 1st Polish Legion formed two elite battalions from a portion of its 2,800 men. The first elite battalion was formed with three 150 man companies of grenadiers and the second was formed with three companies of 150 chasseurs.

The 3rd Battalion of the 1st Polish Legion was captured at the battle of Trebbia on 17 to 19 June 1799 and its soldiers reincorporated into various Austrian regiments. Two of the legion's fusilier battalions succeeded in following the withdrawing French. Later the 1st Legion, in Nice, was reorganized and reinforced. It rose to a strength of about 2,500 men.

On 26 March 1799 the 2nd Legion lost 750 men from the 1st Battalion at Legnano. On 5 April 1799 another 1,000 were lost. The remaining 1,200 infantry and 300 artillerists went to Mantua where they became trapped. The siege lasted 2½ months and when the city capitulated the Poles were handed over to the Austrians. The Austrians incorporated them into the Austro-Galician regiments. The officers were jailed and remained there until the French victory at Marengo. The non-Polish troops taken in Mantua were set free. About 240 of the about 800 Poles succeeded in avoiding incorporation into Austrian regiments by shedding their uniforms and blending in with the rest of the departing garrison. They were reformed in May and sent to Marseilles in late 1799.

On 18 July 1799 the 3rd Battalion, 1st Legion, then in Genoa, absorbed the 600 man depot of the 2nd Legion. The 1st Legion, after its reorganization in Nice, fought at the battle of Novi on 15 August 1799, losing 1,000 men. During the next several weeks the remaining 1,500 legionnaires fought in the Ligurian Mountains and, finally, in the Second Battle of Novi, fought on 6 November. The 1st Legion was then sent to Marseilles, where Dombrowski was organizing eight battalions of the Polish Legion (also known as the 1st Polish Legion as opposed to the 2nd or Danube Legion).

In December 1799 all Polish forces were directed to Marseilles and incorporated into the French army. They received the full pay and allowances accorded to French units. The cavalry regiment was detached and sent to the Armée du Rhin, where it became part of the Legion of the Danube, commanded by General Kniaziewicz.

When the Polish infantry arrived in Marseilles they were rearmed and issued new uniforms. The new uniform had the same cut of jacket, but the cuffs and plastron were of the Polish national color, crimson. The artillery uniform was not altered.

The infantry and artillery were divided into several detachments that were used to fight pirates and the English, who were threatening the French coast with landings in 1800.

The 7th Battalion was re-raised in early 1800 and the 4th, 5th and 6th Battalions were brought back up to nearly full strength by combing the prisoner of war camps for Polish volunteers.

The Polish Demi-brigades, Légion du Danube and Vistula Legion

Légion du Danube

The Law of 8 September 1799 raised the Légio du Danube. The actual formation of the legion (initially called the Légion du Rhin because it was assigned to the Armée du Rhin) began on 8 November 1799 in Phalsbourg. According to the September law, it consisted of a staff, four infantry battalions (10 companies of 123 men each), four cavalry squadrons (2 companies each, 232 men per squadron), and a horse artillery company. It had a theoretical strength of 4,947 infantry, 943 cavalry and 74 artillery.

The actual organization in August 1800 was as follows:

General Staff
- 1 Général de brigade, Chef de la légion
- 1 Adjutant General, Chief of Staff and Vice-Chef
- 1 Captain Quartermaster General
- 1 Sous-lieutenant adjutant to the Legion

Commander
- 1 Captain Adjutant to the Legion Commander
- 1 Sous-lieutenant Adjutant to the Legion Chief of Staff
- 1 Surgeon Major 2nd Class
- 24 Musicians

The infantry staff consisted of:

1 Chef de brigade	4 Standard Bearer Sergeants
4 Chefs de bataillon	1 Drum Major
4 Adjutant-major Lieutenants	4 Senior Drummers
1 Quartermaster Adjunct Lieutenant	1 Master Armorer
4 Adjutant NCOs	4 Tailors
1 Surgeon Major 2nd Class	1 Cobbler
4 Assistant Surgeon 3rd Class	16 Sappers
	50 Total

Each battalion had ten companies, one grenadier, one chasseur and eight fusilier companies. The companies had:

1 Captain	1 Caporal-fourrier
1 Lieutenant	8 Corporals
1 Sous-lieutenant	2 Drummers
1 Sergeant Major	104 Fusiliers
4 Sergeants	123 Total

The cavalry staff consisted of:

1 Chef de brigade	2 Chefs d'escadron
1 Regimental Trumpeter	1 Armorer-spurmaker
1 Adjutant Major Lieutenant	1 Quarter-master Adjunct
1 Master of Uniform Material Lieutenant	1 Cobbler
1 Surgeon Major 2nd Class for both cavalry & artillery	1 Saddlemaker
2 Adjutant NCOs	1 Veterinarian
1 Assistant Surgeon 3rd Class	1 Blacksmith
4 Standard Bearers (Sergeant majors)	20 Total

The cavalry regiment had four squadrons, of two companies each. Each company consisted of:

1 Captain	1 Brigadier-Fourrier
1 Lieutenant	8 Brigadiers
1 Sous-lieutenant	2 Trumpeters
1 Sergeant Major	96 Lancers
4 Sergeants	115 Total

The horse artillery company had:

1 Captain	1 Brigadier Fourrier
1 Lieutenant	4 Brigadiers
2 Sous-lieutenants	30 Gunners 1st Class
1 Sergeant Major	30 Gunners 2nd Class
4 Sergeants	2 Trumpeters
	76 Total

A train company, not included in the original September 1799 organization was organized at the beginning of August 1800 with a theoretical strength of 72 men (1 sous-lieutenant, 1 trumpeter, and 70 artisans and drivers) who wore uniforms of the French train service. Such companies were not introduced into the French army until 3 January 1800.

The cadres of the Légion du Danube came from the Italian Polish Legions. General K. Kniaziewicz was the Chef de légion and was seconded by General Gawronski. M. Sokolnicki commanded the infantry brigade and W. Turski commanded the cavalry. Captain Redel commanded the artillery and the depot, which was organized in mid-September, commanded by Captain Pagowski. By mid-February 1800 the legion stood with an actual strength of 2,700 men.

By the second half of February the depot and all the assigned men were moved to Metz. Since the soldiers did not have uniforms, shirts or even shoes, they marched from Phalsbourg dressed in linen sleeved vests and pants. One third of them were barefoot! By the end of April 1800 the first three battalions, a total of 2,819 men, were organized and under the commands of Chefs de bataillon Fiszer, Drzewiecki and Zeydlitz. They marched to Strasbourg where the depot had also been moved. The line units were, however, shortly later sent to the Kehl fortress.

Though they still did not have proper uniforms, the Légion du Danube found itself engaging the Austro-Galician uhlans at Altenburg and Offenberg.

The actual strengths of the units in June 1800 of the Danube Legion, when its organization was relatively complete, were:

Unit	Men	Horses
1st Battalion	986	
2nd Battalion	920	
3rd Battalion	1,000	
4th Battalion	492	
1st Squadron	212	162
2nd Squadron	230	210
3rd Squadron	185	160
4th Squadron	75	154
Artillery	80	148
Artillery Train	75	150
Total[1]	4,390	885

[1]An additional 318 in depots and 98 in staffs should be added to this, providing a grand total of 4,806.

In August they also finally received uniform supplies and horses for its cavalry and artillery.

Two squadrons of "chasseurs" were organized within the legion prior to 20 February 1800. The cadres of the other two, under chef d'escadron A. Rozniecki, arrived from Dombrowski's Polish corps, then in Italy, on 17 May 1800. Two and a half months later the 1st and 4th platoons of each company of this new regiment were issued lances, making it an uhlan regiment. The 2nd and 3rd Platoons of each company were armed with carbines. This, however, didn't prevent the French commanders from referring to them "dragoons", "mounted rifles" or even "hussars." In November the Legion served with Decaen's division in Bavaria and fought at the Battle of Hohenlinden. On 29 December the depot was moved to Ulm.

After the Treaty of Luneville (9 February 1801) the Danube Legion was sent to Geneva and from there to Italy. Because of the political ramifications of a "Poland" the legion was to be transferred to the newly formed Kingdom of Etruria, under the rule of a Bourbon prince. In May 1801 the legion was sent to Florence, the capital of this new kingdom. This was not a popular move. The soldiers deserted, officers committed suicide and several officers resigned their commissions. When Kniasiewicz resigned, command passed to Jablonowski, but problems continued and the French didn't know what to do with the unit. There was even talk of disbanding it. On 22 December 1801 the legion was transformed into the 3e Demi-brigade Polonaise. It had a strength of 2,918 men. Its cavalry and artillery were amalgamated.

The 1st Polish Legion is Reformed

In early 1800 the debris of the 1st Polish Legion was gathered in Genoa[2] and Nice, while the surviving members of the 2nd Polish Legion were gathered into Marseilles.[3] The Arrêté of 10 February 1800 organized the new 1st Polish Legion. It con¬sisted of four battalions of infantry and a horse battery. The Danube Legion was renumbered as the 2nd Polish Legion. The staff of the 1st Polish Legion consisted of:

1 Général de brigade, commanding
1 Adjutant General
1 Quartermaster General (captain)
1 Chief Surgeon

The infantry staff consisted of:

1 Chef de brigade
4 Chefs de bataillon
1 Drum Major
4 Adjutant NCOs
1 Quartermaster Adjunct
(lieutenant or sous-lieutenant)
1 Chief Surgeon of Infantry
4 Assistant Surgeons
4 Adjutant majors
4 Senior Srummers
1 Master Armorer
4 Tailors
1 Cobbler

[2]A large part of the 1,000 Polish members of the Genoa garrison were captured by the Austrians when the city fell in May 1800.
[3]The 1st Legion's depot was also in Marseilles and had been there prior to 13 March 1800.

Each of the four battalions was organized identically to those in the Danube Legion and had a theoretical total strength of 1,230 men per battalion. The cavalry staff consisted of:

1 Chef de brigade
2 Chefs d'escadron
1 Adjutant major
1 Adjutant NCO
1 Quartermaster adjutant
(lieutenant or sous-lieutenant)
1 Surgeon Major
1 Assistant Surgeon
4 Standard Bearers

1 Staff Trumpeter
1 Master Armorer/Spurmaker
1 Tailor
1 Cobbler
1 Saddlemaker
1 Blacksmith
1 Veterinarian
16 Total

The artillery company consisted of:

1 Captain
1 Lieutenant, 1st Class
2 Lieutenants, 2nd Class
1 Sergeant Major
4 Sergeants

1 Corporal Fourrier
4 Brigadier
30 1st Class Gunners
30 2nd Class Gunners
2 Trumpeters
76 Total

This structure, which mirrored strictly the original organization of the Légion du Nord, was submitted to Dombrowski, who proposed to exchange the cavalry regiment and the horse artillery company for three more infantry battalions and a foot artillery battery. In effect, the Arrêté of 13 March 1800 reorganized the 1st Polish Legion with seven battalions, each with ten companies of 123 men (one grenadier, one chasseur and eight fusilier compa¬nies). The battalion staff had six officers. In addition, there was an artillery battalion with five companies. Each artillery company had four officers and 83 men. The legion had a total theoretical strength of 9,093 men.

The 4th, 5th and 6th Battalions were organized at the end of April in Marseilles with the remnants of the old 2nd Polish Legion. The 1st, 2nd, and 3rd Battalions were organized in Nice in June from the 1st Legion. The 7th Battalion and the depot were organized in Marseilles. The cavalry regiment was transferred to the Danube Legion.

In July 1800 another legion depot/recruiting office was organized in Milan. This Milanese recruiting office also processed the officers of the 2nd Legion then returning from Austrian captivity.

On 23 September 1800 it was decided that the 1st Polish Legion was tao be returned to the pay of the newly reorganized Cisalpine Republic. This was not announced until 1 November 1800. In the second half of October, 1800, the legion was divided into two brigades. The 1st Brigade was commanded by Chef de brigade Strzalkowski and consisted of the 1st, 2nd and 3rd Battalions and all seven grenadier companies. The 2nd Brigade was commanded by General Karwowski and consisted of the 4th, 5th and 6th Battalions, less their grenadier companies. These last three battalions were filled out with released prisoners of war from the former 2nd Legion. The 7th Battalion was still in the process of being formed.

On 1 Germinal An IX (11 March 1801) the 1st Polish Legion consisted of a general staff formed with:

1 Général de division/Chef de légion
3 Chefs de bataillons aide de camp Général
1 Capitaine aide de camp Général
1 Général de brigade
2 Aides de camp Général de brigade
1 Adjutant commandant
3 Aides de camp d'état major
2 Lieutenants assigned to the Quartiermaître Général
1 Chief physician

The legion staff consisted of:

4 Chefs de brigade
1 Chef de brigade d'artillerie
2 Surgeons 2nd Class
2 Baggagemasters
2 Drum majors
1 Master armorer
1 Master cobbler
1 Master tailor
40 Musicians

Each battalion of infantry had a staff of:

1 Chef de bataillon
1 Capitaine adjutant-major
1 Surgeon, 3rd Class
1 Standard Bearer (sous-lieutenant)
1-2 Supernumerary officers

Each of the ten companies in the battalions were organized with:

1 Captain
1 Lieutenant
1 Sous-lieutenant
1 Sergeant Major
4 Sergeants
1 Caporal-fourrier
8 Corporals
2 Drummers
102 Soldiers
121 Total

The artillery battalion consisted of:

1 Chef de bataillon
1 Adjutant Major (Captain)
1 Surgeon, 3rd Class
10 Captains
15 Lieutenants
1 Lieutenant Standard Bearer
550 NCOs and gunners

In addition, there was a depot, consisting of 200 men, and a train company for the artillery that consisted of 70 men. The legion had an actual, not organizational, strength of 10,686 men on 11 March 1801.

Polish Demi-Brigades

The Arrêtés of 11/21 December 1801 united the Polish legions, the 1st Polish Legion in Italy and Danube Legion, and formed them into three demi-brigades. One demi-brigade numbered 3,231 officers and soldiers organized into one grenadier and eight fusilier companies per battalion.

Each demi-brigade had three battaions. The 1re Demi-brigade was formed with the 1st, 2nd and 3rd Battalions of the 1st Legion, the 2e Demi-brigade was formed with the 4th, 5th and 7th Battalions of the 1st Legion and the 3e Demi-brigade was formed with the four battalions of the 2nd Polish Legion (formerly the Danube Legion). The 6th Battalion and the artillery were absorbed into the first two demi-brigades.

The 1st Demi-brigade was organized in Modena and the 2nd was organized in Reggio. Dombrowski was made Inspector General of the Polish Demi-brigades and all former Polish legions were disbanded as of 20 January 1802.

The general staff consisted of:

1 Général de division
1 Général de brigade
1 Adjutant-Commandant
2 Chefs de brigade
12 Chefs de bataillon

The staff of these demi-brigades consisted of:

1 Chef de brigade	1 Drum Major
4 Chefs de bataillon[4]	1 Drum Corporal
1 Quartermaster Treasurer	1 Master Tailor
3 Adjutant-majors	1 Master Cobbler
3 Health Officers	1 Master Gaitermaker
1 Baggage Master	1 Armorer
3 Adjutant NCOs	8 Musicians including one music master)
	30 Total

Each battalion had nine companies, one of grenadiers and eight of fusiliers. The companies were organized with:

[4]One chef de bataillion was assigned to each battalion and the fourth was assigned to support with various administrative du¬ties.

1 Captain
1 Lieutenant
1 Sous-lieutenant
1 Sergeant Major
4 Sergeants
1 Caporal-fourrier
8 Corporals
2 Drummers
64 Grenadiers or
104 Fusiliers
84 Total in a grenadier company
123 Total in a fusilier company

When the horse battery of the Danube Legion was disbanded, its troops, numbering twenty-one 1st Class Gunners and twenty-six 2nd Class Gunners, were amalgamated into the uhlan regiment. The staff of the uhlan regiment consisted of:

1 Chef de brigade
3 Chefs d'escadron
1 Adjutant Major
1 Quartermaster Captain
1 Surgeon 1st Class
1 Surgeon 2nd Class
2 Adjutant NCOs
1 Staff Trumpeter
1 Master Cobbler
1 Master Saddlemaker
13 Total

Each of the four squadrons had two companies, each of which had:

1 Captain
1 Lieutenant
2 Sous-lieutenants
1 Sergeant Major
4 Sergeants
1 Fourrier
8 Brigadiers
96 Uhlans
2 Trumpeters
116 Total

The actual regimental strength on 22 December was 707 officers and men, with only 66 uhlans per company. By 29 April 1802, however, it had grown to 946 men and 1,000 horses.

The legion's artillery was also slightly reorganized. The numbers of 1st Class Gunners was reduced to twenty-one and the number of 2nd Class Gunners was reduced to twenty-six. The 1st Demi-brigade and the cavalry were transferred to the Cisalpine Republic on 31 December 1801. By 29 April 1802, the cavalry regiment's strength had grown again and stood at 946 and 1,000 horses.

The first two demi-brigades were transferred into the service of the Italian Republic, formerly known as the Cisalpine Republic on 21 January 1802. Zaremba gives the date of the transfer as 5 February 1802.The cavalry of the former Danube Legion was transferred on 31 December 1801.

According to Pachonski the Italian army was reorganized on 29 April 1802 and those changes affected the Polish demi-brigades. Their battalions were reduced to eight companies each; one grenadier, one chasseur, and six fusilier companies. The total strength then rose to 3,710 men. The strength of the cavalry regiment was raised to 946 men and 1,000 horses. The total of the two demi-brigades and the cavalry in Italian service rose to 8,366 men. Shortly later the demi-brigades were supplemented by the addition of an invalid and veteran company.

In early 1801, the 2nd Demi-brigade became branded as a subversive unit because of its Masonic activity, which had republican overtones. It was taken back into French service on 10 December 1802 and redesignated as the 114th Demi-brigade.

The 3e Demi-brigade Polonaise departed for Santo Domingo on 17 May 1802 and was redesignated as the French 113th Demi-brigade. It was later joined by the 2nd Demi-brigade (or 114th), which left Italy between 30 January and 4 February 1803. Both units consisted of 3 full battalions.

It is suggested that these two units went because of their republican attitudes and the expense of maintaining foreign units. Yellow fever and other diseases ravaged their ranks and the savagery of the war in Santo-Domingo left few survivors. Both units disappeared from the French army. About 500 men returned to France. Many of the men were captured by the British or sold by the Haitians to the British where they were absorbed into the 5/60th Royal American Regiment of Foot. They were, apparently strongly resistant to the initial pressures, but a deliberately harsh imprisonment and the deliberate violation of all the terms of their surrender by the British soon forced many to enlist in the British army. As the wars continued and the 5/60th was transferred to Spain for service against Napoleon many of these legionnaires deserted the British army to join their fellow Poles in French service.

Polish Legionarie in Santa Domingo 1802-3

Some of the returning survivors were incorporated into various units. About 100 of them were assigned to a "foreign battalion" stationed on Elba. Between February and June 1804, they were transferred back to the 1er Demi-brigade Polonaise.

The 1er Demi-brigade Polonaise remained in Italy and became part of the newly formed army of the Kingdom of Northern Italy. Its morale was not high either and by August 1802 desertion had reduced it to 2,400 men. The first two battalions had to be reinforced by drawing soldiers from the 3rd Battalion, seriously reducing its strength. In May 1803 the demi-brigade stood with two battalions assigned to General Lecchi's Italian-Polish divi¬sion. The 3rd Battalion had remained in various northern Italian garrisons.

The 1er Demi-brigade Polonaise was renamed the "Polish Infantry Regiment" in 1804. In February 1806 the Polish Infantry Regiment participated in the French invasion of Naples. A total of 770 Austro-Polish prisoners, or 26% of the regiment's strength, were incorporated into the regiment, seriously undermining its morale and patriotic spirit. Despite that the regiment continued in the campaign and by April the staff had 15 men, the 1st Battalion - 1,046, and the 2nd and 3rd Battalions - 1,011 men each. In addition, each battalion had a single 3pdr gun assigned to it.

On 4 July 1806, 12 companies from the 2nd and 3rd Battalions (937 men strong) participated in the battle of Maida with a British expeditionary force, losing between 350 and 500 soldiers. In the following encounters the losses mounted and the regiment's strength was reduced to about 400 men per battalion.

On 4 August 1806 the Polish infantry and cavalry regiments serving in Italy were transferred to the service of Joseph Napoleon's new kingdom, Naples. The regiment's 1st and 2nd Battalions totaled nearly 1,000 men. The strengths of both battalions declined to about 400 men per battalion.

The survivors of the regiment were drawn together in February 1807 and reestablished. It contained 78 officers and 1,463 men. On 2 February 1807, they were returned to French service. The losses suffered in the Calabrian campaign amounted to 33% of its officers and 56% of its rank and file. By March 1807, the regiment grew to 98 officers and 2,610 men.

On 22 January 1807 the Polish Hussar Regiment was struck from the Neapolitan army roles and its 586 men and 490 horses were transferred to Silesia. There are indications that part of these troops were, at the last minute, incorporated into King Joseph's Neapolitan guard cavalry.

Joseph Napoleon also kept 1,192 soldiers from the Polish Infantry Regiment, so that only 57 officers, 338 NCOs and about 900 soldiers followed the cavarly into Silesia. These soldiers were to form the nucleus of the Légion Polacco-Italienne.

1st (Kalinowski's) Polish Hussar Regiment

During the last months of 1806 Prince Jan Sulkowski[5] or Antoni Sulkowski, another Polish general, organized another Polish Hussar Regiment in Siewierz. It was initially called a "light cavalry regiment" and by Napoleon's Decree of 12 March 1807, was taken into French pay. The decree renamed the unit the 1st Polish Hussar Regiment and had a decreed strength of 1,043 men.

In April 1807 Sulkowski was caught gathering illegal contributions and was arrested. He escaped abroad and the regiment was passed to Colonel M. Pruszak. Its organization was now based on the Decree of 8 May 1807. Its organization progressed very slowly and on 1 July 1807 it consisted of 42 officers and 348 men. On 28 July the command passed to Colonel J. Kalinowski and the regiment, now known as the Kalinowski Hussars, reached the strength of 529 men.

Unfortunately, the material support promised by Napoleon never materialized and only the 112 man elite company had uniforms and horses, both paid for by Kalinowski. The remainder were in civilian clothes and without mounts. Even the elite company lacked boots and, because of their lack of footwear, they became known as the "poodles". The reason being that, though dressed in furs, they went around barefoot.

On 10 October Maréchal Davout reviewed the regiment, finding it's men barefoot and equipped with only 85 officers horses and 132 mounts for the rank and file. Ten days later Davout asked Berthier to send the hussars 400 infantry great coats and 400 pairs of shoes.

[5]Not to be confused with Joseph Sulkowski, Bonaparte's ADC in Italy and Egypt

On 27 October 1807 Kalinowski's Polish Hussar Regiment was disbanded and the men were transferred to Westphalia where 300 were incorporated into the Polish Hussar Regiment that had served in Italy. One hundred were also assigned to King Jerome's Westphalian Royal Guard. The hundred sent to Kassel eventually rejoined their comrades when they were incorporated into the Vistula Legion cavalry. Colonel Kalinowski rose to the rank of general-adjutant in Westphalian service and eventually returned to Polish service.

Légion du Nord

During the course of Napoleon's lightning campaign against Prussia the French found themselves in possession of a large number of Polish-Prussian deserters and prisoners of war. In order to use them to the best political advantage, on 20 September 1806, Napoleon issued a decree to organize "*une légion polonaise*", which was to be organized under the command of Général de division J. Zayonczek. The decree specified that at least two thirds of the officers were to be Poles, while the rest were to be those who had not served in the French ranks, but were willing to fight for their country. Napoleon also forbad the enlistment of any Polish officers currently serving in the French army. As events would prove, however, both of these instructions were ignored. Two thirds of the officers turned out to be Frenchmen, including former émigrés, and Germans. Napoleon personally dispatched five Polish officers to the new legion from the Armée d'Italie.

Two days later, on 22 September, in a second letter to General Dejean, Napoleon spoke of the 1er Légion du Nord being organized in Juliers (Jülich) and ordered the organization of a second in Nürnberg under the command of Colonel Henry. This was, in fact, Général de brigade H. Wolodkowicz, but his status was, for some unknown reason, unclear at this time. Both legions were to have four battalions each. Napoleon also stated that the colonels issuing proclamations to form these units were not to use the word "Poland" in their decrees.

The 1st Legion had its depot in Jülich, with barracks in Landau, Hagenau and later in Mainz. In the beginning of October 1806 the 1st Battalion, 1st Legion, was ready in Landau, but the other three were still being formed in Mainz. They were later brought up to full strength by the incorporation of Polish prisoners of war from the Prussian garrison of Magdeburg, which capitulated on 8 November.

In the first half of December, the 1st Legion, with 6,425 men, moved to Leipzig and then on to Magdeburg. It was still there on 8 January when an irate Napoleon blasted Berthier as to why it was not yet in Stettin. By February the 1st Legion had joined Ménard's division in Pomerania with a strength of about 5,000 men.

The evolution of the 2nd Legion was not as satisfactory. General Wolodkowicz began organizing it on 9 October 1806 in Nürnberg. By 10 November he had only 77 men. By the end of November it grew to 148 men and by 4 December stood at 164 men. On 9 December the 2nd Legion was moved to Spandau and its organization dragged on.

The 2nd Legion had very few Polish officers and could not compete for rank and file because the volunteers preferred (and were openly enticed by Dombrowski) to join Polish regiments on native soil. Realizing this, on 29 November Napoleon ordered it to march to Posen to be incorporated into the 1st Legion. This decision was formalized by the Decree of 1 March 1807. The next major changes occurred to the legion with the formation of Dombrowski's division and Zayonczek's Observation Corps, which are discussed in the organization of the Polish Army in 1807.

Légion Polacco-Italienne

The Decree of 5 April 1807 redesignated the Polish regiments form Italy as the Polish Legion. It was to consist of a lancer regiment (4 squadrons of 300 men each) and an infantry legion (3 regiments with two battalions each, 9 companies per battalion, 150 men per company having a total of 8,100 soldiers and about 100 men in the legionary staff). The actual reorganization of this force began after the Treaty of Tilsit, when political considerations obliged him to call it the Légion Polacco-Italienne, although this change was never introduced by any official means.

The 1st Regiment of the legion was formed on 7 June 1807. The remaining two began organizing shortly later. By 10 August 1807 the infantry numbered 91 officers and 4,246 men and the lancer regiment had 37 officers and 1,097 men.

The Vistula Legion

The Decree of 11 November 1807 transferred the Légion Polacco-Italienne into the service of Westphalia, but this was reversed by the Decree of 20 March 1808, which brought them back into French service. In a letter to Davout dated 31 March 1808 Napoleon renamed the legion the "Vistula Legion" and directed a reduction in the number of soldiers in its infantry companies to 140 men each. He also stated that the infantry regiments were to be treated on a par with French line regiments and cavalry with the French chasseur à cheval regiments. The legion was still enroute to Paris, so the actual reorganization had not yet begun.

The Legion and its Hussar Regiment went to Metz and Bayonne, where they, and detachments from all other Poles in French service, began organizing the Vistula Legion by the end of May 1808. Later, the Vistula Legion organized its depot in Sedan and established a depot battalion of three companies under a major.

Vistula Legion and 4th Regiment in Spain (Jan Chelminski)

On 11 April 1808 Napoleon issued the organizational decree for the Vistula Legion. It was to contain three infantry regiments, each with two battalions. The number of companies was reduced to six per battalion. This brought the Polish battalions into a close approximation of the organization established by the Decree of 18 February 1808 which put the French in a six company organization.

The Decree of 24 June 1808 established the final organization. The field battalions were now organized with one grenadier, one voltigeur and four fusilier companies of 140 men each. The depot battalion was organized like the field battalions, but had neither a grenadier company nor a voltigeur company. The legion staff consisted of:

1 Colonel	1 Chirurgien-major
3 Majors	6 Chirurgiens
6 Chefs de bataillon	6 Chirurgiens aides
7 Adjutant-majors	14 Adjutant NCOs
1 Quartier-maître trésorier	1 Drum major
3 Officiers payeurs (paymasters)	3 Drum corporals
3 Porte-aigle (eagle bearers)	6 Master artisans
1 Chaplain	18 Musicians
	79 Total

Each of the six companies had:

1 Captain	1 Caporal-fourrier
1 Lieutenant	8 Corporals
1 Sous-lieutenant	121 Soldiers
1 Sergeant-major	2 Drummers
4 Sergeants	140 Total

In addition, the legion had two administrative committees, one for the infantry and one for the lancer regiment.

The lancer regiment was organized like a French chasseur à cheval regiment. The Decree of 24 June 1808 did not address the lancers, so they retained their earlier organization of 43 officers and 1,000 rank and file organized into four squadrons. Each squadron had two companies. Kirkor gives their organization at this time as the following:

Staff

1 Colonel	2 Adjutant NCOs
1 Major	1 Brigadier Trumpeter
2 Chefs d'escadron	1 Veterinarian
2 Adjutant-majors	1 Master Cobbler
1 Quartier-mastre	1 Master Tailor
1 Chirurgien-major	1 Master Armorer/Spurmaker
1 Chirurgien aide-major	1 Master Harnessmaker
2 Chirurgien sous-aide	19 Total

Each company was to have:

1 Captain	8 Brigadiers
1 Lieutenant	108 Lancers
2 Sous-lieutenants	1 Farrier (blacksmith)
1 Maréchal des logis chef	2 Trumpeters
4 Maréchaux des logis	128 Total

The depot was formed in Sedan with three infantry companies and a cavalry company. It had a total of 545 men. In addition, the reorganization left the legion with a very large number of surplus officers serving à la suite, that is, without an assignment or duties.

These first organizational decrees had the effect of reducing the decreed strength of the Vistula Legion from 9,460 men to a more realistic 6,600 men. The Decree of 24 June brought it to a strength of 5,959 men. It should also be noted that French nationals were not permitted to serve in the legion, except as the company clerks (fourriers), battalion adjudant non-commissioned officers and as paymasters. The Poles, apparently, had little concern for administrative duties and, driven to desperation, Napoleon relented on these administrative positions.

At this time the legion's regimental commanders were:

Commander in Chief::	Général de brigade J. Grabinski
1st Infantry Regiment:	Colonel J. Chlopicki
2nd Infantry Regiment:	Colonel S. Bialowieyski
3rd Infantry Regiment:	Colonel P. Swiderski
Lancer Regiment:	Colonel J. Konopka

Between 27 May and 20 June elements of the Vistula Legion arrived in Bayonne preparing for participation in the Spanish campaign. The lancers arrived first and were permitted to retain their lances. The officers, non-commissioned officers and flankers were also issued carbines.

On 8 June Napoleon assigned the 2nd and 3rd Vistula Regiments to General Grandjean's division, effectively destroying the legion concept. General Grabinski no longer had a legion to command and, after a private conversation with Napoleon retired on an unpaid leave, never to return to French service.

At this time Colonel Bialowieyski died and command passed to Major M. Kasinowski. Colonel Swiderski retired and the 3rd Regiment passed to Major J. Szott.

After the battle of Wagram, Napoleon found that he was once again in possession of a large number of ethnic Poles amongst his Austrian prisoners of war. The Decree of 8 July 1809 directed that these men were to form the 2nd Vistula Legion. This legion was to have two regiments with four battalions. Each battalion was to be organized with six companies of 160 men. Its organization began in Saint-Poelten and ethnic Germans and Austrians were also accepted into its ranks. There were, however, insufficient men to fully form a second legion and in September its scope was reduced to two battalions. Both battalions were formed and sent to Sedan in October.

The Decree of 23 July 1809 ordered the raising of every infantry company to a strength of 200 men. This strength was not reached until the end of 1810. The 2nd Vistula Legion did not seem able to complete itself, so it was disbanded by the Decrees of 12/15 February 1810. Its men were incorporated into the 1st Vistula Legion as a 4th Regiment.

In 1810 Bronikowski became a Général de brigade and command of the 4th Regiment passed to K. Tanski, a former major in the 2nd Legion. The regiment, composed of former Austrian soldiers, had not enjoyed a very good reputation and was considered by the rest of the legion as a place of banishment. Tanski resigned his post on 26 June 1810 and on 12 July Colonel S. Estko was designated as his replacement. Estko, however, delayed his arrival until February 1812.

The cavalry regiment consisted of four squadrons, each with two companies. A ninth company acted as a depot. It consisted of 1,171 men, of whom 47 were officers. It had 1,184 horses of which 64 were officers' mounts.

There were three further units that were transferred to French service during this period. The King of Saxony, also the ruler of the Grand Duchy of Warsaw, complained to Napoleon that his treasury could not support the expanding Polish national army. On 16 March 1808 Napoleon decided that the Vistula Legion could, if the need arose, be sent to the aid of the King of Saxony without arousing particular attention. In addition, he authorized the transfer of the 4th, 7th and 9th Polish Regiments from Polish service to French service. They established their depots in Sedan and were organized with two, nine company battalions, and a depot company. Each company had 140 men.

The regimental staff of these three regiments consisted of:

1 Colonel
1 Major
2 Chefs de bataillon
2 Adjutants-major
1 Quartier-maŒtre trésorier
1 Officier payeur
1 Chirurgien-major
2 Chirurgiens aide-major
2 Chirurgiens sous-aide
2 Adjutant NCOs
1 Vaguemestre (baggagemaster)
1 Drum Major
1 Drum Corporal
1 Chef de musique
7 Musicians
1 Master Tailor
1 Master Cobbler
1 Master Armorer
1 Master Gaitermaker

Each company had:

1 Captain
1 Lieutenant
1 Sous-lieutenant
1 Sergeant-major
4 Sergeants
1 Caporal-fourrier
8 Corporals
121 Fusiliers, Grenadiers or Voltigeurs
2 Drummers
140 Total

These units left Poland in May 1808 and arrived in Metz in August. They were sent directly to Spain where the fought until 1811. On 13 December 1808 a royal decree organized four depot companies for these regiments in Lenczyca. Each company consisted of 3 officers, 14 non-commissioned officers, one drummer and 122 soldiers. On 29 October 1808 Napoleon directed that a main depot be formed in Bordeaux. Each regiment was to send one company to Bordeaux for this purpose, thus reducing their field strengths to eight companies. This depot processed new recruits being sent from Lenczyca.

A separate artillery company accompanied the Poles. This company consisted of six 4pdrs, four 8pdrs and two howitzers. In addition, regimental batteries were raised as well.

In 1812 the 4th, 7th and 9th Regiments were withdrawn and incorporated into the Grande Armée for the invasion of Russia where they were destroyed. Each regiment also began forming a third battalion in Posen. The third battalions followed the regiments into Russia and joined them in Smolensk on 10 October.

Shortly after their arrival in France and prior to their departure for Spain they altered their organization to the standard organization of the Polish infantry, which was similar to that established by the Decree of 18 February 1808. Their staff now consisted of:

1 Colonel
1 Major
3 Chefs de bataillon
3 Adjutants-major
1 Officier payeur
1 Chirurgien-major
2 Chirurgiens aide-major
3 Chirurgiens sous-aide

6 Adjutant NCOs
2 Porte aigle sous-officiers (NCO eagle bearers)
1 Chaplain
1 Drum Major
1 Drum Corporal
1 Master Tailor
1 Master Cobbler
1 Master Armorer
1 Master Gaitermaker

Each company had the same strength as it had been assigned in 1810 and stood at:

1 Captain
1 Lieutenant
1 Sous-lieutenant
1 Sergeant-major
4 Sergeants

1 Caporal-fourrier
8 Corporals
117 Fusiliers, Grenadiers or Voltigeurs
2 Drummers
136 Total

The Vistula Legion also adopted this organization during its reorganization in France, and it too was sent to Spain where it fought in the sieges of Saragossa and Segunto. In fact, the Vistula Legion seemed particularly destined to participate in sieges and fought in all of the major sieges in eastern Spain during the early years of the Peninsular War. The next organizational change was the raising of the 2nd Lancer Regiment on 7 February 1811. Its organization was identical to the 1st Lancer Regiment, the one difference being that it had no separate depot company. This gave the regiment a theoretical strength of 43 officers with 59 horses and 1,000 NCOs and troopers with 996 horses. The depot was common for both regiments. The officers were transferred from the 1st Imperial Guard Chevaulégers.

On 18 June 1811 the two lancer regiments were stripped from the Vistula Legion and redesignated as the 7e and 8e Regiments de Chevauléger-lanciers, part of the regular French army.

A third "Polish" regiment was raised on 23 February 1811 when the 30th Chasseurs à Cheval were raised in Hamburg. For a short while they were known as the "chasseurs-lanciers" because they carried lances and dressed as chasseurs, but on 18 June 1811 they were converted into the 9th Chevaulégers, also part of the French army. Though officially known as the "9e Régiment de lanciers Polonaise de la Ligne," they were predominately ethnic Germans.

In preparation for the invasion of Russia the Vistula Legion was withdrawn from Spain in early 1812. The Decree of 3 March 1812 ordered the transformation of the legion into a division. This was to be done by supplementing its four regiment with the organization of a 3rd Battalion for each regiment and the assignment of artillery companies. Command of the division was given to General Claparède and Chlopicki served as a brigade commander. On 14 March the Vistula Legion was renamed "La Légion du Grand Duché de Varsovie." By 5 May, however, it reverted to the "Vistula Legion."

Infantry Czapka voltiguers

On 13 March 1812 Napoleon issued the organizational decrees for the artillery and the third battalions. The decree for the third battalions did not, however, survive. A regimental artillery company was to consist of two guns, an appropriate number of ammunition wagons, an ambulance and a field forge. It was to have:

1 Lieutenant	20 Gunners
1 Sous-lieutenant	2 Artisans
3 Sergeants	40 Train Soldiers
3 Corporals	70 Total

These reorganizations brought the theoretical regimental strength from 1,705 men to 2,622 men and the entire division to a strength of 10,488 men, plus divisional staff. The actual decreed strength was never to be reached.

On 2 April 1812 Napoleon decided to include the Poles in the Young Guard corps under Maréchal Mortier à la suite rather than designating them as Guard.

The third battalions were formed, but on 31 May, after reviewing them in Posen, Napoleon directed that they were not to form elite companies. Napoleon felt their soldiers were too young but, they would follow the main army as far as Smolensk and Gjatsk, joining the main body only during the retreat in the beginning of November.

On 15 June the Vistula Legion, sans 3rd Battalions, had a total of 112 officers and 4,910 men, a far cry from the theoretical strength of 150 officers and 5,175 rank and file. The 4th Regiment was also still serving in Spain.

In July 1812 the Vistula Legion accompanied the Grande Armée into Russia and was attached to the Imperial Guard. Of the almost 7,000 Vistula Legionnaires that entered Russia in the Legion less than 1,500 marched out between December 1812 and February 1813. These men had fought bravely at Smolensk, Borodino, Tarutino, Krasnoe and the Berezina.

On 18 June 1813 the Vistula Regiment was organized from the remnants of the Vistula Legion. It consisted of only two battalions. It was reformed at its depot in Sedan in early 1814 with all of the Poles remaining in French service in an effort to bring it up to strength. The new regiment was commanded by Colonel M. Kosinski and its staff consisted of:

1 Colonel	4 Adjutant NCOs
2 Chefs de bataillon	2 Porte-étandard sous-officiers
2 Adjutants-major	1 Drum Major
1 Paymaster	1 Drum Corporal
1 Eagle Bearer	1 Master Armorer
1 Chirurgien Major	1 Music Master
1 Chirurgien Sous-major	7 Musicians
2 Chirurgien Sous-aides	

Each company had:

1 Captain	1 Sergeant Major
1 Fourrier	4 Sergeants
1 Lieutenant	2 Drummers
8 Corporals	121 Soldiers
1 Sous-lieutenant	140 Total

The regiment has to have two battalions. Each battalion had six companies, one grenadier, one voltigeur and four fusilier companies.

It fought at Leipzig, Hanau, and at Soissons, where it was fought valiantly against the blockading Russian forces. After earning twenty-three Légions d'honneur (two officer and twenty-one cavalier) in Soissons, the legion moved to the Compiègne. They fought at Rheims and Arcis-sur-Aube where Napoleon sought shelter in one of its battalions as it formed square. The legion then went on to fight at the battle of St. Dizier. When the war ended the survi¬vors returned to Poland.

The 7e and 8e Chevauléger-lanciers in French Service

On 18 July 1811 the two cavalry regiments in the Vistula Legion were drawn into the French line cavalry organization and redesignated as the 7th and 8th Chevauléger-lancier Regiments. The Decree of 15 July 1811 established their internal organization as follows:

Staff

1 Colonel	2 Adjutant NCOs
1 Major	1 Brigadier Trumpeter
2 Chefs d'escadron	2 Veterinarians
2 Adjutant-majors	1 Master Cobbler
1 Quartier-mastre	1 Master Tailor
1 Chirurgien-major	1 Master Armorer/Spurmaker
1 Chirurgien Aide-major	1 Master Harnessmaker
2 Chirurgien Sous-aide	20 Total

Each company was to have:

1 Captain	1 Brigadier Fourrier
1 Lieutenant	8 Brigadiers
2 Sous-lieutenants	2 Trumpeters
1 Maréchal des logis chef	108 Lancers
4 Maréchaux des logis	128 Total

On 13 December 1813 Napoleon order the merging of the 7th and 8th Regiments into a new 8th Regiment. The officers of the 7th Regiment sent him a memorandum of protest against this decision and the decree was changed on 18 January 1814. This, in effect, preserved the 7th Regiment. A rebuilt 7th Regiment with three squadrons was formed, but there is considerable question as to the fate of the 8th Regiment. Though it was to have been absorbed by the 7th Regiment, it appears on several orders of battle through the early 1814 campaign and may well not have been disbanded. The Royal Ordinance of 12 May 1814 disbanded the 7e and 8e Chevauléger Régiments.

3e Régiment étranger (Polonaise) and 7e Chevauléger-lanciers in 1815

With Napoleon's return to France during the One Hundred Days, he began to restore his army to its full strength. The first foreign unit he began reorganizing was the Poles. On 23 March he directed that a Polish battalion begin forming in Rheims. The Polish depot at Rheims was established shortly after 28 May 1814 to accommodate the Poles still left in France. It was commanded by Chef de bataillon Golaszewski. The "Poles" in this depot also included a number of native Russians who had served in various Polish regiments. On 11 March 1815 the battalion had 29 officers and 560 non-commissioned officers and men. A further 12 were in hospital and there were 8 women and 5 children carried on the rolls.

The Polish battalion was to have one voltigeur, one grenadier and four fusilier companies. Each company had 3 officers, 14 NCOs, 56 privates and two drummers. The battalion staff consisted of 9 officers, non-commissioned officers and craftsmen. This gave the entire battalion a theoretical strength of 22 officers and 459 men.

The battalion was sent to Sedan, the depot of the now disbanded Vistula Legion. On 23 April it was raised to a regiment by the addition of a second battalion that was to be raised. This battalion was to be formed from prisoners Napoleon expected to take.

The Decree of 11 April directed the formation of cadres for five foreign regiments. Each was to have two battalions. One regiment was to form in Soissons with the Poles.

Disorders broke out in the 1er and 2e Régiments étranger royale and they were disbanded by the Decree of 2 May.

Only a few of these disbanded troops remained to be used in the raising of these new regiments. The 3e Régiment d'étranger royale, or the Irish Regiment, was the only regiment retained and it was renumbered as the 7e Régiment d'étranger. These decrees were followed, in short order, by intensive propaganda campaigns along the various borders in an effort to raise troops for these regiments. However, they succeeded in recruiting only deserters from the foreign armies and a few veterans who had served in the French armies before 1814.

The cadres of these six foreign regiments were very carefully selected from amongst the foreign officers who had remained in France after the First Restoration.

The 3e Régiment was, in fact, raised on 23 April 1815 in Laon. However, the regiment and its depot were quickly sent to Soissons. On 15 June 1815 the Polish regiment had 29 officers and 476 enlisted. The Poles seem to have eventually raised a total of 22 officers and 637 men under the command of Chef de bataillon Golaszewski.

It is known that the 3e Régiment étranger was organized with a staff consisting of:

1 Chef de Bataillon	1 Master cobbler
1 Drum Corporal	1 Health Officer
1 Adjutant-major	1 Master armorer
1 Master tailor	1 Adjutant NCO
1 Quartermastre	9 Total

Each of the companies was organized with:

1 Captain	1 Sergeant-major
1 Fourrier	4 Sergeants
1 Lieutenant	56 Soldiers
8 Corporals	2 Drummers
1 Sous-lieutenant	75 Total

Napoleon also desired to raise some foreign cavalry regiments. These too consisted of many deserters from the various foreign armies, but never amounted to any significant force. Napoleon's first move was to raise, in Soissons, a cadre of Polish cavalry with the issuance of the Decrees of 28 April and 12 May 1815 in an effort to organize a Polish light cavalry regiment. Shortly later, the 7e Chevauléger-lancier Polonais was organized in Soissons with 23 officers, 327 enlisted and 13 horses. They fought on foot in the defense of the bridges in Sévres, just outside Paris on 2 July 1815, earning Davout's praise.

In October the foreign regiments were disbanded, but the 3rd Regiment and the 7th Lancers were not to be disbanded. Those that were still willing to serve were absorbed into the army of the Kingdom of Poland, which served the Czar of Russia. Apparently the 7th Lancers refused this and were disbanded in France.

Uniforms of the Polish Formations In French Service 1795-1815

Infantry of the Lombard/Cisalpine Legion

Shortly after the Lombard Legion was raised, between January and May 1797, its uniform was as close as possible to the traditional Polish uniform. The first battalion of grenadiers and chasseurs wore the "konfederatka", which was a visorless cap with a fur turban and a square top so well known from the czapka, a later military cap. The turban was of black lamb's wool and the square top was of blue cloth piped with the battalion colors: amaranth for the grenadiers and green for the chasseurs. A Polish national cockade was worn and over the cockade was a yellow plume with a horizontal red band.

The uniform consisted of a dark blue kurtka, or jacket, piped with the battalion color. The chasseurs had green lapels, cuffs and turnbacks, while those of the grenadiers were dark blue. Both the grenadiers and chasseurs wore a tricolored belt (top to bottom - red, white and blue). The chasseurs wore blue epaulets with green piping, while those of the grenadiers were red.

The breeches of both battalions were dark blue. They were skin tight and had no side stripes. The bullet pouch was suspended from a white belt worn over the left shoulder. Their haversack was of the standard French issue as was all their other equipment. In some instances, however, captured Austrian and Italian equipment was used.

When the fusilier battalion was raised it adopted the same uniform as the existing troops, except that their cuffs, collar, lapels and turnbacks were yellow.

The artillery wore green uniforms and a konfederatka with a black turban, green top and black piping. The uniform was piped black and the epaulets were dark red.

When the legion was organized into two separate legions, the uniforms were altered. The artillery adopted a green czapka with a red plume, and abandoned the black piping for the blue facings on their coats. Each of the two legions now had three battalions, which were marked with the legion color. It is probable that this new uniform was an attempt by the Cisalpine Government to bring the Poles into conformance with their national unioforms; the Poles were very sensitive to this and resisted such attempts with great vigor.

		1st Legion	2nd Legion
Turnback		Green	Red
Collar		Red	White
Cuffs		White	Green
Plume		Blue	White
	over	Red	Blue
	over	White	Red

The fusiliers also wore a pompon on their czapka, yellow with a red horizontal stripe.

It is important to note that there are conflicting descriptions of the uniforms worn in this period. Kukiel states that the grenadier battalion wore dark blue uniforms with crimson distinctives and the chasseur battalion wore dark green with black distinctives. He states that initially they wore bicorns, but shortly later adopted the "Konfederatkas". There are other as-

Polish Legions in Italy 1797-1802(NYPL)

pects of the preceding description that are inconsistent with the general history of Polish and French uniforms and throw them into question.

With the June 1797 reorganization the legion adopted a new color pattern. The new uniform was to keep the colors of the old legion, amaranth yellow and green, were to be kept by the new 1st Legion. The first battalion was to have cuffs, collar, turnbacks and lapels that were amaranth and a plume. This sequence was introduced on 26 March 1799, that was, top to bottom, blue, red and white. The second battalion was to wear green distinctives and a plume that was red, white and blue. The third battalion wore yellow distinctives and a plume that was white, blue and red. The 2nd Battalion was to have yellow but¬tons, while those of the other battalions were to be white.

The 2nd Legion was assigned the following battalion colors: 1st - black, 2nd - blue, 3rd - pink. The plume sequence was to be the same as in the 1st Legion. The buttons of all the battalions in the 2nd Legion were to be white. The basic color of the uniforms was still, however, blue.

The grenadiers of both legions were to wear red plumes and the chasseurs wore a green plume. Only the fusiliers were to wear the multi-colored plume. The grenadiers were to be issued French bicorns and the chasseurs brimmed hats.

Polish documentation, however, indicates the plume sequence described was not introduced until 26 March 1799. Between October 1798 and March 1799 the plume was, top to bottom, red, white, and blue. The battalion distinctions were derived from the dress of the pre-1796 Polish regimental uniforms. This was because these new Polish battalions were considered, by their members, as the cadres for an eventually restored army of the Polish Kingdom. Thus, for example, the 1st Battalion of the 1st Legion wore the colors of the National Cavalry and the 2nd Battalion wore those of the Wegierski Chasseurs.

On 31 October 1798 the new uniform regulations almost completely removed the battalion distinctions and introduced legion distinctions. The 1st Legion wore amaranth distinctives and the 2nd Legion wore poppy red distinctives. The artillery uniforms were dark green with black distinctives.

The czapka, now worn by all the infantry, was dark green for the rank and file and dark blue for officers. It had poppy red and white pipping and a cloth turban in the former battal-ion's color, i.e. crimson for the 1/1st Legion, yellow for the 2/1st Legion, etc. The czapka lost the black lambskin turban. The grenadiers had poppy red plumes and the chasseurs had green plumes. The fusiliers wore the tri-colored plume that were amaranth, dark blue and white, as described above.

Both officers and the rank and file wore long hair that reached to the middle of their collars. It was in the style known as "à la Kosciuszko". The grenadiers were required to wear moustaches. All officers wore an epaulet on their left shoulder with the traditional Polish rank distinctives. On their right shoulder was a counter-epaulet with a strap in the Cisal-pine colors (red, white and green). The white band of this strap had embroidered on it the words "*Gli uomini liberi sono fratelli*"(All free men are brothers).

In February 1800 the remnants of the Polish Auxiliary Corps of the Cisalpine Republic were transformed into the (First) Polish Legion in French service. The uniform was simplified. Now the infantry wore dark blue kurtkas with crimson distinctives. Their breeches were also dark blue. Their czapkas were dark blue with black lambskin turbans and black leather visors. The fusiliers had white cords and black, six-inch tall woolen pompons. The grenadiers had poppy red cords and plumes and brass grenade front plates. The artillery uniform remained unchanged, except that they had poppy red cords and plumes. The legion also had 40 sappers wearing bearskins. The cockade was the traditional Polish cockade.

Decrees issued by the President of the Italian Republic on 26 June and 26 September 1802 changed the crimson parts of the uniforms to yellow. Some iconographic sources also indicate that a sunburst plaque was adopted on the czapka, but this seems implausible. The cockade was changed to the Italian colors, green replacing the dark blue.

When the 2nd Demi-brigade, renamed the 114th Demi-Brigade, went to Santo-Domingo, its soldiers were issued white linen jackets and pantaloons. In practice the soldiers wore portions of both the new and old uniforms, keeping the dark blue and yellow kurtkas and wearing the white pantaloons. Many discarded the czapka in favor of wide brimmed straw hats. The 1st Demi-brigade retained its 1802 uniforms until 1807.

Cavalry of the Lombard Legion

When the first Polish cavalry regiment was raised, it was out fitted with Austrian equipment captured at Gaete. Its uniform was dark blue and very similar in cut to that worn by the infantry. Their czapka was crimson with a black turban and dark blue piping. The czapka also had a removable visor.

The plumes of the first squadron were, top to bottom, blue, white and red in the first company and red,white and blue in the second company. The first company of the second squadron had a white, blue and red plume, while the second company was red, blue and white.

Their kurtka had crimson cuffs, collar, lapels and turnbacks. The uniforms piping was crimson. The breeches were dark blue and worn inside short black boots. The outside seam of each leg had a crimson stripe.

In addition to company distinctions with the plumes, the lance pennants also indicated company assignments. The pennants were what is known as a swallowtailed pennant:

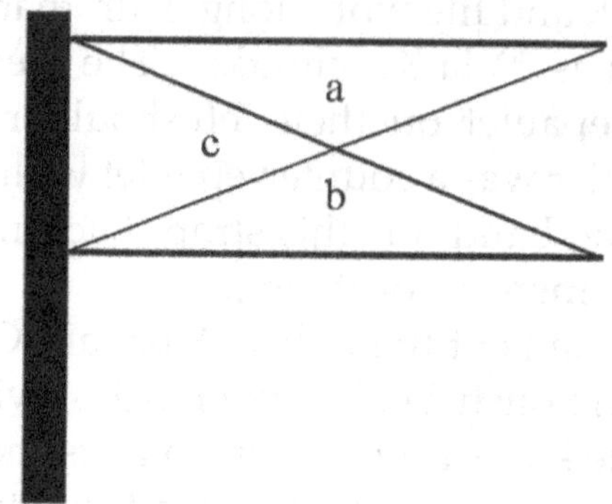

The squadrons and company colors were distributed as follows:

	a	b	c
1st Squadron			
1st Company	Blue	Red	White
2nd Company	Red	Blue	White
2nd Squadron			
1st Company	White	Red	Blue
2nd Company	Red	White	Blue

The horse cloths were of white lamb's wool with crimson wolves' teeth edging.

Infantry of the Danube Legion

The uniform regulations of October 1799 gave the infantry dark blue kurtkas with crimson lapels and square cut cuffs, both piped white. The breeches were dark blue and had a narrow crimson stripe down each leg. The plain metal buttons were yellow. The leather work was all black. They wore short black light infantry gaiters with white edging on the tops and white tassels. The grenadiers wore poppy red epaulets, the chasseurs wore dark green and the fusiliers wore crimson. The cockade and rank insignia were French.

All troops wore a dark blue czapka with a black lambskin turban and black leather visor. It was surmounted by an eight inch tall feather plume that was red for the grenadiers, green for the chasseurs and yellow for the fusiliers. The fusilier officers wore a tricolor plume. The tassel cords were probably of the same color. On 7 January 1800, the plumes were ordered to be made of horsehair, with the top six inches colored poppy red for the grenadiers, green for the chasseurs and crimson for the fusiliers. The bottom two inches were given the following battalion distinctive colors:

1st Battalion - White
2nd Battalion - Blue
3rd Battalion - Poppy Red
4th Battalion - Yellow

Thus the grenadier company of the 3rd Battalion had entirely poppy red plumes. The linen cords were now yellow for everybody and the tassels were of the battalion colors.

Due to a lack of funds and problems with contractors, it was a long time before the more than part of the officer staff had the regulation dress described above. The men still wore their old, mostly Austrian, uniforms or whatever rags they could lay their hands on. The more industrious ones "deserted" to the enemy, where they were issued decent uniforms and shoes, then happily came back. This situation lasted until May 1800 when Kniaziewicz pointed out to his French superiors that his soldiers, soon to face the Austrians, were exposed to unnecessary danger from both the Imperial as well as the French side, and asked for an issuance of French light infantry uniforms. By the end of the month, the Poles received bicorns, long "habits", striped pantaloons or tight breeches, etc. In June the 1st and 2nd Battalions were almost totally dressed in Polish regulation fashion, but the rest continued to wear the French or (the new comer's) Austrian uniforms. Though by 19 August the battle ready units were uniformly clad in the prescribed manner, the problems with uniform supplies continued to plague the legion until the end of its existence.

It is worth mentioning that a contemporary print shows the legion infantry wearing kurtkas with crimson collars and dark blue lapels. The cloth belts were dark blue with crimson edging and square buckles, colored left to right, crimson, white and blue.

When the Danube Legion became the 3rd Polish Demi-brigade, its officers were ordered on 31 March 1802 to wear bicorns with black plumes, the bottom of which had the battalion colors: 1st Battalion - poppy red, 2nd Battalion - blue, 3rd Battalion - white. It is, however, unknown how this regulation affected the uniforms of the other ranks.

In Santo-Domingo, the 113th Demi-brigade wore their old uniforms, combined with white linen like the 114th Demi-brigade.

Danube Legion (Knotel)

Chasseurs/Uhlans of the Danube Legion

As in the case of the infantry, the Legion cavalry received, around May 1800, the uniforms of the French light or horse artillery, with minor modificaiotns. These uniforms consisted of a dark blue hussar style dolman, vest and tight breeches. They had no fur trim on the dolmans. The dolman had poppy red piping and braid. The breeches had red side stripes. Their visored czapkas were black with black leather turbans, yellow cords, poppy red plumes and French cockades.

After receiving lances, before the end of July 1800, the former chasseurs were uniformed in the fashion prescribed by the October 1799 regulations. They wore a dark blue czapka with yellow cords (gold for the officers), black leather turbans, and visors. The French cockade was worn on the left side. The 12-inch tall horsehair plumes were, in accordance with the 7 January reguations, crimson, with a 2-inch bottom in the squadron color.

1st Squadron - White
2nd Squadron - Blue
3rd Squadron - Poppy Red
4th Squadron - Yellow

The yellow cords also had tassels in the squadron colors.

A dark blue kurtka with amaranth cuffs, collar, lapels and turnbacks that were piped white was adopted. The belts were black with gold zig-zag stripes for the officers and white for the troopers. The breeches were dark blue with an amaranth stripe on the outside seams. The lance pennants appear to have been horizontally sectioned, top to bottom, blue, white and red.

In 1802 the uniforms changed again. The uhlans changed their crimson for yellow. The czapka received a white, probably lambskin, turban and white cords. The lance pennant was, top to bottom, red and green with a white triangle. The cockade was Italian. Otherwise the uniform remained unchanged.

Subsequent to this there were a number of minor changes that moved the uniform slowly to a more French style of uniform. In the transitory period between November 1807 and March 1808, when the uhlans passed into Westphalian service, the elite compa-ny had black bearskins with poppy red plumes and yellow bags decorated with white piping and tassel. The bearskins were discarded when the cavalry passed into the Vistula Legion.

Artillery of the Danube Legion

At first, the artillerists were given the uniforms of French sappers, but soon replaced them with French horse artillery uniforms. This consisted of a visored mirliton of black felt that had a black wing piped with poppy red. The cockade was worn half way down the side of the mirliton and was attached to the poppy red plume with a poppy red stripe. The cords, tassels and flounders were poppy red. The gunners wore their hair in long tresses over each temple and were not tied at the end, but secured by a split pistol ball.

They wore a dark blue dolman, vest and breeches. There were 13 rows of brandenburg braid on the dolman with five buttons on each row. The breeches were cut in the Hungarian hussar style. They were skin tight with Hungarian knots on the thighs and poppy red stripes down the outer seams. Hussar style boots were worn that had poppy red trim and tassels.

In March 1800, they finally received their Polish uniforms. The 1799 Regulations prescribed them as identical to the cavalry uniforms, with the exception of the lapels, which were dark blue with crimson piping. The dark blue czapkas had dark blue-white-crimson cords, and 12-inch tall poppy red feather plumes, as specified by the 7 January Regulations. On the other hand, Gembarzewski, after an unidentified source, depicts the artillery uniform as consisting of kurtkas with black collars, lapels and cuffs. Both the kurtka and breeches were piped with poppy red. The side stripes were also poppy red. The czapka was black with a black leather visor, tricolor cords, a French cockade and a poppy red plume. They wore short black boots over their breeches and their sash was poppy red.

The Kalinowski Hussars

Very little is known about the uniform of the Kalinowski Hussars. The only original source, a painting of Lieutenant Dawid Torosiewicz, shows him dressed in a dark blue dolman with crimson piping around the collar and down the middle, silver lace in double strands strung on five spherical buttons and ending in silver tassels. The dolman also has silver epaulets. The cartridge pouch's bandoleer was silver. His breeches are not shown, but they were probably gray.

Légion du Nord

The legion wore a dark blue kurtka with crimson cuffs, cuff flaps, lapels and piping around the collar and turnbacks. Their buttons were white. The czapka was of black felt with a black leather turban. It had a yellow metal sunburst plaque. The plume, pompon, cords and trim were crimson for the carabiniers, yellow for the voltigeurs and light blue for the fusiliers. Their epaulets were of the same color. The cockade was French.

The legionnaires wore white or dark blue breeches and white or black gaiters with black leather buttons. Their overcoats were brown. The uniform also included a white, sleeved vest and a black handkerchief of a "fleecy fabric" around the neck.

The uniforms were manufactured in Prussian military factories captured in 1806. After the capitulation of Danzig, the cloth supplies captured there were used to uniform the legion as well.

The 2e Légion du Nord was uniformed as the first with pink distinctives.

Infantry of the Vistula Legion

The Vistula Legion infantry wore French shakos with a brass "sunburst" plaque being marked with either the regimental number or the Imperial Cipher, "N". The cords were white. A carrot shaped pompon was worn that was red for the grenadiers, green or green and yellow for the voltigeurs, and white for the fusiliers. The grenadiers' and voltigeurs' shakos had "V" side stripes and bands around the crown of the shako. They were red for the grenadiers and yellow for the voltigeurs. However, prior to 1812 the grenadiers wore bearskins with poppy red cords, plumes and patches.

The sappers wore bearskins with yellow sunburst plaques, white cords, and a yellow bag with white wolves' teeth edging and a white tassel.

The sunburst plaques had the Imperial eagle in the center with the regimental number on its breast. On occasion, the plaque had only the regimental number and no eagle. On the bottom edge of some of the plaques there was the inscription "Legia Nadwislanska", but this was not common.

From 1808 to 811, the regiments wore the Polish style uniform of dark blue cloth. The collar, lapels and turnbacks were faced with the regimental color. These were:

Regiment	Collar	Collar Piping	Cuff	Cuff Piping	Turnbacks
1st	Dark Blue	Yellow	-	-	Yellow
2nd	Yellow	Yellow	-	-	Yellow
3rd	Yellow	Dark Blue	Yellow	Yellow	Yellow
4th	Dark Blue	Dark Blue	Yellow	Yellow	Yellow

The fusiliers wore dark blue shoulder straps piped with yellow. The epaulets of the grenadiers were white and those of the voltigeurs were green and yellow. They wore white breeches and knee high gaiters of black cloth. Their equipment was identical to that worn by the French line infantry.

In 1812, a project of new uniform regulations was prepared by Colonel Bardin and the Vistula Legion regimental distinctives were established as follows:

Regiment	Collar	Collar Piping	Cuff	Cuff Piping
1st	Yellow	White	Yellow	-
2nd	Yellow	-	Dark Blue	Yellow
3rd	Dark Blue	Yellow	Yellow	-
4th	Dark Blue	Yellow	Dark Blue	Yellow

It is, however, uncertain if these color changes were implemented.

In 1813 the Vistula Regiment wore a French "habit veste" with the same colors as before. They wore long gaiters reaching above the knee instead of the previous light infantry gaiters. The grenadiers wore dark blue Polish czapkas with white cords, white carrot-shaped pompons and yellow sunburst plaques. These plaques bore the Polish eagle and the inscription "Polk Nawislanski".

Vistula Lancers & the 7e and 8e Régiments des Lanciers Polonaise de la Ligne

The Vistula Lancers wore a dark blue kurtka with yellow cuffs, collars, lapels and turnbacks. The piping on the uniform was also yellow. The elite companies wore white epaulets on their right shoulders and white aiguilettes on their left. The other companies wore pointed shoulder straps that were blue piped with yellow.

They wore a white cummerbund around their waists that had two blue lines. In full dress they wore blue breeches with two yellow stripes separated by blue piping down the outside seams. The "pantaloons à cheval" were also blue and had black leather inserts on the insides and a single yellow stripe down the outer seam.

Both regiments wore a dark blue czapka with a black turban. The dark blue top was piped with white and had the French cockade surmounted by the Maltese Cross. In full dress a white plume was worn. The chin strap was brass and there was no plaque on the czapka.

In 1811 the czapka received the sunburst plaque above the visor and the plume was replaced by a carrot shaped pompon. Those pompons were in squadron colors: 1st - red, 2nd - sky blue, 3rd - aurora and 4th - violet. The elite companies wore a red plume with white cords.

The uniforms of the 7e and 8e Régiments were only slightly different from those worn while part of the Vistula Legion. They wore a dark blue Polish "kurtka." The 7e wore blue piping on yellow shoulder straps, cuffs, collar and lapels. The 8e wore yellow piping on blue shoulder straps, cuffs, collar and lapels.

Their headgear consisted of the traditional square topped "czapka." It had a black leather turban surmounted by a black cloth square peak. It had a "sunburst" brass plaque on its front and a French cockade surmounted by the Maltese cross.

The elite company wore a red plume, white cords, and flounders. The other companies wore white plumes, cords, and flounders. The center companies had a pompon in the squadron color. These squadron colors were: 1st Squadron - red , 2nd - sky blue, 3rd - aurora and 4th - violet.

The elite companies wore white shoulder straps on the right with a white aiguilette on the left. The other companies wore epaulets piped with the facing color. Colonel Bardin's 1812 regulations give the Polish lancers dark blue uniforms with white buttons and dark blue-and-white striped belts. Both regiments wore dark blue soulder straps with yellow piping. The distinctive regimental colors were:

Regiment	Collar	Collar Piping	Lapels	Cuffs	Cuff Piping	Turnbacks
7th	Yellow	Dark Blue	Yellow	Yellow	-	Yellow
8th	Dark Blue	Yellow	Yellow	Dark Blue	Yellow	Yellow

Both regiments wore white leather sword belts and cross belts. Their carbine belt was slightly wider than their bullet pouch belt and the carbine was hung from a swivel hook. The lancers carried the light cavalry saber, but it had two styles of hilt, that of the An IX and the An XI. One hilt was a simple single bar and the second had three bars which provided more protection.

Their carbine was the same as that used by the chasseurs and hussars, the An IX Musketoon. Their lance was 2.65 meters long and made of hardened wood. It was generally painted black and had a white leather strap at the balance point to allow better control of the lance. It had a swallow tailed pennant attached to it with three iron studs. The pennant was 73 cm. long, 38 cm. wide and 37 cm. from the shaft to the notch of the swallowtail.

9e Régiment de Lanciers Polonaise de la Ligne

While designated the 30th Chasseur-lanciers the regiment wore dark blue jackets and breeches with crimson cuffs, sidestripes and piping. There are some unsubstantiated stories about them acquiring the nickname "lanciers rouges" or "red lancers" because of a shortage of appropriate cloth and the use of red cloth for various uniform parts. However, Polish sources do not confirm this.

The regiment wore black shakos with white cords and pompons for the center companies.The elite company wore a brown fur colpack with the white cords and pompon. The colpack had a crimson bag with white tassel and piping. The elite companies wore plain crimson epaulets and the other companies wore white ones. They wore hussar style boots with white trim and tassels.

After being designated as the 9e Lanciers on 15 July 1811 they were issued Polish style uniforms. The czapka consisted of the black leather turban with a red top piped white. There is some question if the sunburst plaque was worn.

The black leather peak was bound with white metal and the chinstrap was of black leather. A black plume with a green tip was worn for full dress, the cords were white and hung from the left to right across the corners of the square top.

The kurtka was dark blue. The cuffs, collar, lapels and turnbacks were "chamois" or a light yellow. The troopers wore dark blue shoulder straps that were piped chamois. Both dark blue and the notorious red cloth were used for breeches. These breeches were often in the baggy Mameluke style. This was preferred by the officers. Those of the troopers were generally the "pantaloons à cheval" with black stripes on the outside seams.

The schabraque was red with a black lace stripe on the edge. There was red piping on the extreme edge of the schabraque. A green portemanteau was carried on the back of the saddle. It was round and its flat ends were trimmed with a stripe similar to that of the schabraque. The lance pennant was either chamoise or white over red, varying between source documents.

Uhlan Uniforms in 1814

The uniforms of the two uhlan regiments organized in 1814 were based on the 1811/12 regulations for the Polish lancer regiments in the French army. The kurtkas were dark blue with poppy red collars, cuffs, lapels, turnbacks and piping on the back seams for the 1st Regiment and crimson for the 2nd Regiment. The buttons were white for the troopers and silver for the officers. The elite companies probably worewhite fringed epaulets, while the center companies wore dark blue shoulder straps piped in the regimental colors. The troopers wore dark blue overalls, reinforced with leather, and decorated with single side stripes of the regimental color down the outer seam. The officers' trousers were either poppy red or crimson, depending on the regiment, with a single wide silver side stripe.

The czapkas were dark blue with black leather turbans, brass sunburst plaques with white regimental numbers in the center, and French cockades. The troopers had round, white pompons, possibly in a carrot like shape for the elite companies, while the officers wore white feather plumes. Their belts were made of cloth, with four white (silver for officers) and three poppy red or crimson stripes. All leatherwork was white, except for the black bullet pouches.

Weapons of the Polish Infantry

The Polish Legions in Italy between 1797 and 1799 carried Austrian muskets of the 1754, 1774 and 1784 models. Some of the chasseur companies, however, were issued rifled carbines. By 1800 they were receiving the French Charville 1777 as well as weapons made in Verona. The Légion du Nord carried old, reworked Prussian muskets of the 1720 and 1782 patterns.

The army of the Grand Duchy between 1807 and 1809 carried 1801 pattern Prussian muskets and a few miscellaneous Russian weapons. Between 1809 and 1811 they still carried principally Prussian muskets, plus a substantial number of Austrian 1807 pattern muskets with rifled barrels. From 1811 through 1814 they were almost completely reequipped with French muskets of the 1793 and 1800/1801 patterns. With the end of the 1812 camaign and the sudden need to replace lost equipment and outfit numerous new recruits, Russian pattern muskets were pressed into service. In addition, large numbers of reseve and garrison units had Prussian 1805 and 1809 pattern muskets made under French supervision in Potsdam.

Battle of Raszyn

Appendix I

Staffing of the Army of the Grand Duchy of Warsaw
Late 1812

Minister of War

Joseph Prince Poniatowski, *Minister of War, Commander in Chief, Chevalier of various orders, Officer of the Legion of Honor.*

Jean Bennet, Colonel, *Secretary General*

Bogoumil Fechner, *Chief of the First Section of Finances*

Joseph Rautenstrauch, Colonel, *Chief of the Second Section of Military Operations*

Jacob Redel, Colonel, *Chief of the Third Section of Artillery and Engineers.*

General Directorate of Administration of War
Joseph Count Wielhorski, Général de division, *Director General*
Valentin Wilkoszewski, *Director Secretary General*
Benedict Doney, *Chief of the First Section of Military Hospitals*
Jean Suchodolski, *Chief of the Second Section of Uniforms*
Henri Deybell, *Chief of the Third Section of Supplies and Forage*

Directors
Antoine Darewski - *Director*
Guilhelm Fiszer - *Director*
Felix Moscicki - *Director of Lithuania*

Commissioners of War
1st Class
Joseph Morawski, Albert Dobiecki, Adam Gorski, Ignace Chmielewski, Jan Dzierzanowski, and Etienne Swiniarski.

2nd Class
Theodor Pzerwic, Felix Wilski, Albert Boyarski, Stanislas Zablocki, Joseph Basson, Vincent Tarczynski, Antoine Borowski, Fortunat Koncza, Joseph Bagowski, Joseph Ryminski, Michel Garlicki, and Martin Zdziarski.

Commissioners of War in Lithuania

Pierre Jaroszewski and Jean Matuszewski

Health Services

Leopold Lafontaine, *Inspector General of Health Services*
Joseph Puchalski, *Inspector of Military Hospitals*

Employed in Divisional Health Services
Charles Kuknel (physician), Onufry Lucy (surgeon), Przybylski (surgeon), and Joseph Skalski (pharmacist).

General Staff for the Inspection of Military Reviews and Conscription

Kajetan Hebdowski, Général de brigade, *Director General*
Joseph Wyszkowski, *Inspector of Reviews, Chief of the Office of Management*
Inspectors of Reviews: Mathias Miroslawski, Floryan Kasinowski, Kajetan Hryniewicz, and Charles Sarnowski (inspector in Lithuania).

Assistant Inspectors of Reviews
Michel Zeydel, Albert Grafen, Pierre Buhut, Theodor Radziejowski, Constantin Jablonowski, Michel Skopowski, François Hampel, Sabin Sierawski, Jean Kozlowski, Fiszer, Pierre Rubieszewski, Joseph Malinowski, Stanlislas Kontecki, and Joseph Grecz (*assistant inspector in Lithuania*)

Military Paymaster: Joseph Wegierski, *Paymaster General*
Divisional Paymasters: Joseph Michalski, Antoine Rose, Adam Wegierski, Jean Ceizyngia

General Staff

Généraux de division (Divisional Generals)
Joseph Prince Poniatowski - *Commander-in-chief of the Army*
Joseph Zajaczek (Zayonshek), Jean Henri Dabrowski, Louis Kamieniecki, Michel Sokolnicki, Stanislas Woyczynski, Joseph Wielhorski, Charles Kniaziewicz, and Amilcar Kosinski.

Inspector Generals of Arms

Inspector General of Infantry (General S. Fiszer, killed in October 1812, at Tarutino)
Alexander Rozniecki, Général de division, *Inspector General of Cavalry*
Jean Pelletier, Général de brigade, *Inspector General of Engineers* (taken prisoner on 3 November 1812 at Vyazma)

Généraux de brigade (Brigade Generals)
Vincent Axamitowski, Joseph Niemojewski, Isidor Krasinski, Kaje¬tan Hebdowski, Maurice Hauke, Luc Bieganski, Michel Piotrowski, Ignace Kamienski, Stanislas Mielzynski, Antoine Prince Sulkowski, Dominique Dziewanowski, Stanislas, Potocki, Casimir Turno, Valen-tin Kwasniewski, Michel Prince Radziwill, Edouard Zoltowski, Joseph Waislewski, Thaddeus Tyszkiewicz, Czeslaw Pakosz, Xaver Kossecki, François Paszkowski, Louis Kropinski, Stephan Grabowski, and Casimir Malachowski.

Adjutants Attached to the Person of His Majesty
Hipolit Bleszynski, Colonel
Mathias Strzyzowski, Major

Titular Adjutants Attached to the Person of His Majesty
Stanislas Potocki, Général de brigade
Casimir Turno Général de brigade
Michel Prince Radziwill, Général de brigade

Command Adjutant Assistant Chief of the General Staff: Joseph Rautenstrauch, Colonel

Command Adjutants of the Divisional Staffs
Colonels: Jean Weysenhoff, Antoine Cedrowski, Basile Wierzbicki, Joseph Szumlanski, François Morawski, and Joseph Nowicki (in Danzig).

Adjutant Colonel attached to the Commander-in-Chief: Antoine Potocki

Chief Adjutants of Squadrons
Stanislas Chlapowski, Adjutant to General Dabrowski
Ignace, Jablkowski, Adjutant to General Zayonshek
Michel Pelczynski, Adjutant to General Kamieniecki
Joseph Gajewski, Adjutant to General Fiszer
Venceslas Gutakowski, Adjutant to General Rozniecki
Jean Kamieniecki, Adjutant to the Commander-in-Chief
Adjutant of the General Staff: Joseph Krasinski, Adjutant to General Kniaziewicz
Lieutenant Colonels: Michel Sobieski, Broszkowski, Stanislas Dönhoff

Regimental Officers

1st Infantry Regiment
Colonel: Stephan Koszarski (from 10/21/12)
Major: Thadee Piotrowski
Chefs de Bataillon: Jacob Leszczynski
Aljzy Biernawski
Onufry Fontanna

2nd Infantry Regiment
Colonel: Jean Krukowiecki
Major: Joseph Szymanowski
Chefs de Bataillon: Jean Hoffmann
Stanislas Zdarski
Louis Boguslawski

3rd Infantry Regiment
Colonel: Ignace Blumer
Major: Mathias STraszewski
Chefs de Bataillon: Stanislas Kurcyusz
Maxim Czaykowski
Samouel Rozycki

4th Infantry Regiment
Colonel: Thadee Wolinski
Major: Cypryan Zdzitowiecki
Chefs de Bataillon: Felix Rylski
Ignace Bronisz

5th Infantry Regiment
Colonel: Stephan Oskierko
Major: Joseph Czyzewski
Chefs de Bataillon: Jean Hoppen
Louis Kaminski
Felix Stokowski

6th Infantry Regiment
Colonel: Jules Sierawski
Major: Ferdinand Boguslawski
Chefs de Bataillon: Kasper Grotowski
Charles Geritz
Joseph Rusiecki

7th Infantry Regiment
Colonel: Paul Tremo (died of wounds early December 1812)
Major: Valentin Borowski
Chefs de Bataillon: Jakob Truszkowski
Antoine Oranowski

8th Infantry Regiment
Colonel: Kajetan Stuart
Major: Henri Dulfus
Chefs de Bataillon: Ferdynand Kossecki
Felix Jerzmanowski
Andree Kruszewski

9th Infantry Regiment
Colonel: Michel Cichocki
Major: Felix Grotowski
Chefs de Bataillon: Joseph Gieyzler
Paul Muchowski
Felix Rynaszewski

10th Infantry Regiment
Colonel: Henri Kamienski
Major: Nicholas Daine
Chefs de Bataillon: François Czyzewski
Jean Kraszyn
Joseph Meier

11th Infantry Regiment
Colonel: Alexandre Chlebowski
Major: Andre Deskur
Chefs de Bataillon: Charles Joneman
Casimir Pomianowski

Pierre Szembek
Joseph Potocki

12th Infantry Regiment
- Colonel: Mathias Wierzbinski
- Major: Ignace Suchodolski
- Chefs de Bataillon: Vincent Bialkowski
  Joseph Polonski
  Andre Bleszynski

13th Infantry Regiment
- Colonel: François Zymirski
- Major: Joseph Obertynski
- Chefs de Bataillon: Nepomucen Kasinowski
  Bartlomiej Lanckoronski
  Leopold Koziobrodzki

14th Infantry Regiment
- Colonel: Euzebi Siemianowski
- Major: Antoine Skalski
- Chefs de Bataillon: Vincent Malinowski
  Jean Winnicki
  Mathias Bittner

15th Infantry Regiment
- Colonel: Kasper Miastkowski
- Major: Leonard Reinhold
- Chefs de Bataillon: Ignace Mycielski
  Joseph Albrecht
  Martin Rybinski

16th Infantry Regiment
- Colonel: Constantin Prince Czartoryski
- Major: Ignace Bolesta
- Chefs de Bataillon: Ignace Dobrogoyski
  Jean Wasilewski
  Martin Cwierczakiewicz

17th Infantry Regiment
- Colonel: Joseph Hornowski
- Major: Jean Kozubski
- Chefs de Bataillon: Igace Proszynski
  Chryzolog Domanski
  Stephan Mazurkiewicz
  Mathias Dabrowski
  Casimir Lux
  Andre Zawadzki

18th Infantry Regiment
- Colonel: Alexandre Chodkiewicz
- Major: Michel Seihr
- Chefs de Bataillon: Stanislas Trebicki

	Slupecki
	Rholand
19th Infantry Regiment	
Colonel:	Tyzenhaus
Major:	Pawlowski
Chefs de Bataillon:	Radwan
	Ryminski
	Gorski
20th Infantry Regiment	
Colonel:	Adam Biszping
Major:	Glaser
Chefs de Bataillon:	Milberg
	Walicki
	Placzynski
21st Infantry Regiment	
Colonel:	Gielgud
Major:	Wegierski
Chefs de Bataillon:	Gorski
	Andrychiewicz
	Laszewski
22nd Infantry Regiment	
Colonel:	Czapski
Major:	Hilchen
Chefs de Bataillon:	Mieszkowski
	Jezierski
	Laszewski

Cavalry Regiments:

1st Regiment (Chasseur à Cheval)	
Colonel:	Constantin Przebendowski
Major:	Louis Montrezor
Chefs d'escadron:	Vincent Adamowski & Mathias Dembinski
Supernumerary:	Constantin Dembowski

2nd Regiment (Uhlan)	
Colonel:	Louis Pac
Major:	Jacob Piasecki
Chefs d'escadron:	Michel Kossecki & one unknown

3rd Regiment (Uhlan)	
Colonel:	Alexandre Radziminski
Major:	Kajetan Rzuchowski
Chefs d'escadron:	Jean Suminski & Jean Deskur

4th Regiment (Chasseur à Cheval)
Colonel: Stanislas Dulfus
Major: Rafal Zajaczek
Chefs d'escadron: François Gorski & Ignace Lubowiecki

5th Regiment (Chasseur à Cheval)
Colonel: Sigismond Kurnatowski
Major: Maxim Fredro
Chefs d'escadron: Thomas Siemiatkowski & Andre Suchecki

6th Regiment (Uhlan)
Colonel: Michel Pagowski
Major: Thadee Suchorzewski
Chefs d'escadron: Martin Lojowski & Casimir Oborski

7th Regiment (Uhlan)
Colonel: Auguste Zawadzki
Major: Antoine Pracki
Chefs d'escadron: Antoine Zaleski & Joseph Konarski

8th Regiment (Uhlan)
Colonel: Dominique Prince Radziwill
Major: Joseph Sokolnicki
Chefs d'escadron : Gabryel Czarnecki & Norbert Obuch

9th Regiment (Uhlan)
Colonel: Felix Przyszychowski
Major: Constantin Krzycki
Chefs d'escadron: Stephan Ziemiecki & Jacob Czosnowski

10th Regiment (Hussar)
Colonel: Nepomucen Uminski
Major: Joseph Rzodkiewicz
Chefs d'escadron: Stanislas Osipowski & unknown

11th Regiment (Uhlan)
Colonel: unknown
Major: Casimir Tanski
Chefs d'escadron: Jean Tomicki & unknown

12th Regiment (Uhlan)
Colonel: Joseph Rzyszczewski
Major: François Brzechffa
Chefs d'escadron: Vincent Borzecki & Adam Nosarzewski

13th Regiment (Hussar)
Colonel: Joseph Tolinski
Major: Alexandre Oborski
Chefs d'escadron: Stanislas Rojewski & Thomas Zalewski

14th Regiment (Cuirassier)
Colonel: Stanislas Malachowski (Captured 11/12)
Major: Casimir Dziekonski
Chefs d'escadron: Ignace Jablonski (Killed at Borodino) & one unknown

15th Regiment (Uhlan)
Colonel: Auguste Trzecieski
Major: Jean Rostworowski
Chefs d'escadron: Joseph Dwernicki & Victor Psarski

16th Regiment (Uhlan)
Colonel: Martin Tarnowski
Major: Michel Korytowski
Chefs d'escadron: Fortunat Skarzynski & Vincent Radziminski

17th Regiment (Uhlan)
Colonel: Tyszkiewicz
Major: Giedroyc
Chefs d'escadron: Strowski & Adam Soltan

18th Regiment (Uhlan)Charles
Colonel: Charles Przezdziecki
Major: Trzcinski
Chefs d'escadron: Ploszczynski & Mamert Dluski

19th Regiment (Uhlan)
Colonel: Rajecki
Major: Kaminski
Chefs d'escadron: Rostworowski & Potkanski

20th Regiment (Uhlan)
Colonel: Obuchowicz
Major: Gutakowski
Chefs d'escadron: Henri Zabiello and Mikoszewski

Artillery and Engineering Staff:
Jean Pelletier, Général de brigade, *Inspector General of*

Artillery and Engineers:
Pierre Bontemps, Colonel, *Director of Artillery*

Jean Mallet, Colonel, *Director of Engineers*
Alexander Alfons, Lieutenant Colonel, *Chief of Topohgraphical Office*

Lieutenant Colonel Under Directors of Fortifications:
Leonard Jodko, Andre Trzeszczkowski, Theodor Kobylanski, and Joseph Reklewski

Foot Artillery Regiment:

Colonel:	Antoine Gorski
Major:	Jean Gugenmus
Chefs de bataillon:	Casimir Uszynski
	Antoine Ploszczynski
	Walewski

Horse Artillery Regiment:

Colonel:	Joseph Hurtig
Major:	Jean Krysinski
	Jean Szweryn
	Joseph Sowinski (lost a leg at Borodino)

Sapper Corps

Commanding Major:	Mathias Kubicki
Chefs de bataillon:	Antoine Salacki
	Artur Potocki

Auxiliary Artillery Battalion:	Lieutenant Colonel: Charles Daret
Invalid and Veterans Corps:	Lieutenant Colonel: Jerome Winner
Military Train Battalion:	Lieutenant Colonel: Felix Hryniewicz

Appendix II - A report by Russian Major Prendel to the Russian Minister of War Barclay de Tolly

May 1811

This transcription of part of the original report is en¬closed because of the interesting insight, that of a contemporary military officer, which it provides into the personalities and capabilities of some members of the Polish General Staff. It is an exact translation and should be understood to be the opinion of its author, Major Prendel.

Généraux de division

Zajonczek, J.	Man of intelligence
Dombrowski, J.H.	Man of spirit and decision
Kamieniecki,L.	Good for nothing
Sokolnicki, M.	Reasonably intelligent, enterprising spirit
Fiszer, S.	To him is accorded no spirit but deceit
Rozniecki,A.	Clear-sighted, enterprising and decisive

Généraux de brigade

Axamitowski, V.	Intelligent and brave
Niemojewski, J.	Insignificant
Woyczynski, S.	Capable
Krasinski,I.	Insignificant
Hauke, M.	Resolute, confidant
Bieganski, L.	Capable
Grabowski, M.	Of iron, immovable.
Piotrowski, M.	A professional
Kamienski, I.	A peasant
Pelletier, J.	Cunning in all things
Mielczynski, S.	Busy with his functions, without knowing how
Sulkowski, A.	Very capable and enterprising
Dziewanowski, D.	Intelligent
Potocki, S.	A zero
Turno, C.	Intelligent, capable, amiable
Kwasniowski, V.	Capable

Aides de camp to the King of Saxony

Colonel Pakosz Cz.	Good and sincere
Colonel Paszkowski F.	False, mean and crafty

Bibliography

Anonymous, Nafziger, G.F. trans. *Operations of the 7th Polish Light Cavalry Division in the Leipzig Campaign*, West Chester, OH: Nafziger Collection, 2007.

Belhomme, Lt. Col., *Histoire de l'Infanterie en France*, Paris.

Bochenski, Z., "Nowe materialy do barwy wojsk Ksiestwa Warsaw skiego, " *Studia i Materialy do Dziejow Dawnego Uzbrojenia i Ubioru Wojskowego 2* (1964)

Bonaparte, N., *Correspondance de Napoléon 1er*, 32 Vols., Paris, Plon, 1861.

Bukhari, E., *Napoleon's Cavalry*, San Rafael, CA, Presidio Press, 1979,

von Chelminsky, J. & Malibran, A. *L'Armée du Duche de Varsovie*, Paris, 1918.

Coqueuegnio, L.C., Nafziger, G.F., trans. *The Légion du Nord, 1806-1808, Memoir of Major Coqueugniot.* West Chester, OH: Nafziger Collection, 2005.

Dal nam przyklad Bonaparte. Wspomnienia i relacje zolnierzy polskich 1796-1815 Ed. Robert Bielecki and A.J.Tyszka, 2 Vols, Krakow, Wydawnictwo Literackie, 1984.

Dundulis, B., *Napoleon et la Lithuanie en 1812*, France, 1940.

de Fedorowicz, W., *1809 Campagne de Pologne depuis le commencement jusqu'a l'occupation de Varsovie*, Paris, 1911.

French Archives, Carton C2-708

Grabowski, A., *Wspomnienia*, Vol 1., Cracow, 1909.

Gembarzewski, B., "Huzar Kalinowskiego z r.1807." *Bron i Barwa 1.5* (1934).

Gembarzewski, B., *Zolnierz polski ubior uzbrojenie i oporzadzenie od wieku xi do roku 1960*, Vol. III, Warsaw, 1964.

Head, M. G., *French Napoleonic Lancer Regiments*, Almark Publicatons, Great Britain, 1971.

Kirkor. S., *Legia Nadwislanska 1808-1814*, London: Oficyna Poetow i Malarzy, 1981.

Kirkor, S., *Pod sztandarami Napoleona*. London, Oficyna Poetow i Malarzy, 1982.

Kikor, S., *Polacy w niewoli angielskiej w latach 1803-1814*, Cracow: Wydawnictwo Literackie, 1981.

Kobielski, S., Polska bron. Bron Palna, Wroclaw: Zaklad Narodowy imienia Ossolinskich, 1975.

Kukiel, M., *Dzieje wojska polskiego w dobie napoleonskiej 1795-1815*, 2 vols., Warsaw: E. Wende i Ska, 1918-1920.

Kukiel, M., *Wojna 1812 roku*, 2 Vols., Krakow: Polska Akademia Umiejetnosci, 1937.

Margueron, *Campagne de Russie*, 4 Vols., Paris, Charles-Lavauzelle, 1897-1906.

Nadolski, A., *Polska bron. Bron biala,* Wroclaw: Zaklad Nardowy imienia Ossolinskich, 1974.

Ochwicz, G., *Rok 1809*, Poznan, 1925.

Pachonski, J., *Jozef Grabinski, general polski, francuski i wloski, naczelny wodz powstania bolonskiego 1831 roku*, Cracow: Wydawnictwo Literackie, 1975.

Pachonski, J. L., *Wojna francusko-neapolitanska 1798-1799 i udzial w niej legionow Polskich,* 2 Vols, Cracow, 1947-1948.

Pawlowski, B., *Historja Wojny Polsko-Austriackiej 1809 Roku*, Warsaw, 1935.

Poniatowski, J., *Correspondance du Prince Joseph Poniatowski avec la France*, Poznan, 1929.

Skalkowski, A., *O czesc imienia polskiego*, Lwow, 1908.

Skalkowski, A., "Oficerowie polscy Stu Dni." *Kwartalnik Historyczny* (Lwow), 29 (1915).

Skalkowski, A., *O kokarde Legionow*, Lwow, 1912.

Skalkowski, A., *Supplément ...la correspondance de Napoléon 1er L'Empereur et la Pologne*, Paris, 1908.

Soltyk, R., *Relation des Operations de l'Armée aux orders du prince Joseph Poniatowski*, Paris, Gaultier-Laguionie,1841.

Staszewski, J., "Mundur 9, pozniejszego 3 p.p. Ksiestwa Warszaw skiego z 1807 r." *Bron i Barwa*, 3.8 (1936)

Staszewski, J., "W sprawie mundurow wojska Ksiestwa Warszawskie go." *Bron i Barwa* 3.5 (1936)

Tyszkiewicz, J., *Histoire du 17me Régiment de cavalerie Polonaise* (Lanciers du Cte. Michel Tyszkiewicz (1812-1815), Cracow: Anczvc, 1904

Ustawodawstwo Ksiestwa Warszawskiego. Akty normatywne wladzy najwyzszej. Ed. W. Bartel, J. Kosim, W. Rostocki, Vol 4., Warsaw: Panstwowe Wydawnictwo Naukowe, 1969.

Wesolowski, M, *Cuirassiers of the Grand Duchy of Warsaw,* unpublished manuscript.

Wielhorski, J., "Lanca." *Studia do Dziejow Dawnego Uzbrojenia i Ubioru Wojskowego* 6 (1974).

Wimmer, J., *Historia piechoty polskiej do roku 1864,* Warsaw, Wydawnictwo Ministerstwa Obrony Narodowej, 1978.

Zaremba, A., "Batalion polski Gwardii w 1813 r."*Bron i Barwa,* (London) 11 (1957).

Zaremba, A., "1 i 2 pulk ulanow polskich w kampanii francuskiej 1814 r." *Studia do Dziejow Dawnego Uzbrojenia i Ubioru Wojskowego* 6 (1974).

Zaremba, A., "Polish Legions of the Napoleonic Period", *Adjutant's Call* (New York) 4.4 (1966)

Zaremba, A., "The 1st and 2nd Regiments of Polish Lancers in the 1814 Campaign", *Adjutant's Call* (New York) 6.34 (1969)

Zych, G., *Armia Ksiestwa Warszawskiego 1807-1812,* Warsaw, Wydawnictwo Ministerstwa Obrony Narodowej, 1961.

Zych, G., *Rok 1807 Wydawnictwo Ministerstwa Obrony Narodowej,* Warsaw, 1957.

Zygulski, Z. Jun., and Wielecki, H., *Polski mundur wojskowy,* Krakow: Krajowa Agencja Wydawnicza, 1988.

Operations of the 7th Polish Light Cavalry Division In the Leipzig Campaign

Translated and Annotated by G.F.Nafziger

Napoleon and Poniatowski at Leipzig (January Suchodolski

Operations of the 7th Polish Light Cavalry Division In the Leipzig Campaign

Translated and Annotated
by G.F.Nafziger

Original work:
PARIS
Imprimerie d'ant. Bailleu
Rue Saite-Anné, No. 71
....
1814

This edition:

Cover Design by Dr. George F. Nafziger
Translated & Annotated by Dr. George F. Nafziger

Notes on this Edition and its Translation

The original work is entitled Journal Historique des Opérations militaries de la 7ᵉ division de cavalerie légère polonaise, faisant partie du 4ᵗʰ corps de la cavalerie de reserve sous les orders de M. le Génèrl de division Sokolnicki; Depuis la reprise des hostilités au mois d'août 1813, jusque'au passage du Rhin, au mois de novembre de la même année [Historical Journal of the Military Operations of the 7ᵗʰ Division of Light Polish Cavalry Forming Part of the 4ᵗʰ Reserve Cavalry Corps from the Month of August 1813 to the Crossing of the Rhine, to the Month of November of the Same Year.]

The unidentified author, who signs himself as Al..... A....., Chef de bataillon du Génie, is unknown.

The translation of this work was relatively straightforward and quick. Names were changed to reflect current spellings. Occasionally words and names were inserted to clarify the passage. When that was done, those words were inserted in square brackets.

The translation does not include the side notes that were found in the original. It seemed inappropriate to retain them. As the translation progressed, it was found that they contributed little to the usefulness of the translation. However, since this is a journal, it was thought appropriate to maintain the format and put the dates in the margin so that the sequence of events would remain very clear.

Introduction

The 7th (Polish) Light Cavalry Division was raised during the summer of 1813. Its assigned regiments participated in the 1812 campaign, but very few of those men actually returned from the campaign and, in 1812, they were not organized into a brigade or division that, as an organization, was identifiable in 1813.

These regiments had to be totally rebuilt. The men that formed them consisted of the small cadres of survivors filled out with new men from the depots. In addition, so few horses had survived the 1812 campaign that one must assume that all the horses and all their equipment had to be replaced.

The rebuilding of these regiments was further complicated by the fact that the Grand Duchy of Warsaw had been overrun by the Russians and defecting Prussians in early 1813. When it came time to rebuild these regiments, their depots were not accessible to them, but in Russian or Prussian hands. The men, horses and material that were used either had to be hurriedly removed as the French fell back across the Grand Duchy before the Allies arrived, or the slipped out and joined the French in eastern Germany after the Grand Duchy was occupied. What was missing was then, by necessity, provided from materials available in Germany, but the Poles had to compete there with the French and every other contingent of the Grande Armée for very limited resources. As a result, you will see comments about the lack of uniforms, etc.

This division the Poles created was critical to Napoleon's fall campaign. His single biggest problem in the 1813 spring campaign had been his near total lack of cavalry which repeatedly allowed the Allies to escape him. The victories at Lützen and Bautzen had almost been pyrrhic in nature, as they lacked a truly decisive result that could have been achieved, if Napoleon had half the cavalry he had lost in Russia.

In addition to the general lack of cavalry, the Poles brought to Napoleon some of the finest cavalry in Europe. One might argue, on an individual basis, if they were as good or better than the notorious Cossacks, but the Cossacks were irregular cavalry and could not stand against regular cavalry. The Poles were disciplined and regulated cavalry that could and did stand up to all of their opponents. This meant that they could and would make a critical contribution to the battles fought at Dresden and Leipzig.

The 7th Division did not fight at many of the major autumn battles, but it was frequently in contact with the Allied cavalry. The 7th Division did, however, perform magnificently at Leipzig, fully living up to its reputation as Polish cavalry and showed itself as good as the Polish Winged Hussars that had fought before the gates of Vienna 130 years earlier.

HISTORICAL JOURNAL OF THE MILTIARY OPERATIONS
OF THE 7TH DIVISION OF POLISH LIGHT CAVALRY

15 August - the 7th Light Cavalry Division was formed from the 17th and 18th Brigades, but this last brigade does not figure in the picture, as it was detached to the Observation Corps under General Dombrowski. It is, therefore, important to note that the history of this division speaks implicitly of the 17th brigade, all the 8th Corps, the cadres of the dislocated cadres, that Prince Poniatowski had brought with him from the Grand Duchy of Warsaw, which were:

1. 1st Chasseur à Cheval Regiment, into which were folded cadres of the 5th Chasseurs and some men of the 4th;
2. 3rd Uhlan Regiment, which were amalgamated from the remnants of the 11th Uhlans.

The force of these two regiments, after a review held on the same day, gave them the following strength:

Units	Men	Horses
1st Chasseurs	510	572
3rd Uhlans	601	663
Total	1,111	1,235

Only a fifth of the corps was equipped with firearms and these were of poor quality. Its swords were provisional, its equipment almost non-existent, and its uniform, despite the sacrifices of the colonels, barely covered the nudity of the soldiers. Uniforms were prepared in Dresden, but the events of war prevented the delivery of most of them. Only the zeal of the commanders and the officers replaced the shortage of these supplies. Other circumstances rendered the situation of this brigade even more difficult and alarming, however, becoming the object of the anxiety for the général de division [Sokolnicki] and it completely justified his expectations. The 2nd Company, 6th Horse Artillery Regiment was attached to the division. It had six cannon - four 6pdrs and two howitzers.

That same day the division left its cantonments at Königsheim and Richnau, where it had, until that point, observed the roads to Friedland and Grottau, to move rapidly by Herrnhut on Rumburg.

17 August - The division took up positions at Nieder-Oderwitz and pushed a reconnaissance down all the roads that debouched from Rumburg on Löbau, Zittau and Georgenthal. A patrol from the 1st Chasseurs penetrated into the city of Rumburg and spread alarm there, capturing two prisoners from the veterans that formed its garrison. This was the first encounter along all the line with the Austrians

19 August - The division moved on Zittau, scouting the roads to Zwickau. Parties of the 1st Chasseurs and 3rd Uhlans encountered strong detachments of Austrian hussars, towards Kirschenstein, charged them, despite their numerical superiority, and drove them back to Kreiwitz.

20 August - The division passed through the Gabel defile and took up positions at Marchersdorf, observing all the defiles to its left.

21 August - It opened communications by Pankratz with Krantzau and Reichenberg, occupied by the advance guard of the 8th Corps. At the same time it pushed reconnaissance forces through Christorf on Böhmisch-Eycha, where it found the Austrian corps of General Neuperg, whose advance posts were at Olschwitz. These latter were driven back, with the loss of a few men, to their lines.

22 August - The position, cut by ravines, ponds, swamps and woods, required the presence of infantry to defend it, so a company of 60 men was assigned. After having posted pickets in the principal defiles, the general left, at the head of two squadrons, to make a reconnaissance by Pankratz and Christorf, on Olschwitz. The enemy held no position and avoided any engagement.

23 August - Despite the fatiguing service that the 7th Division performed, taking into consideration its limited strength and the distance it had to observe and guard, it nevertheless detached two squadrons, with Colonel Kurnatowski, to relieve the post of the 8th Corps in front of Gabel and they sent a reconnaissance as far as Nimes and Böhmisch-Leypa

Polish Eclaireur 1813

24 August - An alarm was given by the post at Pankratz, which was manned by Starzenski's squadron of the 3rd Uhlans. The général de division came up in person with two squadrons. Enemy detachments had come forward in front of the two Westphalian regiments to facilitate their defection.[1] This had not been foreseen or could it be prevented, but the Austrian hussars were driven back beyond Olschwitz.

On the other side, the colonel of the 1st Chasseurs, Kurnatowski, pushed, as he had the night before, reconnaissance forces on Nimes and Böhmisch-Leypa. The 3rd Uhlans lost, in this encounter, four men and four horses, which were wounded and captured at the entry of the village.

25 August - Colonel Kurntowski returned the division's camp. A reconnaissance force was sent to Metzdorf, from where it captured forage from the enemy.

26 August - The enemy made a reconnaissance against the advance posts at Gabel, on the road to Nimes and Böhmisch-Leypa. At the same time they attacked, with superior forces, the ad-

[1]These were the 1st and 2nd Westphalian Hussar Regiments.

vance posts of the 8th Corps at Kratzau. The général de division had it supported by a squadron of the 3rd Uhlans, that he had at Pankratz, and he personally led forward two elite squadrons and 30 voltigeurs on Christorf, to make a diversion. After having forced the enemy to return to his lines, he returned by Metzdorf and Hennersdorf.

27 August - The enemy appeared to have wanted to renew his attacks of the night before on Kratzau. The post at Pankratz was, as a result, reinforced; and a new maneuver made on Christorf and Metzdorf, which was foiled.

28 August - The 7th Division crossed through the Gabel defile and occupied the suburbs of Zittau, so as to observe the roads to Ramburg, Zwickau, Grottau, Friedland and Seydenberg. Chef d'escadorn Starzenski arrived there from Pankratz, moving by Grottau, and captured a convoy of food from the enemy.

31 August - Until that day the division limited itself to sending reconnaissances to the gates of Rumburg and Zwickau, and to scout the other roads with patrols. However, strong enemy forces presented themselves at Seydenberg. Chef d'escadron Madalinski, of the 1st Chasseurs, was detached with 100 men to identify them. He succeeded in flushing out a Russian dragoon regiment, which had advanced to Engelsdorf and moved to take up a position at Hirschfeld, where the général de division had advanced with a squadron to support them.

On the same day the 7th Division furnished an officer and 50 men to escort baggage to Dresden.

1 September - A Russian dragoon regiment came forward at daybreak and, with great impetuosity, attached chef d'escadron Madalinski at Hirschfield, but found the post ready to receive them. They were countercharged and pushed back, with lances at their backs, to Engelsdorf. They left several men on the pavement and abandoned some prisoners to us, including an officer. We had a horse killed and two non-commissioned officers of the chasseurs wounded.

The division then left their cantonments and took up position on the road to Hirschfeld. Chef d'escadron Madalinski received, at the same time, the order to destroy all the bridges that he found on the Neiss as far as Ostritz; which he did through the night and until the moment that the enemy advance guard arrived to capture this post.

2 September - The 7th Division marched out at 4:00 a.m., the left forward to move by Spitz-Cunnersdorf, Alt-Gersdorf and Ebersbach to Kottmannsdorf, where it took up position. Captain Farinelli, aide-de-camp to the général de division, pushed a reconnaissance on Herrnhut, which was already occupied by the enemy's light forces.

3 September - Before daybreak, a squadron of chasseurs moved on Herrnhut, where it encountered a Russian dragoon regiment in the highway, without having had any other engagement beyond one with some skirmishers; it then re-descended by Ober and Nieder-Cunnersdorf to support a squadron of the 3rd Uhlans, which had moved at the same time towards Löbau. This latter was first harassed by 400 to 500 Cossacks and maintained itself in the middle of them until 2:00 p.m., on the Gross-Schweidnitz plateau. However, while swarms of these soldiers came to present themselves on the right flank of the division, from the side of Walsdrof, and on the rear,

from Ebersbach. Chef [d'escadron] Barski, who commanded this squadron, saw himself suddenly enveloped by 1,000 new Cossacks. However, he did not permit himself to be shaken until the arrival of assistance, which was sent to disengage him. Then the fight became more lively, when it was supported by the arrival of a Russian cavalry regiment. Despite the disproportionate numbers, the enemy had more than 50 men hors de combat and we suffered 4 soldiers wounded and one horse killed. The sang-froid of Chef d'escadron Barski and the intrepidity of young Lieutenant Obrewski, caused him to be noted in a distinguished manner on this occasion.

On the other hand, while Chef d'escadron Madalinski held off the main enemy force which had advanced on Ebersbach, Chef d'escadron Rozycki, aide-de-camp to the général de division, was locked in combat with enemy detachments coming to capture the post at Ober-Cunnersdorf, and he succeeded in dislodging them.

Several enemy scouts penetrated on our left into the village of Durr-Hennersdorf, where the commanding general had placed the 6th Uhlan Regiment.[2]

All these attacks were the announcement of the arrival of the main body of a Russian army corps, whose columns, well concentrated and accompanied by a numerous artillery park and several cavalry regiments, defiled before our eyes and moved by the road from Osritz to take up a position behind Löbau.

In this state of things, Colonel Tancarville, chief of staff of the 4th Corps, who had come to reconnoiter during the day, convinced himself the position at Kottmannsdorf (which an army of 60,000 men could successfully occupy) was truly perilous for a thousand poorly armed cavalry with no infantry. Towards evening he sent two companies of infantry to protect the retreat of the division, which was done during the night, in the best order possible, by Friedersdorf and Neusalze, on Schluckenau; at the same time Chef d'escadron Madalinski, who sustained himself at Ebersbach, flanked them by Langegrund and Hempel, following the edge of the Königswald Woods.

4 September - The 7th Division was placed in the second line and in covering the right flank of the 8th Corps, scouting with its patrols from Sebnitz to Rumburg.

5 September - It followed, with the 4th Corps, the movements of the 8th Corps, by Neusalze on Löbau and took up position at Klein-Schweidnitz, facing Herrnhut, and maintaining posts at Nieder-Cunnersdorf, Kotttmannsdorf and Lawalde.

After a rigorous review, in which it marched out, the division presented itself, and it contained an effective strength of 1,085 combatants, with 78 absent, and was put in service outside of the division.

6 September - The post at Lawald was reinforced by 60 horse, to observe the road to Schluckenau, and reconnaissances were pushed beyond Ober-Cunnersdorf.

7 September - The division made a movement toward its center, forming a hook around Gross-Schweidnitz: the 1st Chasseurs faced Schluckenau and the 3rd Uhlans faced Herrnhut; the two elite reserve companies and the artillery in the center, on a hill facing Kottmannsdorf, and which covered with its fire all the streets of the village; a company of infantry lined the woods

[2]The document says the 61st Uhlan Regiment, but there was no such unit. The 6th Uhlans, however, were part of this IV Corps, to which the 7th Division belonged.

where it was crossed by the roads from Rumberg, Herrnhut and Lawalde. These changes were necessitated by the movements that the enemy made on the right.

8 September – With two squadrons of cavalry and a single cannon Colonel Kurnatowski, made a reconnaissance to Schluckenau. It encountered no enemy, but reported important information.

Chef d'escadron Starzenski pushed the same on Rumburg and appropriately seconded Colonel of Hussars Sokolnicki, who was engaged with the enemy beyond Ebersbach.

Chef [d'escadron] Korn reconnoitered the terrain as far as Ober-Ruppersdorf and Chef [d'escadron] advanced to the Cunnersdorf heights to support him, such that almost all the troop was put in movement.

Lithuanian Tartar of the Guard (B. Gembarzewski)

9 September - If the day of the 8th was very fatiguing for the troop. It was very honorable for the 7th Division, which was charged, after the bloody affair of Löbau, with covering the retreat of the 8th Corps, as well as the 4th Reserve Cavalry Corps as far as Bautzen.

From the beginning of the action the division took up a concentrated position closer to the line, covering the right flank. It still had not taken any part in the murderous fight on the left, which stubbornly disputed possession of a mountain, where the enemy had penetrated, initially, without resistance and which dominated the country. Large masses of enemy cavalry moved, nonetheless, on Kottmansdorf, where the mountains and the woods masked their ulterior movement. It was feared that they planned to maneuver by Schönbach to turn us.

The général de division sent this observation to the commanding general and at 4:00 p.m., it was decided to withdraw. We then saw numerous enemy cavalry squadrons move from Nieder-Ottenheim and, under the protection of skirmishers, attempt to force the passes at Klein-Schweidnitz; but the determination of the 7th Division and the fire from its artillery stopped their audacity, and it did not begin its movement, which it did en échiquier, until after all the troops of the 8th Corps had passed through the Olsig defile.

On the other side, Chef d'escadron Jagmin remained forward of Gross-Schweidnitz, opposed, with his imperturbable phlegm, the exuberance of a swarm of Cossacks, who sought to cut off the division They soon found themselves encircled and harassed by numerous bands of all arms. They drove back several very intrepid charges. Canister brought heavy casualties to their ranks; we had two horses killed and four men wounded, whose determination carried them into the enemy pelotons, and who were freed by blows of the lance.

All the officers did their duty. Those of the staff and, notably, the aides-de-camp of the général de division, rivaled the zeal, bravery and intelligence, in carrying orders into the melee. The chefs. by their sang froid, and the soldiers, by their intrepid countenance, fixed the attention of the commanding general and astonished the enemy.

The enemy columns already precipitated into the city. It was urgent to cross the Olsig defile. It had to be done before they debouched. The artillery was brought forward at the gallop to the hills and then showered the road with canister. They stopped the first columns that came out, and forced them to scatter into the gardens. The Krakus, encouraged by the disorder of the enemy columns, attempted to charge, but the terrain did not permit it. The enemy brought forward his guns and put 8 into battery. In less than a quarter of an hour they were reduced to silence by those of the division. This success, which assured the retreat of the corps, was due to the advantage of the position, the celerity with which it was occupied and the zeal of the officers and non-commissioned officers of the artillery, who admitted that the major part of their gunners been in combat for the first time this day.

10 September - The 7th Division continued to cover the retreat of the corps, marching all night by echelons, passing Bautzen and occupying Grobschutz and Doberschau. At 2:00 p.m., the resumed their march and took up position in front of Prisancke.

11 September - The division marched out at 4:00 a.m., and occupied Putzkau, having a company of infantry in front, observing and scouting all the roads to Neustadt and Neukirchen. It furnished strong patrols on Withen and Bautzen, where the enemy began to show himself.

12 September - The 7th Division took up an oblique position: its left was supported on the village of Lauterbach and its right on the hill that separates it from the village of Stolpen. Two companies of infantry occupied the village and the "grand gardes" of cavalry observed the roads to Putzkau and Neustadt. It was on the left flank of the 8th Corps, which camped at Stolpen, and found itself, by this concentrated position, concentrated, in a measure to execute all the movements that may be ordered of it.

13 September - General Excelman's division camps at the side of the 7th Division, in the village of Lauterbach. Towards the evening General Uminski, commanding the advance guard of the 8th Corps, was attacked in his position at Oblaugen-Wolmsdorf by superior forces, and called for support from the 7th Division, Our general went forward with two squadrons to Burckersdorf charging the enemy with so much impetuosity that they were forced to abandon the ground; and the valiant Madalinski pursued them to Neustadt. The enemy suffered a notable loss. The fog, which turned into rain, did not permit the capture of any prisoners; they suffered only the death of an officer's horse killed. On our side, we lost an officer, who was carried away by the ardor of his horse, and was captured, after having stabbed five times by lances; a chasseur and 3 uhlan horses were wounded by Cossack lances.

14 September - The 7th Division crossed to the right of the 8th Corps and established itself on the Alt-Stadt-Stolpen plateau, having its advance posts at Wolmsdorf, observing and scouting the roads to Pinra, Hohenstein and Neustadt. Two companies of infantry were put at its disposition to guard the defiles, as well as the avenues of the villages and the fords at Wesnitz. It pushed, that same day, a reconnaissance to Lohmen and Wehlen.

15 September - Count de Valmy, making a reconnaissance on Neustadt, and finding himself engaged with the enemy, the 7th division moved to the Sturza heights to support this movement.

The enemy deployed a battalion of infantry on the Burckersdorf heights and descended, with a few squadrons of cavalry, into the Hösslich. They were immediately charged by the division and driven back with a notable loss on Hohenstein. We lost four horses wounded, including one officer's horse.

16 September - The enemy sent detachments into the Wesnitz basin to observe the corps' position and weak reconnaissance forces were not sufficient to dislodge them, so the général de division put himself at the head of two squadrons and succeeded in pushing them back, into Hohenstein and beyond the Bockmühl. He profited from this occasion to reconnoiter the progress of the demolition of the redoubts, which the enemy pressed vigorously, and which shortly before the French army had raised.

17 September - A post of 25 men from the division was established at Dobra to assure communications with Pirna, and to maintain mobile vedettes on the Burckersdorf heights.

18 September - The measures taken the night before had contained the enemy beyond the Pollentz. They continued to demolish the redoubts at Hohenstein, and while they made vain demonstrations against the Cunnersdorf and Ehrenberg heights, our parties penetrated into Krun and Bockmühl, and there, grabbed the enemy's beard, while taking provisions of bread, flour and livestock.

19 September - The Duke de Tarento made a movement to close up on the 8th Corps, the 7th Division received orders to be under arms at daybreak. It was accustomed to this; but the enemy, no doubt, having warning of this movement, moved in force to occupy the Burckersdorf heights, and descended on Sturza with cavalry and infantry.

The général de division maneuvered with four squadrons, a company of infantry and two cannon. While two of these squadrons amused the enemy on the right side of Sturza, and the company of infantry slipped, covered by the gardens, into a ravine that led to the Lohmen Woods, and captured it, the général de division emerged unexpectedly from the Bockmühl Woods and by Hösslich , charged the enemy with impetuosity, and forced them to withdraw in disorder on Hohenstein, pursuing them to the suburbs of that city. The enemy left several en on the battlefield. We suffered 5 men and 3 horses wounded with saber blows. The Palatine Hussars showed, on this occasion, much dexterity in cutting the horses bridles.

20 September - The enemy attacked our left by Lauterbach, and a division of Young Guard, which crossed the Elbe, at Pirna, moved to take up position at Lohmen and occupied Dobra and Sturza, the 7th Division pushed reconnaissances on Bockmühle and Hohenstein, in order to make a diversion against the enemy column, so as to mask from the enemy the arrival of the Young Guard.

21 September - The detachment of Young Guard, having evacuated Sturza to concentrate at Dobra, and a detachment of Guard Chevaulegers had a very serious engagement with a large enemy force composed of Austrian hussars, skirmishers, and Cossacks. The général de division moved, by Bockmühle and Burckersdorf, against the Burckersdorf heights, which he occupied and maneuvered so as to precipitously abandon the battlefield to the enemy, who threw them-

selves into Radwalde, where they had infantry. The général de division did not return until that evening.

22 September - The Emperor visited the camp of the Duke of Taranto, the 8th Corps, as well as the 4th Reserve Cavalry Corps also expected to see him in theirs. The enemy, however, unexpectedly showed himself in force on the Sturze heights, so the squadron camped at Helmsdorf, under the orders of Chef d'escadron Madalinski, threw itself on them with intrepidity, which he forced to measure its movements. Another squadron, with a company of infantry, was also sent to support the first; and the général de division moved by echelons with two elite squadrons and two cannons, by Hösslich, right on the Burckersdorf heights. Several charges occurred, in which a peloton of the 1st Chasseurs, commanded by Captain Jezierski, singularly distinguished itself. The enemy was thrown back on Hohenstein, leaving several dead on the battlefield, and 30 wounded. We had an officer and 4 soldiers wounded, plus several horses sabered in the nostrils, as during the day of the 19th, and many snaffles were cut. A squadron pushed to the Radewalde, where one found sufficient provisions, which were obtained without difficulty.

23 September - The 7th Division limited itself to pushing reconnaissances to Bockmühle on Hohenstein, Bruckersdorf and Radewald. They did not encounter any of the enemy and obtained food and forage everywhere with ease. Nonetheless that same night the division received the order to detach 200 cavalry to capture, with main force, all the livestock that could be found in the villages within its range. This measure, repugnant to the hearts of the most hardened, so the général de division put all moderation to it that could be permitted.

24 September - The 7th Light Cavalry Division marched out by Rennersdorf and Neudorf, to move in Fischbach, where it was to unite with the 8th Corps and the 4th Reserve Cavalry Corps. The two corps moved, in the afternoon, on Hartau where the Emperor had the Krakus pass in review, then took the road to Dresden.

25 September - The march of the previous evening had exhausted the horses and troops. Nonetheless, the division was obliged to pass the night in the forest, without forage, and resume its march at daybreak, passing by Dresden and took up a position a mile from the village, on the road to Wilsdruf. It did not have time there to cool down. The 1st Chasseur Regiment left immediately, to move on Tanneberg, along the road to Nossen; and towards 2:00 p.m., all the 4th Corps marched in that direction, and took up a position at Wilsdurf, scouting the roads to Freyberg, Nossen and Meissen. In the absence of His Excellency the Count de Valmy, Général de division Sokolnicki was given command of the corps.

26 September - The 1st Chasseurs pushed to Rosenthal, where it took a post beyond the Nossen; and the 4th Corps camped by echelons in front of the city, observing the road to Freyberg and that to Meissen by Zelle.

That evening, the Count de Valmy arrived at Nossen, and was followed by the headquarters of the 8th Corps.

27 September - The 7th Division, reinforced by an infantry regiment, moved to occupy Colidtz, observing and scouting the roads to Leipzig, Borna and Altenburg.

28 September - The division furnished two strong reconnaissances, each of 150 horse; one on Pomsen along the road to Leipzig; and the other on Frohburg, to scout closer to the posts occupied or threatened by the enemy, so as to obtain positive information on the partisans that infested the vicinity of Altenburg, and which had received considerable reinforcements from Bohemia.

29 September - At 4:00 p.m., all the division moved out under orders from the Count de Valmy; and when it passed Schönbach, it returned on its steps and took up its position at Colditz, leaving a detachment of 50 horse at Pomsen and scouting the roads to Borna and Altenburg.

30 September - The division left its position at Colditz at 5:00 p.m. It maneuvered by Chierbaum, Reichersdorf and Ebersbach, where it spent the first hours of the night in bivouac, awaiting the report of the advance guard, which had gone to assure the Frohburg debouch. A reconnaissance of 50 horse was sent by Laussig on Borna, with orders to stop at Peicha, until the arrival of the reconnaissance from Pomsen arrived at Thierbach, in order to make a concentric movement on Borna and Frohburg.

All these movements were executed punctually, except that of the advance guard. However, it is a fact that there were only eight Cossacks, of which four were on duty at the gate

1 October - The 7th Division arrived, with the day, at Frohburg, and the advance guard at Eschefeld, where the night before the Hetman Platov and Prince Djurgatov had had their headquarters, and which they precipitously abandoned at 3:00 a.m. One found there in the surrounding farms, as with the peasants, still hot bread, and wagons hitched up and charged with provisions that the Cossacks had come to find there and which they abandoned upon the approach of our columns; we also found saddles, bridles and effects in the camp that they had occupied at Eschefeld.

Despite repeated orders, the advance guard did not do its duty on this occasion. Chef d'escadron Korn was sent to take command of it and he pursued the fugitives to Windischleiba. Hetman Platov retired to Altenburg, where he found General Thielmann.

A reconnaissance was, at the same time, sent to Alt-Morbitz, on the road to Penig, and the division placed itself in a manner so as to support its detachments, if the need arose.

Towards the afternoon, the 8th Cavalry Division arrived at Roda. The advance guard of the 8th Corps moved to camp between Roda and Frohburg, and the 8th Corps occupied Grafenheim

2 October - According to information furnished by Chef d'escadron Korn, who always remained in the vicinity of Windischleiba, the colonel of the 3rd, Oborski, leaving at midnight at the head of a squadron of chasseurs, two squadrons of Uhlans, and four companies of infantry arrived, at daybreak, before Altenburg. He pushed back the first enemy pickets, and drove them back to their camp, beyond the city. A regiment of Cossacks, forming the Hetman's guard, presented a ferocious resistance. They wanted to charge our scattered squadrons; but the intrepidity of Chef d'escadron Madalinski, at the head of his squadron of chasseurs, fell on their flank with such boldness, that they were put to rout and he pursued them, with a lance at their back, until they were beyond the Saara Bridge, where they reached the retreating columns of Thielmann and disordered it. More than 160 of the famous Don Cossacks were made hors de combat. Around

40, including 3 officers were captured. They were all of a superb stature and uniform, and all natural figures. One could have thought they saw ancient Sythians still defying their conquerors. They pulled their beards and nothing could calm the rage that we found among our prisoners. "We are dishonored," they said. "Never since our regiment has existed has it suffered such a humiliating check." The chasseurs and uhlans took from them a booty of a few thousand ducats, and remounted on excellent horses.

On the other side, Captain Starzenski, sent on a reconnaissance with 50 horse on Alt-Morbitz, charged the post of Austrian hussars below Goldne-Plug, and penetrated to Schönbach. According to his report 800 to 900 hussars were deployed, by echelon, from that point to the Penig, and an equal number camped behind the city, under the orders of Colonel Mentzdorf, to maintain communications between Altenburg and Chemnitz, where they expected, as well as at Zwickau, the arrival of large army corps.

Général de division Sokolnicki perceived the possibility of throwing back these various detachments, and judged that the occupation of Penig, as the principal debouch on the Mulde, could be of great importance for the success of the subsequent operations of the Grande Armée. He solicited the honor and obtained the authorization upon the return of the Prince from his race to Altenburg.

3 October - At 2:00 a.m., the général de division put himself at the head of what remained available to him in the camp; that is; 6 squadrons of chasseurs and uhlans, 8 companies of infantry and 2 light cannons. A total of 1,225 combatants.

General Michal Sokolnicki (unknown)

Arriving before daybreak at Goldne-Plug, Sokolnicki had Captain Starzenski charge. Starzenski had maintained himself before the pickets of hussars and Cossacks that guarded the avenue of Langen-Leiba. In his charge he was supported by 2 squadrons of chasseurs and lancers and by 2 companies of voltigeurs, under the orders of Chief of Staff, Major Jabtkowski. The first parties were thrown back and dispersed.

Captain Starzenski pursued those fugitives who retreated down the road to Waldenburg and Major Jabtkowski chased them, from position to position, units reformed to the extent that they could move in echelons. However, they did not form definitively until were in front of and behind the suburbs of the city.

The main body of the [enemy] detachment appeared, along with these fugitives, on the rear of the plateau, which sloped downwards and the ground before the old city was furrowed with deep ravines. Regimental Adjutant Jabtkowski charged them with such great enthusiasm, that he forced them into a disordered retreat.

The voltigeurs took the bridge, which linked the two villages, at bayonet point and captured the new village.

Chef d'escadron Korn, with his squadron of chasseurs, pursued them, with the lance to their backs, to a point beyond Hartmannsdorf, where the hussars rallied on the edge of the woods. They suffered significant losses due to cowardice of the Cossacks, who ran away first, and only stopped beyond Röhrsdorf, on the road to Chemnitz. We had a few men, among the flankers, who were seriously wounded, and five horses killed.

On no occasion, perhaps, has one better seen what the straightforward determination of a handful of brave soldiers, submissive to orders, can do against a troop in rout, even though it is more than tenfold their number. Lieutenants Sokolnicki and Matona lost their horses in this action and the former was wounded.

The city of Penig was built in a very pronounced bend formed by the Mulde. Its banks, as it descends, are very steep, close together, and wooded, and the bed is fordable almost everywhere, not cluttered by rocks that make the passage difficult. A raised hill covered the side of Chemnitz and it dominated, at a distance of three or four cannon shots [6-8,000 paces], the sector was formed by the two branches that mounted and descended the right bank. This position is commanded by a vast plateau, which borders the left bank to Lunzenau, and extends beyond Wechselburg. The road that leads to Chemnitz crosses through the middle of that hill, while the old road followed the hollow of a deep and narrow gully.

This position merits being studied, to draw everything possible out of it. Two cannon, with a company of grenadiers, were placed on the hill, and two companies of voltigeurs occupied the intervals which separated the bank of the Mulde. A large group of cavalry pickets were established, by echelons, to the Mulde during the day and brought back during the evening.

The rest of the division bivouacked behind the old city, guarding the side facing Waldenburg, and a company of grenadiers occupied the new city.

Captain Lewinski, staff officer, was sent by Lunzenau to Mittweida to advise General Lauriston of the operation that was to be executed.

4 October - According to the report of Captain Starzenski, who remained in observation of Wolpersdorf, a detachment of 500 to 600 men, hussars and Cossacks continued to occupy Waldenburg. A corps of 2,000 cavalry, with 8 cannon, moved on the same point, coming from Gasnitz, under the orders of the Russian Prince and Hetman Platov in Morana.

Colonel Kurnatowski, with two squadrons and two infantry companies, were sent to reconnoiter them. The enemy flankers did not stand before ours. At 3:00 p.m., the enemy had, almost without resistance, evacuated the city and moved by Calenberg on Liechtenstein.

We learned that very large enemy force was assembling at Zwickau expecting the arrival of Prince von Schwarzenberg, as well as the headquarters of the Russian and Prussian armies; that the advance guard, commanded by General Mohr, from General Graf Klenau's corps, found itself at Langfeld, marching on Chemnitz, where there were 2,000 men at most.

This news was transmitted, at the same time, to the King of Naples [Murat], to Prince Poniatowski and to Count Lauriston. The latter informed Sokolnicki, by his aide-de-camp, that he would make a strong reconnaissance the following day on Chemnitz and invited him to second this movement.

5 October - Considering the position of the enemy and that of Count Lauriston, defeating or dispersing Colonel Mentzdorf's detachment, placed in the vicinity of Röhrsdorf, was honestly nothing more than a hunting party.

Colonel Kurnatowski received orders to move from Waldenburg by Lange-Thursbach and Limbach, where the commander of the 3rd [Uhlans], Zdanowski, moved them from Mittel-Throna, which it occupied. The general then came in person, with four companies of infantry, two cannon and two of the elite squadrons [of Uhlans], at Hartmannsdorf, while Chef d'escadron Korn broke up the enemy to make them leave the woods.

This operation, however, was thought to be daring and the general was given orders to retreat with all his force on Penig. He received no reinforcements from the rest of his division, though he repeatedly requested repeatedly them and whose presence at Frohburg was perfectly useless. Count Lauriston was the only one who sent him his regards in the most flattering terms. To consol himself the general united a large group of officers and citizens of the city in the chateau and they danced part of the night.

6 October - The operation of the previous night was unsuccessful and the reconnaissance by Lauriston was also not a success, so one naturally expected some enterprise on the part of the enemy. At 3:00 a.m., Sokolnicki sent his artillery to the plateau on the left bank, dominating the hill and covering the road to Chemnitz on the flank. He took all appropriate measures to assure his retreat in case he was forced back by superior forces.

In effect, events soon justified this precaution. From daybreak, five or six squadrons of hussars and Cossacks charged to the foot of the hill, with a veritable fury, where they sought to capture our cannons. The guns, masked by the branches of the trees on the plateau, opposing the right bank, began to fire canister and the enemy disappeared with losses and in confusion. They were pursued by the Guards to Muhla, were they reformed.

At 8:00 a.m., General Mohr's advance guard moved on the Muhla heights. Two battalions formed in attack column and moved to within shot range of the cannon. They were greeted [by cannon fire]; several shots struck the mass and stopped their further movement. The cavalry tried to advance and was no more fortunate in its enterprise. Four cannons move down the flank and we fired several wasted shots at them. Four battalions formed in attack columns and remained immobile more than an hour under arms. Finally, towards noon, General Mohr resumed [his movement down] the road to Chemnitz.

The retrograde movement of the enemy was the result of a attack made by General Count Lauriston. The general judged that it was appropriate for him to make, a reconnaissance, to support by his movements to the flank of the change of front made by the 5th Corps. He pushed, in person, as far as Hartmannsdorf and his advance guard maintained itself on the Mulda until the evening. Upon his return, the good inhabitants of Penig, to make a truce with the anguishes of fright, delivered themselves into joy, and willingly illuminated the city.

At the sound of the cannon, the rest of the division advanced as far as Goldne-Plug, and the 8th Corps took up a more concentric position between Frohburg and Rochlitz.

7 October - The enemy returned, with larger forces than the day before, to attack the city of Penig. He appeared to fly to an assured victory and attempted to carry the defile with main force.

Four strong battalions, preceded by 6 cannon, advanced in an attack column and at the *pas de charge*[3]; 12 battalions, with as many guns and 16 squadrons of cavalry followed, part in line and part in columns on the flank.

[3]The pas de charge is a cadenced march of 120 paces per minute. On occasion, this work will speak of the Austrians and Russians using the pas de charge. In those instances it was a quick pace, but not quite as fast as that of the French and Poles.

The general had the advance posts fall back to the city and let the first [enemy] columns approach to half cannon range [1000 paces]. Then he unmasked his batteries, which spread death into the formidable masses and forced them to maneuver to the left flank so as to avoid this fire; while the enemy artillery, which made a terrible din, didn't cause us the least loss.

A regiment of Croatian [light infantry] slipped up to the Mulde gorge covered by ravines and turned the flank of our advance posts.[4] Some of their companies penetrated into the interior of the city. It was necessary to relieve our brave soldiers. Two companies of grenadiers, with Major Kossecki, of the 1st Regiment, at their head, crossed the passage and attacked with bayonets to join their comrades. There, they formed in line, while plunging canister fire swept and scattered the Croatians, who were advancing in line on the hill, and disordered them. They left more than 200 dead on the ground and suffered as many wounded. We also took 30 prisoners. The enemy cavalry shook out to dislodge our grenadiers from the hill, but the fire of the artillery and the pelotons stopped them on the edge of the hollow road and forced them to withdraw. Such was the advantage of the position, where the artillery had the greatest effect possible and was itself beyond reach. Our loss consisted of:

Unit	Killed	Wounded
1st Infantry Regiment	43	63
1st Chasseur Regiment	4	7
3rd Uhlan Regiment	2	9
Total	52	79

This included 3 officers wounded. In the artillery and cavalry 10-11 horses were hors de combat.

The general waited impatiently for the arrival of his reserve, consisting of four companies of infantry, four light cannons and 450 horse, and to which he had sent repeated orders at Laugenleuba, where it was supposed to be. However, it had taken the road to Wechselburg, where it found the Count de Valmy, and in confusion it moved back to Bruchheim, near Gottheim, where Prince Poniatowski was to be found.

When, the enemy came to occupy Altenburg, and moved in force from Zweikau. The 5th Corps had began its movement on Rochlitz, parties of skirmishers had followed it and began to show themselves at Hohnkirche, vis-à-vis Lunzenau. The enemy masses augmented vis-à-vis Penig and we lacked munitions. People were sent to Rochlitz to find some, but they did not return.

In this crisis the general saw himself completely isolated on the extreme end of the Army of the King of Naples. It evacuated the right bank of the Mulde, destroyed the bridge between the two cities and limited itself to maintaining the plateau on the left bank as far as Rochburg. Brave Chef de bataillon Fontana, with two companies of voltigeurs, descended the Mulde, by echelons, as far as Lunzenau to destroy the bridge there and to establish a post, while detachments of cavalry observed the roads to Waldenburg, Altenburg and Frohburg. Finally, at 11:00 a.m., he received orders to retire on Wechselburg, and he occupied a dominating position above Neider-Elsdorf, which was more advantageous. He supported his right on Ober-Elsdorf, with an observation post in the small woods behind Dittmannsdorf, and two companies of voltigeurs at Lunzenau. The advance guard was in front of Neider-Elsdorf.

---

[4]These Croatian light infantry are the famous Grenzers

The enemy did not see this movement until the main body of the corps had passed through Arensdorf. A few pelotons of cavalry passed the ford above the city and followed weakly the scouts of the rearguard. Their infantry did not begin to show itself on the left bank of the Mulde until after we were established in our [new] position where we were joined towards evening by the members who had to that point been separated from the skeleton of division that was commanded by Général de Division Sokolnicki. If they had joined sooner, the general intended to operate directly by the right flank, and, favored by the gullies, to cut off and remove everything that he found on this bank.

8 October - All the reconnaissance reports sent during the day were in agreement.

1. That the enemy had only a regiment of Croatians, of some 2,000 men on the left bank of the river.
2. That he had only sent over a squadron of hussars and about 50 Cossacks.
3. That there was nothing but cavalry on the hill and all along the road to Muhla.
4. That General Mohr, with his entire division, were camped behind the village and awaiting the arrival, at Chemnitz, Klenau's corps, whose advance guard he commanded.

Knowing, that the King of Naples [Murat] placed a high importance on the Penig defile, General Sokolnicki, despite his losses and the fatigues he had suffered, claimed this honor and requested, with insistence, the authorization [to defend it]. He obtained this authorization towards noon, along with the ammunition he lacked and the news that, to support his movements, the Count de Valmy wished to establish himself, with the 8th Division, at Ober-Grafenheim.

The general divided up his troop into two columns. He left the center and left in position under the command of Colonel Kurnatowski, with orders, when the signal was given, to move rapidly by Rochsburg on the plateau that dominated the Penig hill. He left, himself, with the right, moving in two pieces, and moved by the road running to Dittmannsdorf, without the enemy perceiving it.

The signal given, the infantry formed and moved, at the pas de charge, on the left flank of the Croatians who camped in front of Alt-Penig. Two companies of grenadiers penetrated, weapons in hand, to the bridge and captured it at bayonet point. The cannons maneuvered with the cavalry to protect its movements and Colonel Kurnatowski arrived on the plateau at the moment when he agreed, to protect, with his artillery, our columns that had already crossed the debouch.

The Croatians were thrown into the river, losing many casualties. We took 60 prisoners from then and several hussars were dismounted by the infantry's bayonets. Colonel Oborski pursued the fugitives with the aggressiveness that was natural for him, throwing them from the hill and maintaining himself there, despite the stubborn resistance of the numerically superior enemy and whose forces augmented constantly by the arrival of new columns.

A considerable mass of enemy cavalry, preceded by 6 cannons, descended at a full trot the side of the Muhla. It could not, however, damage them and it was pounded by our batteries placed on the plateau.

General Mohr did not delay in crowning the Muhla heights with all his forces. They were, truthfully, very imposing, but incapable of shaking us. Eighteen to 20 battalions of infantry, preceded by 10-12 cannon, deployed in line and descended the side, as if on parade.

It was too late to be able to undertake anything and he resumed his first position, limiting himself to advancing 2 or 3 battalions of Croatians or jagers, who slipped through the gorges and the woods, and disturbed us all night.

We barricaded the gates to the city, blocked all the avenues, destroyed the bridge and spent the night under arms. The two banks of the Mulde to the entry of the city presented a spectacle of continual fire.

9 October - The night had exhausted the troop and consumed a great portion of the infantry's cartridges. Some companies entirely lacked ammunition and dawn became the signal for a stubborn and murderous fight. The enemy had placed fourteen guns into battery, to which our six guns responded with equal activity and reduced two of them to silence. However, soon they ceased fire because of an absolute lack of ammunition. The caissons had been sent to find ammunition on Rochlitz and they had not returned.

Towards 10:00 a.m. the Count de Valmy made a demonstration on the road to Frohberg. One waited to see him occupy the Schleisdorf position, as much as one had seen a strong enemy column, of all arms, moving from Hoyersdorf on Neukirchen, vis-à-vis Lunzenau, where only a small picket had been left to guard the uncovered bridge. The enemy could have cut us off without resource and isolated us from the army, which stretched from Rochlitz to Frohburg, where the advance guard of the 8th Corps was engaged with the forces coming from Altenburg; and this was the advance guard of the Grande Armée, which marched on this point from Zwickau. The Count de Valmy wanted to send Général de Brigade Sierawski, with two battalions of the 16th [Infantry Regiment], to relieve the 1st [Infantry Regiment], which had consumed all its cartridges and which had more than 160 men hors de combat.

This sudden exchange shook the enemy. The new companies, lead by the valiant Major Bolesta, chased the Croatians in position there, from the gorge and forced them to move on the hill, where the canister exterminated them. However, this triumph did not last long. The enemy masses and their resources augmented to the measure that ours diminished. Everything announced the arrival of General Klenau's corps.

It was necessary to order the retreat. This measure was difficult for the brave soldiers, who had maintained themselves with vigor against the forces more than tenfold [their size]; but it was commanded by necessity and by prudence. The retreat of the two companies of grenadiers that still guarded the right bank at the entry of the city was the most difficult to execute. It was necessary to pass over a plank, or over the ford, under the nearly point-blank fire of enemy skirmishers and under the explosions of bursting howitzer shells.

We simulated a few attacks with main force on various points to attract the enemy's attention to those points. A battalion had orders to descend the river to Rochsburg, and to fire continuously during its march; and while another battalion made a crossed peloton fire, two cannons fired plunging fire in to the gorge with their last rounds of canister.

It was thus that the two companies were disengaged a loss of about 35 men of 148. This reunited battalion followed the movement of the 1st Regiment, which had threaded through two ravines, running towards Arensdorf and Neusorge and the Count de Valmy executed, at the same time, his retreat by Laugenleuba on Grafeinheim.

As soon as our fire ended, the enemy placed eight guns in battery on the hill and his skirmishers, passing over the fords, spread like a torrent over the plateau; however the cavalry, immobile until that time on the edge of the Neusorge Woods, received the order to send forward three squadrons of chasseurs and uhlans. General Sokolnicki personally led this force against the enemy. Chefs d'escadron Madalinski and Barski charged with an impetuosity worthy of their habitual bravery and threw then back into the river, where a large number of them, escaping the lances were drowned. Sokolnicki did not leave the plateau until the last peloton of the rearguard and then resumed its position at Schleisdorf.

Arriving there, he found, two infantry regiments below Hohenkirchen formed in line: a dragoon regiment, two squadrons of Austrian hussars, with one hundred Cossacks and six cannons. It was the column that had been seen in Hoyersdorf, and which, a half hour earlier, had been able, without firing a shot, to debouch by Lunzenau and take our rear. It had been held, for a couple of hours, in uncertainty, and this time was necessary to reunite all of the detached forces on the flanks.

Towards evening the 7th Division reunited, at Ober-Grafenheim, with the 4th Cavalry Corps, where the advance guard skirmished with parties of Cossacks and hussars that came, by intervals, from the Meysdorf Woods.

During the 8th and 9th, the 7th Cavalry division lost only 9 men dead, 15 wounded and around 30 horses as casualties, 2 gunners and a sergeant major of artillery wounded and 5 artillery horses hors de combat.

The most notable loss, however, was that of the infantry. The 1st Regiment, with 920 combatants, lost 200 men as casualties, including 4 officers; the 16th Regiment, which had come to relieve the 1st, had lost more than 110, including 3 officers, out of a total strength of 850 men.

The general greatly regretted one of his attached officers, Captain Dowait, a young man of great devotion, who died during the retreat, after having transmitted orders to General Sierawski.

It would be difficult to cite all the notable acts that marked these two days and to count all those who have acquired the rights to high praise. All the commanders of the corps made examples. All the officers imitated them with envy and there was not a soldier who did not wish to be in the first action. The artillery covered itself with glory and the officers of the staff distinguished themselves by their activity, by their audacity and by the precision with which they transmitted orders. One cannot, among the latter, an honorable mention of Captains Valentin, engineer of the division, and Farinelli, aide-de-camp to general Sokolnicki. These officers, full of merit, were indefatigable and their zeal was marked the most noble distinction.

One cannot estimate the enemy losses, since they remained in control of the battlefield, but any man of war will say, 1.) That in a stubborn and continuous battle lasting 10 hours, and with equal chances, the losses are almost always in proportion to the numbers engaged, and 2.) When the preponderant forces attack a troop with fury, they barely stop to consider numerical strengths, they do not stop on their impetuous path and that they do not allow themselves to be dislodged, even if attacked repeatedly, from the posts they have penetrated, before having suffered very considerable losses.

One has the certainty that the enemy had successively engaged more than 8,000 men in the battle and, in considering, 1.) that in the presence of an army of more than 30,000 men, they were chased out of the city and ravines five times, and pursued with bayonets in their backs; 2.) That all the fights occurred under the canister fire of six cannons and that they dismounted two of the enemy's guns, who had 14 in position; 3.) That the enemy cavalry was completely inactive, while ours made several charges that were as successful as they were beautiful, 4.) And finally, that the enemy became master of the positions because we wished to abandon it to them. Certainly, we can persuade ourselves that, in the most moderate terms, the enemy must have lost 2,000 to 3,000 men hors de combat.

These details are, perhaps, too long, but this is about noting the importance of the contributions the 7th Division made in this circumstance; and that it is no less important, under the reports of the art, to see what one can undertake with a handful of determined men, who the same spirit enlivens, and who are proud of the motive to which they devote themselves.

10 October - The 4th Reserve Cavalry Corps, reunited, executed a forced march by Lannig, as far as Otterwisch and Gross-Buch. It stopped a couple of hours, in passing by Lauterbach, where it found the advance guard of the 8th Corps, as well as the division of General Berckheim. It took up position there, facing the parties of Cossacks that hotly pursued it, while the 8th Corps was engaged on the side of Borna. This stop gave the troops the self-assurance that they had lost by having been cut off from the main body of the army.

This same night the 7th Division furnished, two reconnaissances forces to the King of Naples [Murat] and Prince Poniatowski; that is, one by Melbus to Espenheim, the other by Thierbach on Borna. It provided, at the same time, an escort for the reserve artillery park of the 8th Corps, to conduct it to Pomsen.

The Count de Valmy, tormented by sharp pains of a chronic illness was unable to continue service and handed command of the 4th Reserve Cavalry Corps to Général de Division Sokolnicki. The corps now consisted of the 7th and 8th Polish Divisions, or instead, the 17th and 19th brigades, with the 20th Brigade enroute, as it had been, on leaving Bohemia, detached to the 1st Corps, while the 18th Brigade continued to be assigned to General Dombrowski. Thus the 4th Corps was limited to about four regiments, having about 2,150 cavalry troopers and 12 cannon, followed by an administrative train, giving it a corps of 2,500 to 3,000 men.[5]

General Jan Sierawski

11 October - After the news reported by the reconnaissance to Thierbach, returning at 3:00 a.m., the 4th Corps left its position before daybreak and moved to camp, first behind Thierbach, on the road to Melbus, then at Klein-Zossen, between the confluence of the Eyla and the Wehra with the Pleiss, and in the second line of the 8th Corps.

The Count de Valmy obtained authorization to go to Leipzig to recover his health, and Prince Poniatowski and Murat, after having related their satisfaction to General Sokolnicki for his conduct at Penig, confirmed him in command of the 4th Cavalry Corps. All the orders were, subsequently, addressed in this manner.

12 October - The King of Naples [Murat] ordered a retrograde movement on Leipzig, so the 4th Cavalry Corps put itself in position at midnight, in front of Muckern, with a post of 200 men at Rötha. It remained under arms all night, until all the units of the corps had defiled and taken up their positions behind Göselbach and Gröbern. It then followed the movement of l'Hériter's division, which put itself in line with the other army corps. A brigade of Genera' Berckheim

[5]The original document says 25,000 to 30,000 men, but this is an obvious typographical error.

alone rested forward.

About 1,000 Cossacks, followed by a few squadrons of Prussian hussars, presented themselves immediately after our entry into the village, where they enetered without resistance, because one had neglected to protect the streets with infantry. The 4th Corps received orders to dislodge them and they succeeded in a spectacular manner. Several very successful charges occurred in the Sestowitz plain, where they enemy left about 30 dead and suffered about 50 wounded, some of whom fell into our hands.

Two battalions of infantry were put at the disposition of General Sokolnicki and he occupied, with part of the corps and two cannon, the position on the left bank, from Crosterwitz to Magdeborn, and they maintained themselves there despite the stubborn enemy attacks.

13 October - Towards 2:00 p.m., a strong enemy column moved to establish itself at Rötha, and its grand guards faced ours at Zehmen. Another column from Zwenckau, with six cannon, established itself at Klein-Stödel, on the left bank of the Pleiss, and, despite the woods that covered us, the fired 200 to 300 shot and shell at us, which did no damage, but which forced us to change front.

14 October - During the night, the King of Naples [Murat] moved closer to Leipzig. The 8th Corps took up position behind the Lössnig valley and the 4th Cavalry, with the Krakus, which were on this day put under the command of Sokolnicki, covered the retreat of the army.

The enemy cavalry did not delay in following us. A very hot engagement occurred on the right wing, before arriving at Markkleberg. The light artillery did marvels and stopped several enemy columns that charged with remarkable impetuosity. The Krakus comported itself with distinction and the 4th Cavalry Corps moved to pursue these advantages, when Berckheim's division, which found itself on the heights in front of Wachau, by an unexpected retreat, uncovered our left flank and forced us to limit the élan of our troops, who had already chased the enemy from the Auerhayn farm.

Then the 4th Corps established itself at Dölitz and Dösen, having the Krakus in the interval. The left of the corps covered, thus, the front of the 2nd Corps of Marshal the Duke de Bellune [Victor] who supported his right on the 8th Corps of Prince Poniatowski.

15 October - The emperor came to visit the right of the Grande Armée, the 4th Cavalry Corps deploys in line. All the staffs, united, move as body to compliment Poniatowski on the marshal's baton, which he is about to receive.

16 October - At daybreak the 4th Cavalry Corps deployed in line of battle on the heights that commanded the Wachau plain, having its grand guards in front of the village, it covered, thus, the front of the 2nd Corps of Marshal Duke de Bellune [Victor], while the Krakus covered that of the 8th Corps.

Masses of the enemy, preceded by a formidable artillery, descended the small hill, by Gossa, to flood the Wachau plain. General Sokolnicki saw that this village, which formed a salient angle, a hook, in the line should be regarded as the key to the success of the battle and that it had not been provided with an infantry garrison. He immediately sent Captain Vezyck, his aide-de-camp, to Marshal Victor, to inform him, and while he waited, the general had his batteries fire canister on the village, which the enemy skirmishers had already occupied. Thus, he facilitated the infantry of the 2nd Corps as they occupied the village and had the honor of beginning the fire all along the extended line and in the center of the line. Towards noon, from the height where he had been placed behind Wachau, Sokolnicki saw the hesitation in the movements of the columns that came from Crosterwitz and Gröbern, to attack our right by Markkleberg, so he seized the opportune moment to charge them with his cavalry. He had pass the stream and the bottom of the valley that bind this last village with Wachau, the intrepid Chef d'escadron Madalinski, with orders to fall, in extended order, on these scattered enemy battalions, while Colonel Kurnatowski, at the head of his brave chasseurs, marched by echelons, but at the trot, to support them. This charge succeeded beyond all hopes. The chasseurs tore to pieces more than 1,500 men of the most beautiful Hungarian infantry. They capture about 600 prisoners and the 8th Corps carries Dölitz with bayonets.

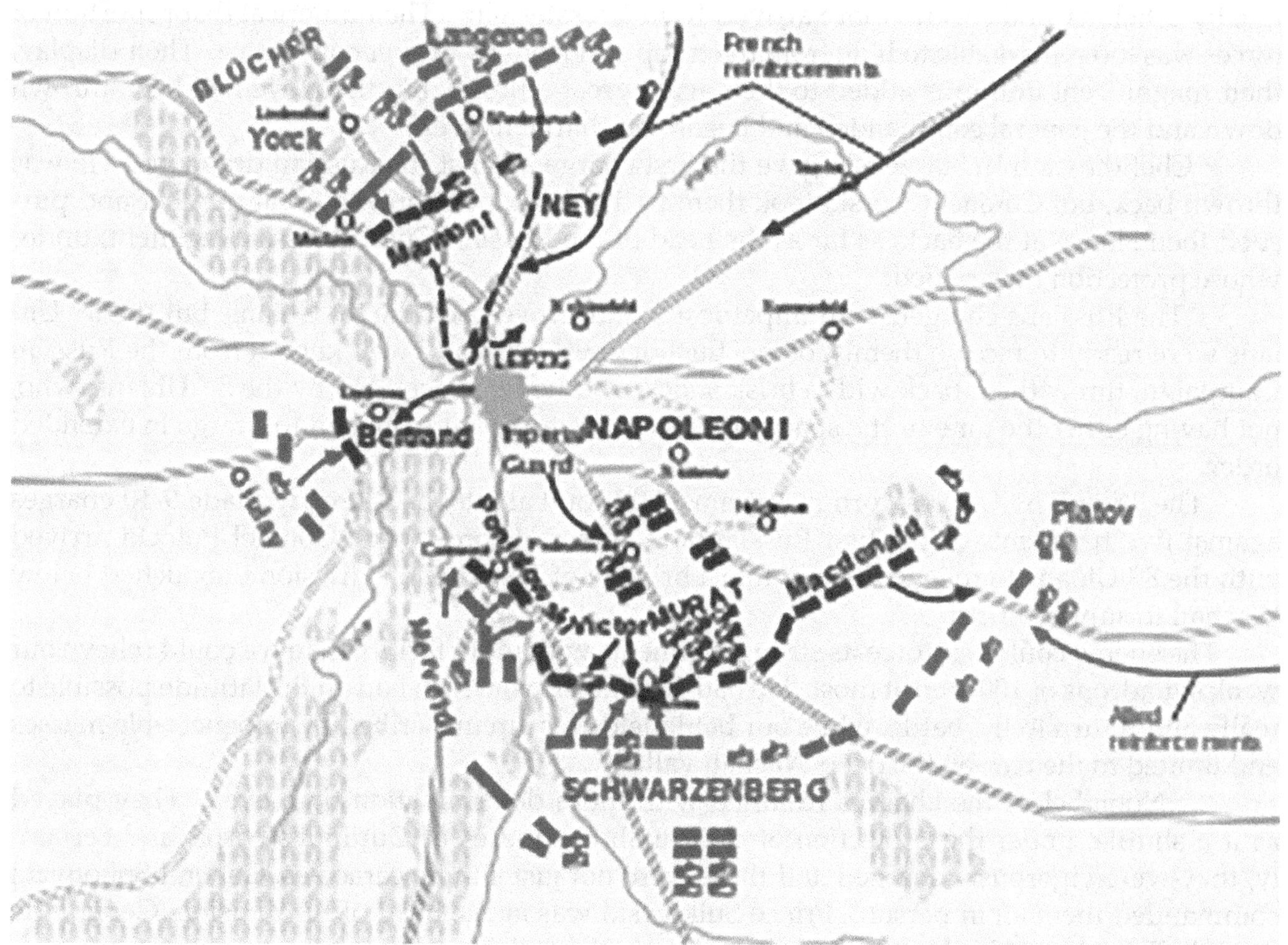

It was at the moment of this brilliant charge that Murat arrived on the Wachau heights. The satisfaction that he expressed on this first success gave him the desire to see it renewed and he ordered General Sokolnicki to advance all his cavalry beyond the valley.

Then the 8th Division made a movement to its right flank to close with the infantry of the 8th Corps, in order to support it in case of need. The Krakus were in the second line and the chasseurs, after having brought in their prisoners, moved to their side. Only the 3rd Uhlans remained to cover the 12 light cannon that stood on the Wachau heights. The 8th Corps formed its battalions in square on the plain. They were indispensable on the right to protect themselves against the enormous masses of enemy cavalry that arrived at the gallop from Görbern. However, the King's orders held them back.

While the 3rd Uhlans crossed the valley near Wachau, and that they moved to the side protected by the squares of the Duke de Reggio [Oudinot], Sokolnicki put himself at the head of the 6th Uhlans and moved in the center along the road that led from Dösen to Gröbern. At the same time he had the rest of Prince Sulkowski's division advance by echelons. Captain Valentin had carried to Sulkowski the order to advance to the valley, and a moment of hesitation had delayed the march.

In arriving at this culminating point of the plain, he contemplated for a moment the depth of the enemy cavalry columns. Sixteen Austrian and Russian cavalry regiments were formed in line by echelons, and several more arrived from Crossterwitz. The numerical disproportion of forces was too remarkable to hide from the troop and from its proper conscience. Their display, their magnificent uniforms added to their again great attitude; but the glove had been thrown down and the general commanded and began the charge himself.

Chef d'escadron Starzenski gave the first charge against the Russian dragoons. He was thrown back, but Colonel Oborski took them in the flank, overthrew a great number and pursued them, lance at the back, as far as the head of the Russian Guard Hussar Regiment, under whose protection they rallied.

The Russians charged with impetuosity and drove back the 3rd Uhlans, but the 6th Uhlans were ready to receive them. Colonel Suchorzewski, already well known from the Russian Campaign, threw them back with a brisk shock, and he was seconded by the 3rd Uhlans, who, not having either the time or the space necessary to reform were obliged to charge in extended order.

The 3rd and 6th Uhlans, forming at most 800 combatants, had already made 9-10 charges against five regiments of the first Russian and Austrian force when Colonel Potocki arrived with the 8th Uhlans to relieve them, while a brigade of Berckheim's division debouched below Wachau to support them.

The enemy could reinforce its strong regiments with more facility than we could relieve our weak squadrons of 100 men at most. He had 10 of all arms, which had all the latitude possible to really and return to the battle, while our battlefield was circumscribed by impenetrable masses and limited to the rear by the deep Wachau valley.

Nonetheless the charges resumed with more determination than ever. They played as if a shuttle, under the protection of the battalion squares of Oudinot's corps; and certainly, they were vigorously charged and these were not just simple caracoles. General Sokolnicki commanded them all in person. Prince Sulkowski was at the head of his division. Général de Brigade Tolinski had his horse killed under him in the melee, and the Valiant Colonel Suchorzewski received several saber blows to the head. We profited from a calm moment to bring him away and to reform in line, when a very large regiment of the Russian Guard Cossacks appeared on our right and formed to envelop us. The Krakus, which had already passed the valley and supported their right on the infantry of the 8th Corps, opposed them. They charged the Russians with a firm resolve and put them to route before they were formed.

At the same time, two superb regiments of Austrian cuirassiers arrived, with their coats covering their armor. The 3rd Uhlans, thinking them to be dragoons, charged them frontally and broke their lances on the Austrian cuirasses. Emboldened by this success, the Austrians pursued our broken squadrons to the foot of the valley. However, Colonel Kurnatowski fell on them with such violence that he put them to a complete rout. We knocked down a large number [of them] with the shafts of the lances. Three squadrons were cut off and sought a path to escape over the Dösen plateau. It was there that they encountered the [Russian] Guard Dragoons and gave trophies of arms to General Letors.

The cavalry of the 4th Corps also suffered substantial casualties. The 3rd and 6th Uhlans were reduced to less than half; and as they had broken their lances, they then formed in the second line of the Dösen plateau. The 8th had nearly 200 men hors de combat and the 1st Chasseurs had more than 120. These two regiments remounted the valley and formed the second line. The Krakus filled the interval that separated them from the 8th Corps, which stood at Dölitz. The light artillery, which was inactive during the charges, was placed between these two lines.

New masses of forces began to appear on the side of Gröbern and Crosterwitz, Sokolnicki moved to the summit of the small hill that dominated the Auerhayn farm, to observe it more closely. It was the reserve of Count von Merveldt, who moved in mass, and a quick pace on Dölitz.

He found, on returning, one of his batteries established forward of the valley, without any support and completely at risk. As a result he advanced the 1st Chasseurs and ordered his artillery to retire as soon as it made its first canister discharge. This was executed, but nothing prevented the guns from being assailed by the masses of infantry that a ridge hid from their view and that the current of the stream in the valley, whose steep banks, made it difficult to move the horses and caissons.

A battalion of Austrian jägers advanced rapidly to capture the guns, but the chasseurs, accustomed to breaking them, charged them and, despite the difficulty of the terrain, forced them to retreat. However, several [artillery] horses fell in this situation. Tangled harnesses and broken advance trains only permitted us to bring away two cannons and three caissons. The remaining four were spiked and the abandoned caissons emptied.

This feat of arms was the last of the day for the cavalry of the 4th Corps. It wished to persuade itself that its proud continuance and the lesson that it had given the enemy cavalry had prevented the latter from taking an active part in the unfortunate efforts of the Count von Merveldt at Dölitz.

At night fall the 4th Corps took up a position with the 8th Army Corps, to the right of the village of Dösen, with advance posts, which were its grand guards, beyond the Wachau valley.

All special praises here are superfluous. Everyone did well, everyone took part in the battle. One does not wish to exclude anyone and the citations would be too numerous. Among the officers of the staff, Captain of Engineers Valentin had a horse hors de combat under him. The others were more or less struck by enemy weapons.

17 October - This day was not remarkable for the 4th Corps, except for the arrival, towards evening, of the 18th Brigade, which had to that point, been detached to General Dombrowski. It had been sent on a reconnaissance beyond the Elster and was cut off from its corps by superior enemy cavalry forces. This explanation was questionable, since, on one side General Bertrand had swept all the left bank of the Elster, and on the other, the Duke Ragusa [Marmont] maintained himself on the Partha; There were some irregularities in the actions of Général de rigade Krukowiecki, who commanded, nonetheless, in view of the immense losses that the 4th Cavalry Corps had suffered the eve, considering, besides, that this brigade belonged on the right of the

7th Division, and when its presence had become urgent, Prince Poniatowski ordered General Sokolnicki to put it in line and to employ it as an integral part of the 4th Reserve Cavalry Corps.

18 October - While the 8th Corps took a more concentrated position below Leipzig with the Grande Armée, and placed itself on the Cunnewitz dams, the 4th Cavalry Corps formed its squadrons in echelon from the Wachau valley to the banks of the Lössnig, leaving its grand guards and its vedettes, formed from the Krakus, in front of the valley. General Sokolnicki remained with his picket forward of the rearmost echelon to observe the enemy's movements.

At 8:30 a.m., he saw the entire enemy line shake out and move down the sides of Gossa and Auerhayn with the most imposing attitude. Its left moved from Crosterwitz in attack columns and its right extended to Klein-Pössna, a space of three full leagues.

On the other side, the hook formed by the Imperial Guard around the tobacco mill in front of Thornberg, presented in all its majesty above the lines, where the cadre, tightly closed, restored all the pride of its of its intrepid countenance. This aspect was the only omen of victory.

Given to the most profound meditation in the middle of this panorama, whose spectacle would be inimitable, we were awoken by the approach of some enemy scouts, who fell with an astonishing impetuosity on the Krakus who remained in the picket line, and who, according to the last order they had received, withdrew and recrossed the valley.

They were hotly pursued. Already four squadrons had crossed the stream and came up the other side. They were allowed to close to within range of a carbine shot.

Sokolnicki wanted to have them charged by the 18th Brigade, which had yet to furnish any service in the corps, and was less fatigued. But such was his astonishment, when he learned that General Krukowiecki, without awaiting orders, had crossed the Lössnig dams and, even more so, he had taken with him, be it by example or by persuasion, part of the 19th Brigade, such that he remained isolated on an immense plain, with its only picket escort in reserve, and the Krakus in front.

The 17th Brigade, more accustomed to its commander, was still within range to support. He had them advance and Colonel Oborski threw back, with his impetuous shock four squadrons of Austrian dragons that were stopped. The Krakus fell on them with a fury and, with their lances, threw a large number of them into the stream. It was at this time that Prince Sulkowsi arrived by the commanding general to learn his intentions. They were not difficult to divine and he sent the order to the 8th Division to return on its steps.

As the first check had reduced to hesitation the columns of enemy cavalry which descended into the Valley, Colonel Kurnatowski had the time to arrive with two cannon on the Dösen plateau and General Tolinski, to recross the Cunnewitz dams and to put his brigade in line at the foot of the plateau. In addition, General Kurkowiecki reached the dams at Cunnewitz, and placed himself aside the Imperial Guard Cavalry, to the rear of Prostheida. Orders were carried to him by the first aide-de-camp Rozycki, but it is possible that this officer, who by an excess of zeal, despite a still doubtful convalescence, had arrived from Leipzig to take part in the chances of the day, had not been able to reach his destination, since from this moment, one had lost him from view.

The enemy then made new efforts to cross the valley and they descended into it with a battery of eight guns. While one did not see any column come out of Wachau, General Sokolnicki believed that it was is duty to maintain his position, and to delay, as much as possible, the march of the enemy. He ordered a new charge and the 3rd Uhlans, which was now reduced to a cadre, but totally composed of brave men, had the glory of capturing four guns that had already crossed the stream with their caissons. The Krakus had a good measure of some Austrian dragoons, putting a large number hors de combat. The four other cannon regained the far side with part of the horses of the first, but they brought forward horses and carried away our prize. This feat of arms was the last that crowned the services of the 17th Brigade in this campaign.

The enemy masses began to come out of Dölitz, Wachau and Liebervolkowitz. All the echelons recrossed the Lössnig dams. The artillery of the 4th Corps alone took an active part in the fight that was engaged on all the line. It commanded the Lössnig dams, and the general personally directed them, as well as four 12pdrs of the 8th Corps, which Prince Poniatowski put at his disposition. More than 40 enemy cannon were opposing us and, under their protection, several very vigorous infantry attacks were made to dislodge them. These attacks were all driven back with canister and held the enemy cavalry in a fluctuation that did not permit it to decide any movement.

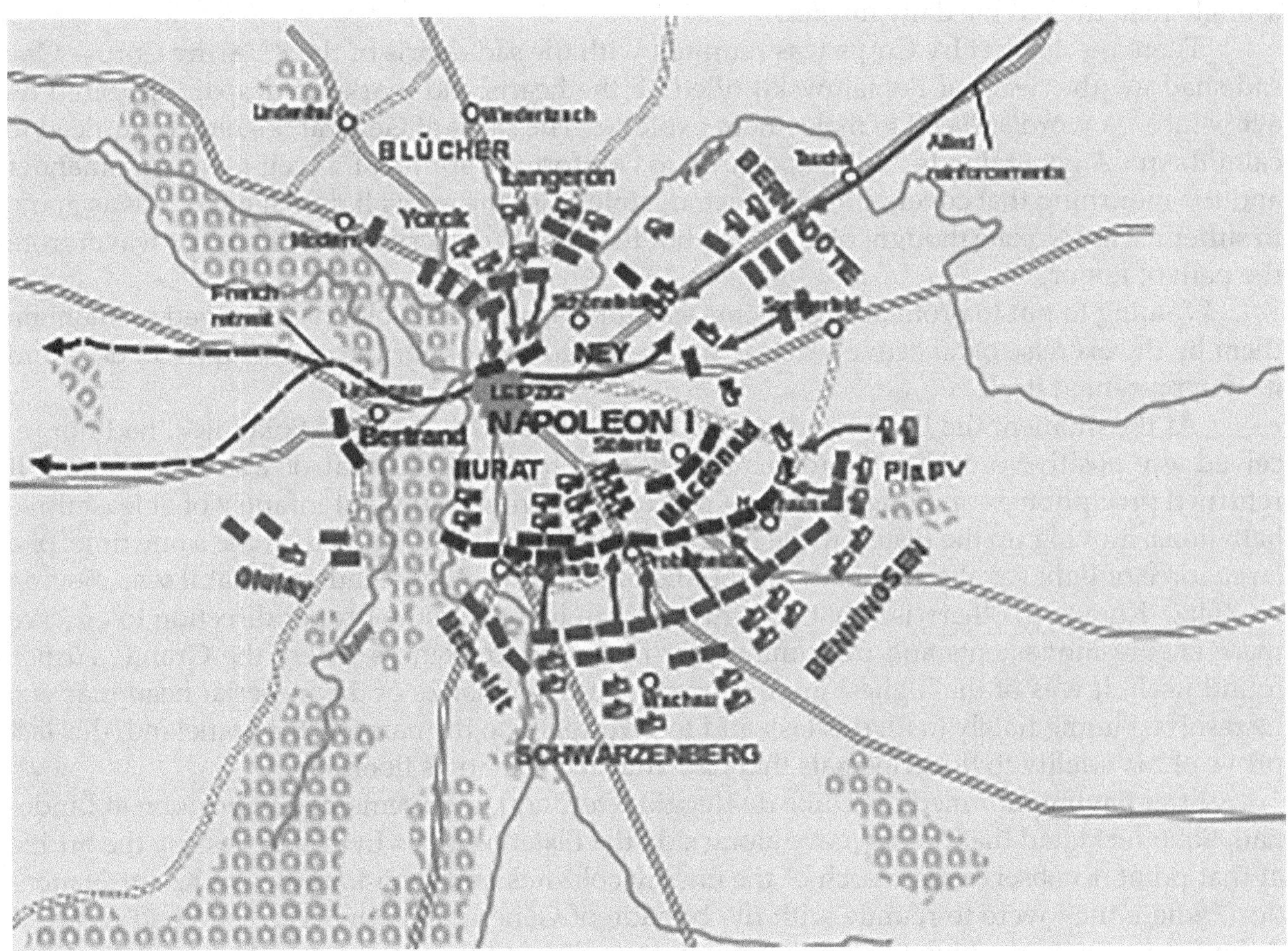

The Polish artillery had already emptied its caissons twice, which it sent to exchange in Leipzig, when towards 5:00 p.m. General Drouot, aide-de-camp to the Emperor came with the Guard artillery to replace that of the 4th Reserve Cavalry Corps and it pounded the presumptuous masses that sought to wipe us out by the force of their inertia.

Sokolnicki saw several meritorious gunners fall by his sides, as well as officers of great devotion, among others Lieutenant Labrouère, nephew to General Lauriston, a young man of the great promise. Two adjoints to the staff, Chefs d'escadron Lascaris and Podkorodynski, were grievously wounded: the first had a shoulder carried off. Captains Wemzyck and Farinelli, his aides-de-camps, had their capotes torn to shreds by the explosion of a howitzer shell. Others were dismounted and, in addition, the artillery lost 20 horses to shot. All the superior and subaltern officers of the 3rd Uhlans fought in the ranks a simple soldiers, who they animated by their example. Everyone of them merits special distinction.

19 October - At 2:00 a.m., the 4th Reserve Cavalry Corps received the order to leave and move by Leipzig to Lindenau. The Krakus were also included and put under the orders of Général de Division Sokolnicki. Prince Poniatowski only kept a single squadron of the latter and a picket of lancers for his escort.

This order was punctually executed and with the day, the 4th Corps took up position on the old road to Lützen, on the slide of Plögnitz, having an observation post at Klein-Zscocher. Not a single man missed the daily muster.

There the 4th Cavalry Corps was reunited with the sad debris of the 8th Army Corps. One sad shadow [the death of Poniatowski] filled all the hearts and marks of despair appeared on every face. A word sufficed to make them explode. The cares of General Sokolnicki sufficed to calm them. A general outpouring appeared to comfort the spirits of a well-loved commander and the mourning that covered the homeland, stole from the eyes all damage that it was going to suffer itself. No one thought of anything but his duty and everyone swore to not waver from the path of honor.

Wanting to put to profit arrangements as happy as sublime, Sokolnicki judged to maintain them by the exercise of an active service: him resolved to look for the opportunity to do it and it soon presented itself.

At the moment the Emperor departed for Markranstädt, General Sokolnicki had not received any positive order on the march that he was to make, so a patrol was sent Eythra. It returned precipitously and informed us of a strong Austrian column of infantry of at least three battalions, moving up the Elster by the road to Zwenckau. It had learned, at the same time, of a large force of light cavalry that had, during the night, moved by Pegau and that it was moving on Zeitz. Knowing, otherwise, that no army column had taken the proper direction to observe these enemy movements and presuming that in the circumstances where the Grande Armée found itself, it was of the highest importance to cover the flanks of the imperial headquarters, he resolved immediately to fill this task and to give again, to the name of his homeland, this last prove of his fidelity to the principals that had attached him to its liberator.

After having informed the Duke de Reggio [Oudinot], who remained in position at Lindenau, Sokolnicki had the Krakus move along side the Elster as far as Eythra to destroy the bridge at that point, to observe the march of the enemy columns and then to move on Knaut-Nauendorf, where they were to reunite with the brigade of General Krukowiecki, who had received orders to move by the highway on that point, to maintain through the march communications between the Krakus and the army corps, and, after having left an observation post there, to move with the Krakus to take up a position in from of Schkeitbar, at the fork of the roads to Pegau and Zwenckau.

At the same time the 4th Cavalry Corps, having about 800 men and 18 cannon, followed the road from Ribbach to Schkeitbar, where it took a military position proper to cover Markranstädt, where the Emperor was to be found.

From his arrival, he made a report to the King of Naples [Murat] of the reasons that had caused him to choose this position and to depict to him the sad condition of his compatriots, he implored him to look in his sensitive and faithful heart for some remedy to the torments of exasperation that were increased by the uncertainty of their subsequent fate. Colonel Tancarville, Chief of Staff to the 4th Corps, with whom he had shared all the work, wished that he be charged with submitting this report and to plead the cause of the unfortunates abandoned to themselves.

After having expedited Colonel Tancarville, Sokolnicki visited all the posts and returned to sleep. Then, at about 2:00 a.m., he was brought two Austrian prisoners, taken in the advance posts by the Krakus. One of them was a Pole from Galicia.

The Death of Poniatowski (Horace Vernet)

According to their disposition, he was positive:

1. That they were a party of three Austrian battalions composed of grenadiers and jägers, who had crossed the Elster at Zwenkau, and were moving, by a forced march, to Weissenfels, and that to this end, they sought to gain the road that led there by Kaja, as the most isolated and least obstructed. Finally, that having attained there without passing through any village, and the troop already out of breath, the stopped there to rest for a few hours;

2. That they had no artillery with them, nor cavalry; having preceded them, and moving alone by Pegau on Naumburg;

3. That they were in an open plain, and were not supported by a village, or wood, or stream, or ravine.

These circumstances have been well detailed, presented to General Sokolnicki a very easy opportunity to destroy, without firing a shot, three entire battalions.

In effect, on an immense plain and without any obstacle, it sufficed to turn part of the Krakus on the side of Gross-Schkorlop, and to move to the flank a few squadrons by Meihen on the road to Kaja and to march on them with two cannons in front, to make them lay down their weapons. The moon was magnificent Sokolnicki gave the order to the troop to put itself under arms in the greatest silence. He sent the two prisoners to the King of Naples [Murat], with his engineering officer, Valentin, and immediately went to the advance posts to make dispositions. He was surprised when he found neither the 18th Brigade, nor the Krakus, both of which General Krukowiecki had taken with him to Lützen! However, this general, who, in the preceding days, had already given the measure of his spirit of insubordination, in quitting a post of honor, without any regard for the security of the camp, had spread seditious oaths. He attempted to persuade these brave men, who had never failed their duty, that it no longer agreed to them to continue to fight against the enemy that they had so often faced; he sought to alarm their conscience to the same goal that had caused them to pour out their blood; and he supported these maxims by personal motives that made him avoid the meeting the Austrians, as their deserter. Whatever his motives were, it is true to say that, by the tumultuous cries and the disorder that followed them he warned the enemy, who, on their side, precipitously decamped. The general personally went to the position where the three battalions had been and found there a few scattered fagots that they had not burned. It was known that they had changed direction and moved by Eisdorf and Gross-Gorschen on Naumburg.

General Jan Krukowiecki

20 October - After such a debut, one expected even more violent actions from a man whose bad spirit had led him out of his sphere. Sokolnicki wished to ward off the scandal by an act of vigor; but General Krukowiecki, considering the storm that was going to fall on his head, tried to escape it by an extraordinary act. Having had the whole time to consider it, he had to resort to the expediencies, paid for audacity; and succeeded beyond all expectations.

Without awaiting the arrival of the column at Lützen, and without having the least authorization, [Krukowiecki] had the imprudence to penetrate as far as the door to the Emperor's coach, and of announcing himself as a delegate of all the Poles in the corps to demand Prince Sulkowski be placed at their head.

General Sokolnicki presented himself shortly after to confound the imposter and to claim the command of the Poles in favor Général de division Dombrowski, as the most senior, and because all the Poles were accustomed to considering him as their natural guide to find the road to their homeland. But the trick had made a too great an impression, so it was listened to. Sokolnicki was surprised by the sovereign's confidence. The choice didn't answer [the concerns of the troops] as expected and was the germ of the nearly complete dissolution of a corps that that only good spirit had, to that point, sustained. From this moment, which retraced the perfect image of the famous veto[6] , there was no longer a corps, nor soul, nor spirit. It was an errant tribe, whose dislocated members marched at random. Everyone pressed to go home, and many preferred running the chance of attempting to return. Some of the most judicious made efforts to raise their spirits. Colonels Morawski and Redel, in particular, demonstrated their zeal in this regard; but the example of the commander only justified, in the eyes of the weakness, a measure that exasperation alone could dictate.

This finishes the history of the 4th Reserve Cavalry Corps, which, from this point to the crossing of the Rhine, performed no military act and took no part in the military events that occurred during the retreat of the Grande Armée. It is to an impartial and judicious public to weigh on which side are the true services and the good duty. In what settings it agrees to it to classify the integrity of the principles, of the devotion, honor, the fidelity and the most absolute disinterestedness; all the proofs finally of the nobility and the purity of intentions that a clear and complete patriotism alone can inspire and direct towards a determined goal.

To calm the agitation that such an unjust and impolitic act could not fail to provoke, the Emperor had accorded 150 decorations of the Legion d'honneur to the 4th Cavalry Corps. The lists of those who had most warranted them, were formed with the greatest care. The major part of the soldiers had already been listed in those presented by the Count de Valmy and by Prince Poniatowski, before the affairs of 16 and 18 October, but an arbitrary partiality had frustrated a great number of the brave, to place the names of those on the list that had no right to be there. Among these was the 18th Brigade, which had taken no part in the work of the 17th and 19th Brigades, and which had largely been recommended for the services, which they had rendered under the orders of General Dombrowski. In addition, General Krukowiecki solicited the commanders cross [of the Legion d'honneur], after having obtained it in the rank of "officer" and he obtained this higher decoration. The acts reported above witness how [little] he merited it.

Général de division Sokolnicki was equally placed on this list. First, by the Count de Valmy, then by Prince Poniatowski, and in the last instance, by Prince Sulkowski. But as it didn't agree to him to appear on a list where favor, and not justice, had placed the names, he erased his name from it with his own hand, in the presence of the whole corps, in reposing, in this regard, on the return to a sovereign's principles to which he had rendered real and singular services.

Finally, the Emperor judged it necessary to address himself to his adopted children, and sought to return calm to their spirits. He succeeded in rallying them around the fasces of glory

[6]This is a reference to veto that existed within the Polish government, whereby any single noble in the assembly could object to any proposed law and veto it. This process resulted in a near paralysis of the Polish government for years and directly contributed to the destruction of the Polish state.

and honor, which alone could in their eyes retrace again the image of their homeland[7], while the choice of a general who, at first, showed them the indirect road to return to their foyers, brought back them to the order that a temporary ardor had caused them to forget.

---

[7]Four days before the battle at Hanau, on a hillock far from the road, in a circle of Polish officers, the Emperor Napoleon spoke to them, and one of them recorded the following passages:

"One has given me a report of your intentions: as Emperor, as general, I cannot but praise your behavior: I cannot reproach you. You have acted loyally towards me; you have not wished to abandon me without my saying anything, and the same you have promised me to accompany me to the Rhine. Today I wish to give you good advice. Tell me, where you wish to go? With your king, who perhaps himself has no asylum..... I have given him to you as your sovereign because the other powers did not want to see at the head of your nation who had more energy. It was necessary to give you a German, so as to not excite the jealousy of your enemies; and as he is an honest man, my particular friend, I have made him your Duke, that he might be the organ of my wishes... As for you, you are the masters to return to your homes, if it is your intention. Two or three thousand men, more or less, all of you brave, will change nothing in my affairs. However, do you fear that your brothers, that posterity will not reproach you if Poland no longer exists!.... If you abandon me, I will have no more right to speak for you, and I believe that, despite the disasters that have occurred, I am still the most powerful monarch in Europe. Things can take another face. And besides as you exist by treaties, until is another one, your political existence is not wiped out. If I am constrained to sacrifice you, one will mention you in the next peace treaty. Then you can return tranquilly to your homes... Now you return with your hat off; who knows if one day you will return with arms in your hands? I have always supported your existence and to give you proof, read the Moniteur, it will show you a peace treaty made with the Emperor of Austria, by which he ceded Galicia to me in exchange for Illyria..... If I didn't hold so strongly to you, I could have made the peace at Dresden, by sacrificing you... You always nourished hope in the most critical time: today, if it abandons you, one will accuse you of flightiness and weakness....."

They all cried that they were ready to follow the Emperor anywhere. That one wished only to know how he regarded the Polish corps in the circumstances of that day. "I regard you," responded His Majesty, "as the troops of the Duchy of Warsaw, as allied troops, as representatives of your nation. You have your relations with the Minister of Foreign Affairs."

At these words, [there erupted] cries of "vive l'Empereur," that one would not abandon him, and His Majesty departed.

Appendix I - IV Reserve Cavalry Corps[1]

6 July 1813

IV Cavalry Corps

7th Light Cavalry Division: Général de division Sokolnicki

18th Light Cavalry Brigade: Général de brigade Krukowiecki (Detached to I Corps)
- 2nd Polish Uhlan Regiment
- 4th Polish Chasseur à Cheval Regiment

17th Light Cavalry Brigade: Général de brigade Tolinski
- 1/3rd Polish Uhlan Regiment (19/208/276)[2]
- 2/3rd Polish Uhlan Regiment (8/195/232)
- 3/3rd Polish Uhlan Regiment (9/199/237)
- 4/3rd Polish Uhlan Regiment (4/144/112)
- 1/13th Polish Hussar Regiment (19/164/221)
- 2/13th Polish Hussar Regiment (7/102/109)
- 3/13th Polish Hussar Regiment (8/105/120)
- 4/13th Polish Hussar Regiment (8/127/138)

Artillery:
- Polish Horse Battery (6/106)

8th Light Cavalry Division: Général de division

19th Light Cavalry Brigade:
- 1/1st Polish Chasseur à Cheval Regiment (20/181/262)
- 2/1st Polish Chasseur à Cheval Regiment (7/119/140)
- 3/1st Polish Chasseur à Cheval Regiment (8/141/163)
- 4/1st Polish Chasseur à Cheval Regiment (11/98/106)
- 1/6th Polish Uhlan Regiment (20/182/272)
- 2/6th Polish Uhlan Regiment (8/141/166)
- 3/6th Polish Uhlan Regiment (9/148/168)
- 4/6th Polish Uhlan Regiment (11/126/87)

20th Light Cavalry Brigade: Général de brigade Weissenhoff
- 1/8th Polish Uhlan Regiment (20/231/298)
- 2/8th Polish Uhlan Regiment (11/167/202)
- 3/8th Polish Uhlan Regiment (11/170/203)
- 4/8th Polish Uhlan Regiment (15/164/161)
- 1/16th Polish Uhlan Regiment (19/193/262)
- 2/16th Polish Uhlan Regiment (11/130/159)

[1]This return is drawn from an order of battle constructed for the entire Grande Armée using material found in the following catons in the French Section historique de l'armée de terre - Cartons C2- 537, 538, 539, 540, 541, 542, 543, 544, and C2-708.
[2]Numbers are officers, men, and horses.

3/16th Polish Uhlan Regiment (11/118/143)
4/16th Polish Uhlan Regiment (12/129/162)
Artillery:
1st Polish Horse Battery (8/161) (4-6pdrs & 2-24pdr howitzers)

1 August 1813

IV Cavalry Corps[3]

Commander-in-Chief: Général de division Kellermann, Count of Valmy
Chief of Staff: Adjutant Commandant Tancarville

7th Light Cavalry Division: Général de division Sokolnicki

17th Light Cavalry Brigade: Général de brigade Kwasinski
1/2/3/4/1st Polish Uhlan Regiment (40/529/637)
1/2/3/4/3rd Chasseur à Cheval Regiment (46/562/682)
18th Light Cavalry Brigade: Général de brigade Krukowiecki
Detached to 27th Division
Artillery:
Polish Horse Battery (6/125)(4-6pdrs & 2 howitzers)

8th Light Cavalry Division: Général de division Sulkowski

19th Light Cavalry Brigade: Général de brigade Tolinski
1/2/3/4/6th Polish Uhlan Regiment (42/591/666)
1/2/3/4/8th Polish Uhlan Regiment (49/701/831)
20th Light Cavalry Brigade: Général de brigade Weissenhoff
1/2/3/4/13th Polish Hussar Regiment (40/444/744)
1/2/3/4/16th Polish Uhlan Regiment (51/552/712)
Artillery:
Polish Horse Artillery Battery (8/161)

[3]This return is drawn from an order of battle constructed for the entire Grande Armée using material found in the following cartons in the French Section historique de l'armée de terre - C2-543 & 544, XP-3 and Carton AF IV*-1334 from the French National Archives

10 November 1813

27th (Polish) Infantry Division, VIII Corps

Commanding Officer: Général de division Dombrowski

Brigadiers: Généraux de brigade Zolkowski & Tolinski

2nd Polish Infantry Regiment (32/128)
4th Polish Infantry Regiment (40/397)
Combined Polish Regiment (74/678)
1st Polish Infantry Regiment
8th Polish Infantry Regiment
15th Polish Infantry Regiment
16th Polish Infantry Regiment
12th Polish Infantry Regiment
14th Polish Infantry Regiment (27/88)
1st Polish Chasseur à Cheval Regiment (28/191/188)
2nd Polish Uhlan Regiment (45/384/392)
3rd Polish Uhlan Regiment (28/191/188)
4th Polish Chasseur à Cheval Regiment (26/203/229)
6th Polish Uhlan Regiment (30/196/213)
8th Polish Uhlan Regiment (48/369/402)
13th Polish Hussar Regiment (17/113/112)
14th Polish Cuirassier Regiment (5/93/40)
16th Polish Uhlan Regiment (4/27/10)
Krakus Regiment (21/257/288)
Polish Artillery (15/447)
Polish Sappers (9/60)

Index

Operations of the Polish Army
During the 1809 Campaign
By Roman Soltyk
Annotated and edited by George F. Nafziger

A History of the Polish
Revolution of 1830
Joseph Hordynski

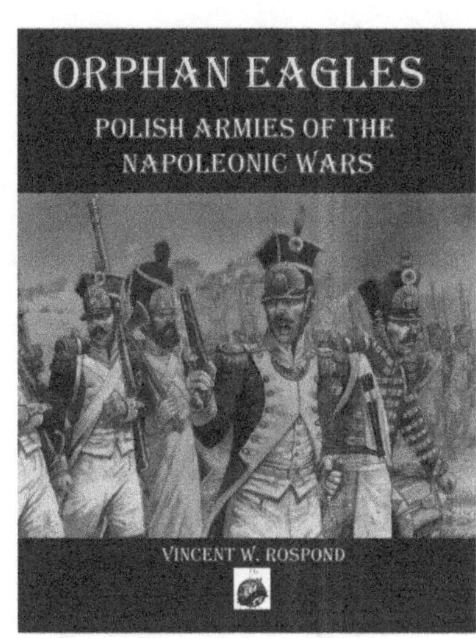
ORPHAN EAGLES
POLISH ARMIES OF THE
NAPOLEONIC WARS
VINCENT W. ROSPOND